LINUX
UNWIRED

*Roger Weeks, Edd Dumbill,
and Brian Jepson*

Beijing · Cambridge · Farnham · Köln · Paris · Sebastopol · Taipei · Tokyo

Linux Unwired
by Roger Weeks, Edd Dumbill, and Brian Jepson

Published by O'Reilly Media, Inc., 1005 Gravenstein Highway North, Sebastopol, CA 95472.

O'Reilly & Associates books may be purchased for educational, business, or sales promotional use. Online editions are also available for most titles (*safari.oreilly.com*). For more information, contact our corporate/institutional sales department: (800) 998-9938 or *corporate@oreilly.com*.

Editor:	Brian Jepson
Production Editor:	Sarah Sherman
Cover Designer:	Emma Colby
Interior Designer:	David Futato

Printing History:

April 2004:	First Edition.

 This book uses RepKover™, a durable and flexible lay-flat binding.

ISBN: 0-596-00583-0

[M]

Table of Contents

Foreword

This is a book about two revolutions: free software and free wireless networking.

The first revolution was born in 1991, when a lone Finnish hacker named Linus Torvalds used the GNU Project's free C compiler to build Linux, a free Unix-like operating system kernel. One of the hallmarks of this kernel was its release under the GNU Public License, which guaranteed that anyone would be able to customize and improve the Linux kernel to suit their computing needs, and that those improvements would be shared with the other users of the Linux kernel.

Today, Linus Torvalds is virtually a household name, and his brainchild has gone on to star in millions of personal computers, web servers, supercomputing clusters, embedded devices, mainframes, and more. Bolstered by the success of Linux and its BSD-derived cousins, a globe-spanning Free Software movement has taken hold, spawning thousands of community-supported projects, and fundamentally altering how software is made and distributed in the 21st century.

Although the second revolution has been lurking in the background for years, it received a major boost in 1999 from the publication of the IEEE 802.11b standard, a specification for wireless data networking that made use of the 2.4 GHz microwave band, which had long been considered "junk" spectrum in the U.S. As consumer 802.11b devices hit the market, more and more people were able to use computers and access the network from an ever widening array of locales—living room couches, conference rooms, coffee shops, and even sunny park benches.

Meanwhile, ordinary individuals were discovering that, using nothing more than off-the-shelf radio hardware and the right antennas, they could build wide-area—and even metropolitan-area—IP network infrastructure for the first time ever, without the need for costly or restrictive government licenses. The result has been a quantum leap in ubiquitous computing, with millions of 802.11 devices in use across the world. The newer IEEE 802.11a and 802.11g standards are now implemented to offer even more possibilities for free data networking.

The operative word at the heart of both of these revolutions is the word "free," but the concept it refers to is freedom. Trivially, they offer the opportunity to download an operating system free of charge or perhaps to escape the tyranny of Ethernet cables. But on a deeper level, these revolutions promise basic freedoms of action and of speech—the freedom to employ your computing hardware to communicate with others as you see fit, and not merely as commercial interests dictate. Unlike many of the technical choices available to you today, Linux and 802.11 serve to enhance your freedom and expand your options, rather than to constrain them.

As the title implies, *Linux Unwired* guides you through configuring and using Linux with the 802.11 protocols, as well as Bluetooth, IR, cellular data networking, and GPS. Ultimately, though, this is a book about freedom. This book shows you how to harness the combined power of these technologies to expand your options and your technical horizons.

Welcome to the revolution(s). May you do good work!

—Schuyler Erle
February, 2004

Preface

Take a trip to the computer store, buy a Wi-Fi card, and insert it into your Linux notebook. You will probably hear two beeps; are they both happy beeps, or is one of them an angry beep? It's possible that you will receive a happy beep, but with the variety of hardware, firmware, and software drivers for Wi-Fi cards, it's quite likely that you will receive the angry beep. Next, go through this exercise with a Bluetooth adapter, cell phone, and some other random wireless hardware.

This book is all about hearing the happy beeps.

Wireless networks are popping up everywhere; from Wi-Fi hotspots to cellular data plans, you can connect to the Internet virtually anywhere. You can even cut more cables with technologies like Bluetooth and Infrared. Linux is already an amazing operating system, and combined with wireless, its strengths are amplified.

But things really shine when you combine wireless technologies. This book also discusses using wireless technology in combination, whether you want to share your Wi-Fi connection to Bluetooth devices or map out Wi-Fi networks with a Global Positioning System (GPS) device.

What This Book Covers

This book explains how to use the following wireless technologies with Linux:

Wireless Fidelity (Wi-Fi)
Wi-Fi is short-range wireless networking that supports raw speeds up to 54 Mbps (about 20–25 Mbps actual speeds). It's an affordable replacement for wired Ethernet, and includes the 802.11b, 802.11g, and 802.11a protocols. Chapters 1 through 6 discuss Wi-Fi.

Bluetooth

Bluetooth is a wireless cable-replacement that allows you to get rid of USB and serial cables. You can use it to connect a Personal Digital Assistant (PDA), such as a Palm or Pocket PC, to Linux; create an ad-hoc network; or transfer files between computers. Bluetooth is covered in Chapter 7.

Infrared

Infrared has been available for a long time, and in some cases, it's the only way that two devices will talk to each other, particularly with older PDAs. Infrared uses light waves that are just outside the range of visible light. Infrared is covered in Chapter 8.

Cellular networking

Although Wi-Fi is fast and reliable, it disappears the moment you leave its useful range. Cellular networks cover large areas, reach speeds between 40 kbps and 100 kbps, and even work reliably while you are in a moving vehicle. With unlimited data plans starting at $19.99 a month from some providers, cellular data plans can be a useful complement to Wi-Fi. Chapter 9 covers cellular data.

Global Positioning System (GPS)

Use a GPS to figure out your location in two or three dimensions. Plugged into a Linux computer, a GPS device becomes a source of location data that can be combined with freely available maps to plot locations of wireless networks, figure out where you are, or map out whatever interests you. GPS is covered in Chapter 10.

Conventions Used in This Book

This book uses the following abbreviations:

Hz, kHz, MHz, and GHz

Hertz (cycles per second), kilohertz (one thousand hertz), megahertz (one million hertz), and gigahertz (one billion, or 10^9 hertz)

bps, kbps, Mbps

Bits per second, kilobits (1,024 bits) per second, and megabits (1,048,576 bits) per second

KB/s, MB/s

Kilobytes (1,024 bytes) per second and megabytes (1,048,576 bytes) per second

MB

Megabytes (1,048,576 bytes) of hard disk or RAM storage

mW
> Milliwatts; one thousandth of a watt of power output

This book uses the following typographic conventions:

Constant width
> Used for listing the output of command-line utilities

Constant width italic
> Used to show items that need to be replaced in commands

Italic
> Used for emphasis, for first use of a technical term, and for URLs

...
> Indicates text that has been omitted for clarity

  This icon indicates a tip, suggestion, or general note.

  This icon indicates a warning or caution.

Comments and Questions

Please address any comments or questions concerning this book to the publisher:

> O'Reilly & Associates
> 1005 Gravenstein Highway North
> Sebastopol, CA 95472
> (800) 998-9938 (in the U.S. or Canada)
> (707) 829-0515 (international or local)
> (707) 829-0104 (fax)

To ask technical questions or comment on the book, send email to:

> *bookquestions@oreilly.com*

O'Reilly has a web site for this book where examples, errata, and any plans for future editions are listed. You can access this site at:

> *http://www.oreilly.com/catalog/lnxunwired*

For more information about this book and others, see the O'Reilly web site:

> *http://www.oreilly.com*

Acknowledgments

Roger Weeks

Writing this book would not have been possible without the backing and inspiration of my wife, Cynthia. Despite a house sometimes too cluttered with geek gear, long technical conversations, and more than one late night, she's always there for me.

Many thanks also to Schuyler Erle, who not only got the book approved by O'Reilly, but somehow managed to convince them that I should be the author.

All of the "Cats" should be thanked publicly for their amazing amounts of knowledge, friendship, and hard work: Rob Flickenger, Schuyler Erle, Adam Flaherty, Nate Boblitt, Jim Rosenbaum, and Rich Gibson. Without them, significant parts of the West Coast would be very boring, and the wireless community would be much poorer.

Finally, many thanks to Brad Silva for excellent hardware advice and soldering skills.

Edd Dumbill

I would like to thank Marcel Holtmann and Maxim Krasnyansky for their devoted work on the BlueZ Linux Bluetooth stack and, of course my wife Rachael for her patient support.

Brian Jepson

My thanks go out to Schuyler Erle and Rob Flickenger for helping to develop the original outline of this book and for technical review. Thanks also to Adam Flaherty for technical review. I'm very grateful to Roger and Edd for being such great coauthors.

I'd especially like to thank my wife, Joan, and my stepsons, Seiji and Yeuhi, for their support and encouragement through my late night and weekend writing sessions, my occasional trips around town in a car full of Wi-Fi and GPS equipment, and the various milliwattage that soaked through the walls of my home office while I worked on this book.

## CHAPTER 1

Introduction
to Wireless

Wireless networks use radio waves to move data without wires and they have been around in one form or another for decades. *Teletype*, or telex, systems were established worldwide in the early 1920s. These systems used copper lines to connect two or more teletype machines. Government investments in military radios lead to innovations in radio; *teletype over radio* (TOR), or *radioteletype*, replaced many teletype systems, particularly in third-world countries that lacked copper-wire infrastructures. In many parts of the world, TOR is still used as the primary communications medium for governments. TOR uses the *high frequency* (HF) radio band. We'll cover the types of radio bands later in this chapter.

In 1970, Norm Abramson, a professor of engineering at the University of Hawaii, developed a radio-based communications system known as ALO-HANET. This was the world's first wireless *packet-switched* network, which allows multiple devices to transmit and receive data simultaneously. The research behind ALOHANET was used by Bob Metcalfe to develop the Ethernet standard for wired networking.

Presently, there are many types of wireless networks in use around the world. The *802.11* protocol set, popularly known as Wi-Fi, includes wireless network standards that allow data transmission up to a theoretical 54 Mbps. The *Global Positioning System* (GPS) uses a wireless connection from a receiver to a series of satellites to fix a location precisely on the planet. There are several wireless networking standards in the mobile-phone world, including *General Packet Radio Service* (GPRS) and Code Division Multiple Access (CDMA) 1xRTT (1x Radio Transmission Technology). Subsequent chapters will discuss all of these in detail.

Radio Waves

Radio waves are created when electrically charged particles accelerate with a frequency that lies in the *radio frequency* (RF) portion of the electromagnetic spectrum. Other emissions that fall outside of the RF spectrum include X-rays, gamma rays, and infrared and ultraviolet light. When a radio wave passes a copper wire or another electrically sensitive device, it produces a moving electric charge, or voltage, which can be transformed into an audio or data signal.

Radio waves can be depicted mathematically as a sinusoidal curve, as shown in Figure 1-1.

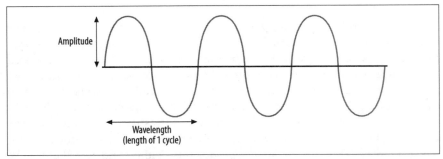

Figure 1-1. A sine wave representing a radio wave

The distance covered by a complete sine wave (a cycle) is known as the *wavelength*. The height of the wave is called the *amplitude*. The number of cycles made in a second is known as the *frequency*. Frequency is measured in Hertz (Hz), also known as cycles per second. So, a 1 Hz signal makes a full cycle once per second. You should be familiar with this unit of measurement: if your new computer's CPU operates at 2 GHz, the internal clock of your CPU generates signals roughly at two billion cycles per second.

 Note that frequency is inversely proportional to the wavelength: the longer the wavelength, the lower the frequency; the shorter the wavelength, the higher the frequency. The wavelength of a 1 Hz signal is about 30 billion centimeters, which is the distance that light travels in one second. A 1 MHz signal has a wavelength of 300 meters.

Radio Frequency Spectrum

To regulate the use of the various radio frequencies, the Federal Communications Commission (FCC) in the United States determines the allocation of frequencies for various uses. Table 1-1 shows some of the bands defined by the FCC (see *http://www.fcc.gov/oet/spectrum/table/fcctable.pdf*).

Table 1-1. Range of frequencies defined for the various bands

Frequency	Band
10 kHz to 30 kHz	Very Low Frequency (VLF)
30 kHz to 300 kHz	Low Frequency (LF)
300 kHz to 3 MHz	Medium Frequency (MF)
3 MHz to 30 MHz	High Frequency (HF)
30 MHz to 328.6 MHz	Very High Frequency (VHF)
328.6 MHz to 2.9 GHz	Ultra High Frequency (UHF)
2.9 GHz to 30 GHz	Super High Frequency (SHF)
30 GHz and higher	Extremely High Frequency (EHF)

You can get a more detailed frequency allocation chart from *http://www.ntia. doc.gov/osmhome/allochrt.pdf*. The following conversion list should help you understand this chart:

- 1 kilohertz (kHz) = 1,000 Hz
- 1 megahertz (MHz) = 1,000 kHz
- 1 gigahertz (GHz) = 1,000 MHz

Wireless networks use a variety of radio frequencies. Table 1-2 shows some common wireless network protocols and the corresponding radio frequencies.

Table 1-2. Frequencies used by various wireless networks

Frequency range	Wireless network
2.45 GHz	Bluetooth
2.4 to 2.483 GHz	802.11, 802.11b, 802.11g
5.180 GHz to 5.805 GHz	802.11a
1.2276 and 1.57542 GHz	GPS

Radio Wave Behavior

Radio waves, similar to light waves, exhibit certain characteristics when coming into contact with objects.

Reflection occurs when a radio wave hits an object that is larger than the wavelength of the radio wave (see Figure 1-2). The radio wave is then reflected off the surface.

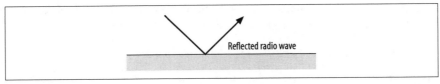

Figure 1-2. Reflection of a radio wave

Refraction occurs when a radio wave hits an object of a higher density than its current medium (see Figure 1-3). The radio wave now travels at a different angle—for example, waves propagating through clouds.

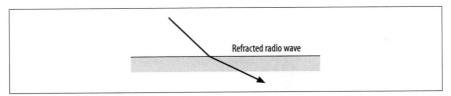

Figure 1-3. Refraction of a radio wave

Scattering occurs when a radio wave hits an object of irregular shape, usually an object with a rough surface area (see Figure 1-4), and the radio wave bounces off in multiple directions.

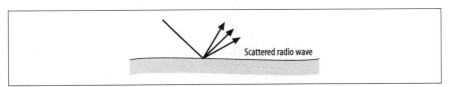

Figure 1-4. Scattering of a radio wave

Absorption occurs when a radio wave hits an object but is not reflected, refracted, or scattered. Rather, the radio wave is absorbed by the object and is then lost (see Figure 1-5).

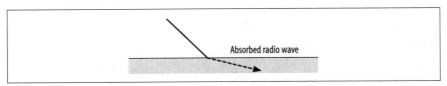

Figure 1-5. Absorption of a radio wave

Diffraction occurs when objects block a radio wave's path. In this case, the radio wave breaks up and bends around the corners of the object (see Figure 1-6). This property allows radio waves to operate without a visual line of sight.

Radio Interference and Absorption

Radio waves are subject to interference caused by objects and obstacles in the air. Such obstacles can be concrete walls, metal cabinets, or even raindrops. Generally, transmissions made at higher frequencies are more subject to radio absorption (by the obstacles) and larger signal loss. Larger frequencies have smaller wavelengths; hence, signals with smaller wavelengths tend to be absorbed by the obstacles that they collide with. This causes high-frequency devices to have a shorter operating range.

For devices that transmit data at high frequencies, much more power is needed in order for them to cover the same range as compared to lower-frequency transmitting devices.

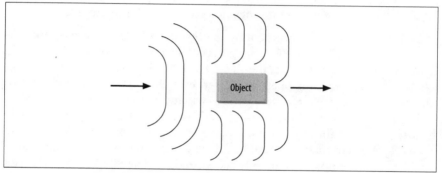

Figure 1-6. Diffraction of radio waves

Connections Without Wires

There are many types of wireless networks, such as Cellular (wide-area wireless networking), Wi-Fi (local and wide area wireless networking), and Bluetooth (cable-replacement and short-range wireless networking). All of these networks run with Linux. Here is a list of tasks you can complete with Linux and wireless networks:

Build your own wireless access point. At home, use a Linux box as your wireless access point and secure firewall for a broadband connection, and use a Linux notebook as a wireless client. To control who uses your access point, build a captive portal. It's also possible that your broadband connection is wireless and uses a point-to-point directional wireless network.

Synchronize your contacts . At the office, keep your contacts list from your Linux desktop synchronized with your cell phone using Bluetooth or an infrared port.

Use a cellular network and GPS for the ultimate road warrior experience.

On the road, use your Linux-powered PDA to check email from a wireless hotspot. Connect your cell phone and laptop, and use a high-speed data network where there is a digital cell signal. Hook a GPS receiver to your laptop and find that out-of-the-way hotel.

Wireless Alphabet Soup

While it is not the sole focus of this book, there are several chapters that deal entirely with "Wi-Fi," or *Wireless Fidelity*. This phrase is trademarked by the Wi-Fi Alliance, a group that consists of nearly all 802.11 manufacturers. The Wi-Fi Alliance does product testing and certification for interoperability.

802.11 was defined as a protocol by the *Institute of Electrical and Electronics Engineers* (IEEE) in 1997. This protocol specification allowed for 1 and 2 Mbps transfer rates using the 2.4 GHz ISM (Industrial, Scientific, and Medical) band, which is open to unlicensed public use. Prior to the adoption of this standard, there were various wireless network vendors manufacturing proprietary equipment using both the 2.4 GHz and the 900 MHz bands. The early adopters of the proprietary technologies and 802.11 were primarily the manufacturing and health care industries, which rapidly benefited from their employees' mobile access to data. The 802.11 standard uses spread spectrum modulation to achieve high data rates. Two types of modulation were specified: Frequency Hopping and Direct Sequence. 802.11 also uses the *Carrier Sense Multiple Access* (CSMA), which was developed for Ethernet in 1975 with the addition of Collision Avoidance (CA)— referred to as CSMA-CA.

In 1999, the IEEE adopted two supplements to the 802.11 standard: 802.11a and 802.11b. The 802.11b standard is also referred to as High Rate DS and is an extension of the Direct Sequence Spread Spectrum type of modulation specified in 802.11. 802.11b uses 14 overlapping, staggered channels, each channel occupying 22 MHz of the spectrum. This standard's primary benefit is that it offers data rates of 5.5 and 11 Mbps in addition to the 12 megabits provided by 802.11. 802.11b has been widely adopted around the world, and its products have been readily available since 1999.

However, 802.11a products did not begin shipping until 2001. 802.11a utilizes a range in the 5 GHz frequency and operates with a theoretical maximum throughput of 54 Mbps. It provides for 12 nonoverlapping channels.

Products based on this protocol have not seen the adoption rate of 802.11b products for several reasons. At higher frequencies, more power is needed to transmit. The power of 802.11 radio types is limited; therefore, 802.11 and 802.11b have longer range transmission and reception characteristics than 802.11a. Because of its higher frequency, 802.11a is absorbed more readily by obstacles, reducing range and throughput.

In June of 2003, the IEEE ratified a third supplement to the 802.11 standard: 802.11g. This standard continues to operate in the 2.4 GHz band with backward compatibility to 802.11b, but it raises the theoretical maximum throughput to 54 Mbps. In early 2003, there were many products released prior to the ratification of the standard. The standard was delayed several times as the subcommittees in the IEEE worked out interoperability issues between 802.11b and 802.11g.

Operating Modes

There are two main client operating modes in the 802.11 family of standards: Infrastructure and Ad-Hoc. Two additional modes, Master and Monitor, are discussed in later chapters.

Infrastructure Mode requires the use of a wireless access point. At a minimum, this is a device with a radio that operates in Infrastructure Mode and has a connection to a wired network. This is also known as the Basic Service Set (BSS). There is also an Extended Service Set (ESS) for use with multiple access points.

A typical 802.11b access point consists of a radio, external antenna, and at least one Ethernet port. There are many variations on this theme, with models sporting 4-port Ethernet switches, connectors for other external antennas, and higher-power radios.

When operating in Infrastructure Mode, an access point is the master of any client radios that are associated with the access point. The client radios are also operating in Infrastructure Mode, in a different sub-mode. The access point is programmed with a *Service Set Identifier* (SSID); this is the network name for the access point. The access point broadcasts the SSID as an advertisement of the network name.

Clients operating in Infrastructure Mode identify an access point by these SSID broadcast frames. Once a client is associated with an access point, the access point manages all communication over the radio link. When multiple clients are associated with a single access point, the access point has a set of algorithms for controlling traffic to and from the access point radio.

Ad-Hoc Mode, or peer-to-peer mode, is designed specifically for client-to-client communication. To use Ad-Hoc Mode, you need at least two radio clients. In this example, let's say we have two Linux notebooks with PCM-CIA radio cards. Both cards are configured to work in Ad-Hoc Mode, and both clients must use the same SSID. Ad-Hoc clients do not advertise themselves with the same broadcast frames used by an access point.

While Ad-Hoc Mode is very useful for client-to-client communication, it introduces a difficult situation known as the *Hidden Node* problem. Ad-Hoc Mode does not provide an access point to control communications between other client machines, so any client using Ad-Hoc Mode may decide to transmit data on its own rather than being told when it is clear to transmit. Figure 1-7 illustrates the problem.

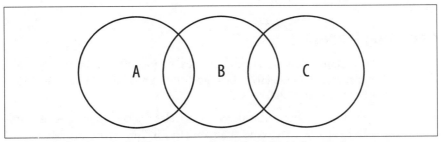

Figure 1-7. A Hidden Node problem with three clients in Ad-Hoc Mode

As shown, node A can hear node B, but it cannot hear node C. Node C can also hear node B, but it cannot hear node A. Because 802.11 is a shared-access physical medium, only one device can transmit at any given time. The Hidden Node problem is that node A and node C cannot hear each other, and neither node will detect a collision. Hidden Node issues reduce throughput in this example by at least 50%.

Wi-Fi Hardware

As discussed previously, to make a Wi-Fi network, you need a minimum of two radios, whether you operate in Ad-Hoc or Infrastructure Mode. For PC hardware, there are three physical types of radio interface cards available: PC Card, PCI, and MiniPCI.

Of the three, the PC Card is by far the most common, because notebook PCs are widely deployed, and most have at least one card slot; notebook users are the most common users of 802.11 networks.

MiniPCI cards are the up-and-coming form factor. Many notebook manufacturers have built MiniPCI cards into their motherboards, which enables you to install network cards without using a PC Card slot.

At one time, PCI cards were not as common as the other types of radios, but they are staging a comeback with new offerings from Linksys and D-Link. Many manufacturers, such as Linksys and D-Link, produce some PCI cards now, which actually consist of a MiniPCI or PCMCIA card on a larger PCI card.

There is a fourth option for a growing number of notebook and PDA users: built-in Wi-Fi. Intel is marketing their Centrino chipset that integrates an 802.11b radio on the motherboard, and most notebook manufacturers offer Centrino notebooks. Similarly, other CPU manufacturers such as Via will be integrating wireless into their chipsets. Finally, there are a number of notebook and PDA models that feature built-in radios. Sony, for example, sells a Vaio notebook with an Orinoco radio built in and also sells the Clie handheld PDAs with optional Wi-Fi.

As of this writing, more and more dual- and tri-mode cards are available. These cards allow you to access 802.11a/b/g networks with a single radio. The maker of a radio chipset decides the level of support—as of this writing, support for these cards is still in flux under Linux. We'll cover this in more detail in the next chapter.

Wireless access points are also available now in dual- and tri-mode. There is a wide range of access points on the market, which range from units geared specifically for home users with built-in firewalls, 4-port switches, and web-based configuration to models aimed at the corporate market with support for authentication protocols such as RADIUS and LDAP, the ability to run via *Power Over Ethernet* (POE), and connectors for external antennas.

Another category of access point is the "hotspot in a box." With the rising popularity of Wi-Fi hotspots in cafes, hotels, and airports, many manufacturers have developed access points that are an all-in-one solution. These boxes provide the radio and Ethernet of a normal access point, but also have some form of authentication and payment system, which range from a web-based login to a printed coupon that the store clerk delivers to the customer.

Antennas

Although a discussion of the physics of antennas is beyond the scope of this book, antennas are obviously a very important part of any radio. Depending on the type of antenna, radio coverage is narrowly focused or widely distributed, which makes a great deal of difference when building or connecting to 802.11 networks.

Briefly, antennas are transducers that convert radio frequency electric currents to electromagnetic waves that are then radiated into space. Antennas are *polarized* according to the plane of the electric field radiating from the antenna. A vertically polarized antenna has an electric field that is perpendicular to the Earth's surface. Likewise, the electric field of a horizontally polarized antenna is parallel with the Earth's surface.

There are several types of antennas used for Wi-Fi networks. The most common antenna is the *integrated* antenna, followed by *omnidirectional* and *directional* antennas

Integrated antennas

Most PC Card radios have integrated antennas inside the enclosure of the card. A typical integrated antenna design has two very small antennas—really just a solder trace or small piece of foil—located at right angles to each other for *diversity*. Diversity antennas are designed so that one antenna or the other is used to transmit and receive, but never at the same time. The card switches automatically between antennas to choose the stronger signal. The antennas are horizontally polarized, and this layout produces an antenna that has a somewhat omnidirectional pattern in a horizontal beam.

Omnidirectional antennas

If you have a radio card or access point with a single external antenna attached, you are likely looking at an omnidirectional, or *omni*, antenna. Omnidirectional antennas, as the name implies, are designed to send and receive signals 360 degrees around the antenna. Figure 1-8, which is a sample antenna gain pattern for a commercially produced omnidirectional antenna, shows that the 360-degree pattern is not circular at all. Notice that the antenna has pronounced gain at 0 and 180 degrees, but hardly any gain at 90 and 270 degrees.

While the theoretical beamwidth of an omnidirectional antenna is 360 degrees horizontally, the vertical beamwidth of most omni antennas is less than 8 degrees. See Figure 1-9 for a side view of a typical omni antenna. Notice that if the antenna were mounted high enough, someone directly under the antenna itself would have very poor signal quality.

Most omnidirectional antennas are of the "rubber ducky" type—a rubber- covered antenna, which ranges from a few inches long for a low-gain model to several feet for high-gain types.

Directional antennas

Although patch antennas are similar to sector antennas, they are considered directional antennas. Patch antennas generally have horizontal and vertical beamwidths that are similar. An example shown in Figure 1-10 shows the gain patterns for a patch antenna.

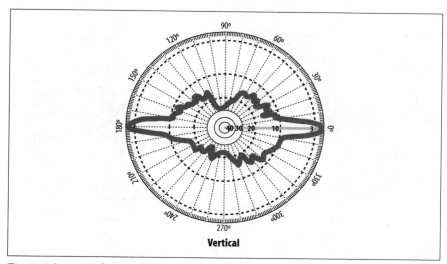

Figure 1-8. A sample omnidirectional antenna gain pattern

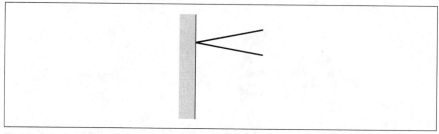

Figure 1-9. A side view of an omnidirectional antenna beamwidth

Yagi antennas are also directional antennas and are designed for highly directional applications. They typically have a beamwidth of less than 30 degrees; most of them look like a PVC pipe or a "Christmas tree" pointed at its target.

Finally, parabolic dish, or grid, antennas are the most highly directional antennas used in the 802.11 world. If you've seen a satellite dish, you've seen a parabolic dish antenna. These antenna types are suited for sending wireless network signals over several miles. As shown in Figure 1-11, the gain pattern is very tight.

Another antenna type widely used in outdoor applications is a sector antenna. These antennas are generally available with horizontal polarization and antenna patterns from 90 to 180 degrees. They are rectangular with a flat profile.

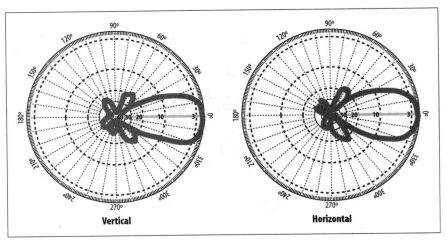

Figure 1-10. A sample patch antenna gain pattern

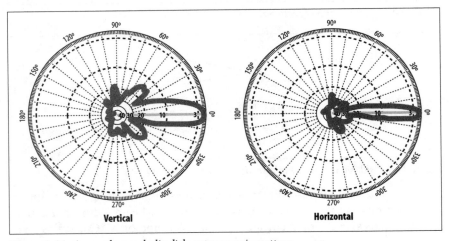

Figure 1-11. A sample parabolic dish antenna gain pattern

Bluetooth

Bluetooth is a low-power radio technology aimed at replacing cables for connecting devices. It was originally developed by the Swedish telecommunications manufacturer Ericsson and then formalized by an industry consortium.
The name is taken from a Danish king, Harald Bluetooth, who ruled Den-
mark and Norway in A.D. 936.

The standards for Bluetooth define a low-power radio with a maximum
range of 300 feet. The radios are actually on a transceiver microchip to keep

---

size and power consumption to a minimum. Bluetooth uses the 2.45 GHz band of the ISM radio spectrum and divides the band into 79 channels. To further reduce any crosstalk into other ISM bands, Bluetooth devices can change channels up to 1,600 times per second.

Bluetooth is becoming widely available on mobile phones and PDAs, and one of its "killer" applications is hands-free wireless headsets for mobile phones. Bluetooth is also a popular way to "tether" a notebook computer to a cellular phone, which allows you to connect to the Internet even when an 802.11 network is not available (because current cellular data speeds are much slower than Bluetooth, Bluetooth's relatively slow speeds are not the limiting factor). Bluetooth adapters are available for PDAs, desktops, and notebooks. There are some printers and keyboards available that use Bluetooth to communicate with the host device as well.

Compared to Wi-Fi, Bluetooth speeds are not impressive, but they are quite useful for transferring small amounts of data. Download speeds can max out at 720 kbps with a simultaneous upload speed of 56 kbps. Every Bluetooth device can simultaneously maintain up to seven connections, making a personal Bluetooth LAN a real possibility.

Cellular Data

With the rise of digital cellular phone networks, it became possible to use these networks to transfer data rather than just voice. There are several differing and competing technologies available.

Cellular Digital Packet Data (CDPD) was one of the first data networking technologies available for mobile phones. CDPD utilizes unused bandwidth in the 800–900 MHz range normally used by mobile phones. Data transfer rates max out at a theoretical 19.2 kbps. Today, CDPD is obsolete, and cellular carriers are actively trying to phase it out.

General Packet Radio Service (GPRS) is an add-on technology to existing Time Division Multiple Access (TDMA)–based GSM mobile phone networks. Timeslots in the GSM network are normally allocated to create a circuit-switched voice connection. With a GPRS-enabled network, the timeslots are used for packet data as needed. This by design creates a very slow data network with high latency and, theoretically, the speed of a 56 kbps modem. AT&T Wireless, T-Mobile, and Cingular Wireless use this technology. In 2003, an enhancement to GPRS, Enhanced Data Rates for Global Evolution (EDGE), was partially rolled out in the United States by AT&T Wireless and Cingular. In theory, EDGE can triple the data rate of GPRS, but you need an EDGE-capable handset, such as the Nokia 6200, to use it.

1xRTT stands for Single Carrier Radio Transmission Technology and is part of the CDMA2000 family of protocols, which includes successors to 1xRTT such as Single Carrier Evolution Data Only (1xEV-DO). It is built on top of the CDMA-based mobile phone networks and allows for ISDN-like data transfer speeds up to 144 kbps (1xEV-DO is capable of much higher speeds). Sprint's PCS Vision and Verizon's Express Network use this technology. As of this writing, Verizon Wireless is experimenting with 1xEV-DO in two U.S. markets, with testers obtaining data rates between 500 and 800 kbps.

Infrared

The electromagnetic (EM) spectrum contains many different wavelengths of which the RF spectrum is a small part. Another part of the EM spectrum is infrared light. This light has a longer wavelength than visible light, but a much shorter wavelength than radio or microwave radiation. Infrared is usually linked to body or mechanical heat, as many objects above room temperature emit infrared radiation. These emissions can be seen by night vision equipment.

Infrared is used in television remote controls, because the signal does not interfere with the TV transmission. Remote controls and Infrared Data (IrDA) equipment utilize light-emitting diodes to emit infrared radiation that is then focused by a lens into a narrow beam. The beam is modulated on and off to encode the data transmission.

The IrDA Association publishes specifications that are used by PDA, notebook, and mobile phone device manufacturers for the infrared ports on their devices. IrDA devices typically have a maximum throughput of 4 Mbps. While most mobile devices still have IrDA, many manufacturers are replacing these with Bluetooth.

## CHAPTER 2

Wi-Fi on Your Linux Box

Wireless support on Linux has come a long way. With modern Linux distributions, you may not need to recompile your kernel to receive support for your Wi-Fi card. You probably won't need to install driver software or even touch a command line. However, this isn't always the case, especially as new cards come on the market, so you should still have a good understanding of how Wi-Fi works under Linux. This chapter starts out with an explanation of what you need to do with some common distributions and a common radio card, and then gets into the details you need to know to take things a little further, including radio chipsets, drivers, kernel compilation, the PCM-CIA subsystem, and the Linux wireless tools.

Quick Start

If you haven't purchased a Wi-Fi card yet, and are happy with 802.11b (about 5.5 Mbps real-world speed versus about 20 for 802.11a or g), pick up either a Lucent/Agere/Avaya/Proxim Orinoco Silver or Orinoco Gold (see "Lucent WaveLan/Orinoco" later in this chapter). If you've purchased a different card, it may work out of the box with Linux. But if it doesn't, the rest of this chapter describes chipsets and drivers in enough detail for you to find your way. Unfortunately, the orinoco_cs driver does not support monitor mode, which passive monitoring tools such as Kismet require. See Chapter 3 for information on monitor mode and available patches for orinoco_cs. If you want to use monitor mode with an unpatched driver, we suggest that you use a Prism or Atheros-based card.

When you install Linux for the first time, load the modules for *all* the built-in network interfaces, especially any wired Ethernet adapters you might use in the future to avoid a particular situation where your Wi-Fi card is assigned and configured as eth0 during installation, but the system later detects the onboard Ethernet and assigns it to eth0 (bumping up your Wi-Fi adapter to eth1 and messing up the configuration files that think eth0 is your Wi-Fi adapter).

You must install the wireless tools package, which is described in "Installing the Wireless Tools" later in this chapter. The name of this package in all the Linux distributions in the following list is *wireless-tools*.

We tested the Proxim Orinoco Classic Gold (pictured in Figure 2-1) with several Linux distributions on an IBM ThinkPad A20m with onboard Ethernet (eth0), and this is what we found:

Debian 3.0r1
> We used disk 5 (kernel 2.4.18-bf2.4) to boot the installer and installed the base system using disk 1. During installation, the card was recognized and configured properly using orinoco_cs and the eth1 adapter.

SuSE 9.0
> We used the free download version of SuSE 9.0 and installed everything over FTP. The installer did not automatically detect the card, so we had to use wired Ethernet for the installation. However, when we booted the system for the first time, SuSE found the card and configured it automatically using the orinoco_cs driver as wlan0 (the default for orinoco_cs would be to use eth1).

Mandrake 9.2
> The card was automatically detected during installation. We configured it by clicking Configure under Network & Internet when the installer reached the summary screen. Mandrake offers advanced options, including SSID (WIRELESS_ESSID) and WEP key (WIRELESS_ENC_KEY). Mandrake used orinoco_cs and the eth1 adapter for this card.

RedHat 9
> The RedHat installer detected the card using the orinoco_cs driver and set up the card as eth1. However, the card was not configured correctly on first boot. We edited */etc/sysconfig/network-scripts/ifcfg-eth1* and set ONBOOT to no, which corrected the problem. (Linux should always defer configuration of PCMCIA adapters until the *pcmcia rc* script runs.)

Gentoo 1.4
> We performed a stage 3 install of Gentoo. After booting the installer, we tried to start PCMCIA with */etc/init.d/pcmcia start*, but it insisted on

loading the prism2_cs driver, which did not work at all. However, after we installed Gentoo, built a kernel with genkernel, and rebooted, Gentoo correctly loaded the orinoco_cs driver (which saw the card as eth1).

Figure 2-1. The Orinoco Classic Gold card

 If you're connecting to a network that uses WEP or one that doesn't broadcast its SSID, you may need to use the wireless tools, described later in this chapter, after installation is complete. However, if the Linux distribution supports advanced options (as does Mandrake 9.2), you should be able to connect to the network during the initial installation. For more information on using WEP with Linux, see Chapter 4.

Chipset Compatibility

While there are many vendors selling Wi-Fi hardware, the radio chipsets come from a relatively small set of manufacturers. With a few exceptions, radio chipset support under Linux is quite good, and getting better.

Before getting into the nuts and bolts of radio chipsets, there is one online resource that you absolutely need. Jean Tourrilhes at Hewlett Packard is the author of the Linux Wireless Tools (covered later in this chapter). He also maintains an extensive web page that includes the Wireless LAN How-To. The page is located at *http://www.hpl.hp.com/personal/Jean_Tourrilhes/index.html*.

For information regarding a specific radio chipset and driver support in Linux, look on the Devices & Drivers page: *http://www.hpl.hp.com/personal/Jean_Tourrilhes/Linux/Linux.Wireless.drivers.html*. The page is updated frequently and has extensive information on many esoteric wireless devices and drivers.

Common Chipsets

Although there are probably less than 50 manufacturers of Wi-Fi radio chipsets, this book simply does not have the space to cover each of these manufacturers in detail. We cover the five most popular manufacturers and their chipsets, which, in reality, produce 80% of all 802.11 hardware.

Intersil Prism II

Before it became a part of Intersil, a company called Harris developed the Prism I reference standard for 802.11, based on an AMD AM930 processor core. This chipset is 802.11 only, so we won't cover any details of driver support, but they are available on Jean Tourrilhes' web site, listed in the previous section.

At one point, Prism II has been the most widely available and popular 802.11b radio chipset. Intersil licensed the chipset and reference designs for Prism II to a large number of vendors. A partial list of vendors using Prism II radios in their access points, PCMCIA cards, PCI cards, USB adapters, and Compact Flash (CF) cards includes:

- Compaq
- Nokia
- Proxim
- D-Link
- Linksys
- Netgear
- SMC
- Senao/Engenius

Nearly all of these vendors have products using other radio chipsets. Unfortunately, many products have kept the same name and sometimes even the same part number, while changing the underlying radio chipset. A good case in point: the D-Link DWL-650. This radio card initially shipped with a Prism II chipset and was very popular, because it worked in a Linux box. However, D-Link changed chipsets when it released the DWL-650 Version 2, choosing an ADMtek chipset. It is very difficult to tell from the packaging which version of the DWL-650 you are purchasing.

Although you have a very good chance of finding an 802.11b radio card that uses a Prism II chipset, there is no guarantee that the chipset is inside your card. This applies to every other card manufacturer as well. Once you've decided on a radio card, research online to make sure you know which chipset it uses.

Several manufacturers licensed the Prism II reference design from Intersil and based their products around this design. These manufacturers include Lucent, Symbol, and Aironet/Cisco. However, the radios designed by these manufacturers use different firmware and are not compatible with Prism II drivers, although some cards may appear to work: the driver will load, but the card may function only partially or not at all.

Lucent WaveLan/Orinoco

The original Lucent WaveLan radios developed at AT&T (before Lucent was spun off as a separate company) were 900 MHz radios, later followed by 2.4 GHz radios in the Industrial, Scientific, and Medical (ISM) band. These cards used an Ethernet MAC chip onboard, rather than a MAC chip that met standard 802.11 specifications.

The history of WaveLan is of name changes, mergers, and acquisitions. Lucent released a newer version of the card, the WaveLan IEEE, which met the 802.11 specifications, and then later upgraded the card to support 802.11b (based on the Prism II reference design, discussed previously). Not too long afterward, the WaveLan brand was renamed to Orinoco. Lucent then spun off this part of its company into a separate company named Agere. Another Lucent spin-off called Avaya also sells radio cards using the Orinoco chipset. Most recently the end unit sales of Orinoco have been acquired by Proxim, while Agere still manufactures the radio chipsets.

Lucent/Agere was one of the few vendors not only to manufacture the radio chipset, but to sell end-user equipment in the form of radio cards and access points.

In addition to the Lucent, Agere, and Avaya brands, which use the Orinoco chipset, the Apple AirPort line of products is based on the WaveLan IEEE chipset but is not compatible with Linux drivers for Orinoco. Other vendors that sell radios using the Orinoco chipset include Enterasys, Elsa, Buffalo, HP, IBM, Dell, Sony, and Compaq. Again, many of these vendors also produce radios using chipsets from other manufacturers.

Aironet/Cisco

The original Aironet radios were similar to the original Lucent WaveLan: they started at 900 MHz and then moved to 2.4 GHz. Again, they were not initially compatible with the 802.11 standard. Aironet produced the 4500 (802.11) and 4800 (802.11b) series of radios, based on the Harris Prism chipset, but with proprietary firmware.

The story of Aironet is also one of acquisition: Cisco purchased Aironet in March of 2000. Prior to the purchase, Aironet had released the 4800B family of radio cards, including ISA, PCI, and PCMCIA versions, based on the Intersil Prism II chipset. These radios were renamed as the Cisco 340 series of cards. Cisco has since released the 350 series of radio cards that feature 100 mW of transmit power (as opposed to the 30 mW offered by the majority of radios). The 350 family also includes a MiniPCI form factor radio card.

 The majority of consumer Wi-Fi radio cards have radios that feature 30 mW of transmit power. Notable exceptions to this are the Cisco 350 cards, the Senao/EnGenius 100 and 200 mW cards, similar 100/200 mW cards from Zcomax, and a few models from D-Link.

Symbol

Symbol developed frequency-hopping radios in the 2.4 GHz band called Spectrum24. In a slight twist, Symbol made sure its products were 802.11-compliant from the beginning. Symbol came somewhat late to the 802.11b market, but it released a new line called Spectrum24 High-Rate. Again, these cards are based on the Intersil Prism II chipset with custom firmware. Both 3Com and Intel sell OEM versions of these cards.

Symbol sells mostly PCMCIA cards but also offers a PCI card. Symbol main strength is integrated products—it offers PDAs with built-in wireless and barcode readers for industrial, medical, and manufacturing applications. Symbol also has one of the few CF implementations of 802.11b. Versions of these cards are also available and sold as an OEM package by Socket Communications.

Atmel

Atmel was the first to market a USB 802.11b chipset. However, that chipset did not include a radio, so various radios can be used with this chipset, including the Intersil Prism II radios. Linksys and D-Link both sell USB radio adapters based on the Intersil chipset. SMC and 3Com both sell PCMCIA cards using the Atmel chipset.

Atheros

Atheros is unique in that its chipsets are not based on the Intersil Prism II reference designs. It was the first to market 802.11a chipsets. For quite some time, any 802.11a radios available for purchase were built using the Atheros chipset. Atheros has since introduced dual-mode 802.11a/b radios with its ar5211 chipset and tri-mode a/b/g radios using their ar5212 chipset.

Proxim, SMC, Linksys, and D-Link all sell 802.11a, as well as dual- and tri-mode radio products using the Atheros chipset. The primary form factors are PCMCIA and MiniPCI. Linksys and D-Link both sell PCI dual- and tri-mode radios; however, they consist of a PCI card with a MiniPCI radio onboard.

Broadcom

Broadcom has both 802.11b and 802.11g radio chipsets. It has completely ignored the Linux community despite the many references to Linux on its web pages. No Linux drivers are available for Broadcom radio cards as of this writing. Cards based on the Broadcom 802.11b chipset include the Dell TrueMobile 1180 and the Linksys WMP11 (previous versions of this card used the Intersil Prism II chipset). Cards based on the Broadcom 802.11g chipset include the Linksys WPC54G and WMP54G.

Determining Your Radio Chipset

As previously discussed, determining the chipset your radio uses can be difficult, because many equipment vendors use chipsets from several different manufacturers. An excellent example is Linksys. Its 802.11b PCMCIA cards use the Prism II chipset. However, the Linksys USB 802.11b adapters use the Atmel chipset, while its 802.11g PCMCIA cards use a Broadcom chipset, and its dual-mode 802.11a/802.11g PCMCIA and PCI cards use the Atheros chipset. The bottom line is that you should determine your card chipset type before installing drivers.

To determine the chipset of a radio card, refer to the following methods:

- If your radio card is PCMCIA or Cardbus, and you have the pcmcia-cs package installed, or are using the kernel tree PCMCIA, use the `cardctl ident` command. This shows vendor identification strings for the cards that are currently inserted in the PCMCIA slots. This works regardless of whether you have a driver loaded for the card. Here is an example output of the command on a system with two Orinoco cards:

  ```
  # cardctl ident
  Socket 0:
  ```

Linux, Driver Support, and the GPL

There are a few fronts on which the proprietary approach of a few hardware vendors clashes with the spirit of the Linux community.

Companies that manufacture many of the unsupported Wi-Fi cards refuse to divulge enough information on their radios and firmware for the open source community to effectively build drivers.

Also, there are a number of drivers available that are available only in binary form. The company that manufactures the radio chipset releases most of these drivers. The madwifi driver for the Atheros chipsets, developed by Sam Leffler with the cooperation of Atheros, is a good example. The original driver was developed for BSD but wasn't released, because the Atheros hardware does not enforce valid operating modes that comply with FCC regulations.

As a solution, Atheros developed a *Hardware Abstraction Layer* (HAL), in binary form, that sits between the hardware and the driver and regulates the hardware to meet FCC requirements. Unfortunately, the binary HAL is available only for i386 architecture, and source is not available.

As such, the madwifi driver is viewed in the open source community as a "black sheep" project, and many people refuse to use the driver, because a large portion of it does not have source publicly available. There is a completely open source driver for the Atheros chipsets under development; see the "madwifi" section later in this chapter.

Finally, there are issues with some vendors that have released products based on Linux and other open source software products. The open source community has made recent discoveries that show that some vendors appear to be violating the GNU General Public License under which the operating system and tools software were published. As of this writing, this is an unresolved matter.

```
        product info: "Lucent Technologies", "WaveLAN/IEEE", "Version 01.01",
        ""
      manfid: 0x0156, 0x0002
      function: 6 (network)
    Socket 1:
      product info: "Lucent Technologies", "WaveLAN/IEEE", "Version 01.01",
      ""
      manfid: 0x0156, 0x0002
      function: 6 (network)
```

Here is an example output of the command on a system with a single Senao Prism II–based card:

```
# cardctl ident
Socket 0:
  product info: "INTERSIL", "HFA384x/IEEE", "Version 01.02", ""
  manfid: 0x0156, 0x0002
  function: 6 (network)
```

- If your radio card is PCI, use the command `lspci -v` to show the vendor identification string. Bear in mind that this command shows you all of the devices on your PCI bus, so for some systems this may return a list several pages long.

- If your radio card is USB, you can usually find the vendor identification strings for any USB device by using the `dmesg` command to show output generated during the boot process. You might also find the same information in */var/log/messages*.

These commands usually let you know the manufacturer of the chipset. However, some manufacturers have obfuscated their vendor identification strings, so you still may not find a valid chipset ID.

An excellent resource that is published on the pages of the wlan-ng driver is the WLAN Adapter Chipset Directory (*http://www.linux-wlan.org/docs/wlan_adapters.html*). This is compiled and updated regularly by the maintainers of wlan-ng, AbsoluteValue Systems, Inc.

All radio devices are required to have the FCC ID printed on them. A final option is to get the FCC ID from your radio card and look it up on the FCC web site (*http://www.fcc.gov/oet/fccid*). Using this web site, the FCC ID NI3-SL-2011CD from the back of a Senao 100 mW 802.11b card returned a single entry for Senao in Taiwan. If you select this entry by choosing the link for Detail, you are again presented with a number of documents provided to the FCC by the manufacturer. In this particular case, select a PDF document titled "Operational Description," which reads:

> The SL-2011CD WLAN PC Card utilize the Intersil Prism II Direct Sequence Spread Spectrum Wireless Transceiver chip set.

Four Steps to Wi-Fi

To use a Wi-Fi card on your Linux system, you need several things:

- The correct driver software for your Wi-Fi card
- The Linux Wireless Tools software
- If your system uses a PC Card interface for the Wi-Fi card, the pcmcia-cs software package must be installed and configured **OR**
- Your kernel must have kernel PCMCIA support compiled in. You may need to recompile your kernel, depending on your system and distribution.

If you installed your Linux distribution on a notebook or laptop, there's a good chance that you already have at least part of the necessary packages to make a configured and operational Wi-Fi network card. Current versions of Red Hat, Debian, and SuSE with 2.4 kernels all include a "notebook" option during the installation process that installs kernel PCMCIA support.

You have two options for PCMCIA support in Linux: the pcmcia-cs package or kernel PCMCIA support. All 2.4.x distributions of the Linux kernel include the option for compiling in PCMCIA support, which removes the need for the external pcmcia-cs package. However, there are some valid reasons to use the pcmcia-cs package rather than the kernel PCMCIA support, which we discuss later in this section.

Kernel PCMCIA support is based on the pcmcia-cs package. The pcmcia-cs README for Version 2.4 kernels, found at *http://pcmcia-cs.sourceforge.net/ftp/README-2.4*, has several good questions on this topic:

> Q: Are these two versions of PCMCIA both going to continue with active development?
>
> A: The kernel PCMCIA subsystem should be the focus for ongoing development. The standalone pcmcia-cs drivers are still being maintained but the focus has shifted from adding functionality, towards mainly bug fixes.
>
> Q: Which should I use / which is better? The kernel PCMCIA, or the standalone PCMCIA?
>
> A: It rarely matters. The client drivers should generally behave the same. At this point, most current distributions use the kernel PCMCIA subsystem, and I recommend sticking with that unless you have a particular need that is only met by the standalone drivers.

Your Linux distribution may not install the Linux Wireless Tools or the pcmcia-cs packages by default. You must select these packages during the installation process or add them at a later time.

    You don't need to install both kernel PCMCIA and pcmcia-cs.

The same is true for many wireless drivers. Most current Linux distributions give you drivers for some common Wi-Fi cards, including the orinoco_cs driver for Lucent WaveLan/Orinoco cards. However, if you need the hostap, wlan-ng, or madwifi drivers, you must install these from source, or optionally from a binary package that a third party has made available.

Linux Wi-Fi Drivers

We can't cover all Wi-Fi radio cards, their features, and the available drivers for them. We'll discuss several of them briefly and cover the four most useful drivers for Linux in more detail at the end of this chapter:

Hermes AP

Hermes AP is a patched version of the orinoco_cs driver that allows you to use the "tertiary" code available for Orinoco cards, which allows them to act as an access point. You can find the driver at *http://hunz.org/hermesap.html*.

hostap_cs

This is a driver for Prism II cards but with a few features not found in other drivers. You can find the driver at *http://hostap.epitest.fi*. See "hostap_cs" later in this chapter.

madwifi

This driver supports the Atheros 802.11a/b/g radio cards. You can find this driver at *http://sourceforge.net/projects/madwifi*. See "madwifi" later in this chapter.

orinoco_cs

This driver supports Lucent WaveLAN IEEE, Lucent Orinoco, Symbol Spectrum 24, and Apple AirPort (but not AirPort Extreme) cards, and is included with most recent Linux distributions. This driver also supports Prism II cards, but most features of the Prism II chipset are not supported. You can download the driver from *http://www.hpl.hp.com/personal/Jean_Tourrilhes/Linux/Orinoco.html*. See "orinoco_cs" later in this chapter.

prism54

The prism54 driver supports cards based on Prism GT, Prism Duette, and Prism Indigo chipsets. You can find this driver at *http://prism54.org/*.

wlan-ng

This is another Prism II driver. It does not support the wireless-tools package, but it does come with its own utilities. You can download the driver from *http://www.linux-wlan.org/*. See "wlan-ng" later in this chapter.

Configuring and Compiling Your Kernel

There are a number of reasons why you should consider compiling your own Linux kernel from source:

- Many drivers require certain features to be compiled into the kernel that are not available in stock distribution kernels. For example, the madwifi driver requires not only radio support and the wireless tools, but also PCI Hotplug and ACPI support, which must be compiled into the kernel.

- Other drivers, while not requiring experimental kernel features, still require a configured kernel source. A *.config* file must exist in the root of your kernel source and must be the file that was used to configure and compile your running kernel. Some Linux distributions do not include this file, which makes it difficult for you to install kernel drivers.

- You should know how to compile a Linux kernel. If you have used Linux for any length of time, or if you plan to, kernel compilation teaches you a great deal about Linux.

Compiling the Linux kernel from source is not a trivial undertaking. While you don't need prior experience building system-level software, you do need a basic understanding of Linux filesystems, editors, and other concepts. See the following resources for some good basic Linux backgrounders:

- The Linux Kernel HOWTO, part of the Linux Documentation Project (*http://www.linux.org/docs/ldp/howto/Kernel-HOWTO/index.html*)
- *Running Linux*, Fourth Edition (O'Reilly)
- *Understanding the Linux Kernel*, Second Edition (O'Reilly)

To configure and compile a Linux kernel, you must obtain the following items:

- A working Linux system
- The correct compiler, libraries and tools
- The kernel source

A working Linux system should be fairly modern if you are planning on compiling modern kernel code. For instance, do not attempt to compile a 2.4 kernel tree using a Linux system based on a 2.0 or prior kernel. Any recent distribution of Linux should have the kernel version and tools necessary for compiling your own kernel.

In each kernel release, the README file in the kernel source specifies the version of the gcc compiler needed to compile successfully. For example, the README for kernel 2.4.22 states:

> Make sure you have gcc 2.94.3 available. gcc 2.91.66 (ecgs-1.1.2) may also work but is not as safe, and gcc 2.7.2.3 is no longer supported.
>
> Compiling and running the 2.4.xx kernels requires up-to-date versions of various software packages. Consult /Documentation/Changes for the minimum version numbers required and how to get updates for these packages.

The Changes document goes into great detail on versions of software, including gcc, that are required for successful compilation of the kernel source. Make sure your system has the correct versions of the tools specified. Failure to do so may mean that your new kernel will not compile, or that bugs will be introduced into your kernel.

Kernel source can be obtained from many places. The major distributions include kernel source in package format—RPMs, Debian packages for apt-get, or dpkg. Other kernel source RPMs built by third parties can be found at *http://www.rpmfind.net*. The ultimate repository for all Linux kernels is kernel.org, accessible via FTP or HTTP. Here you can find source for any kernel version you want, all the way back to the 1.0 kernel from 1994.

The latest stable kernel is Version 2.4.23, and it can be downloaded directly by using this URL: *http://www.kernel.org/pub/linux/kernel/v2.4/linux-2.4. 23.tar.bz2.* You'll want to save this compressed file in */usr/src.*

To find the latest kernel source, look in the major/minor version subdirectory (such as *v2.4*) for a file starting with LATEST-IS. For example, a file named *LATEST-IS-2.4.23* tells you that kernel 2.4.23 is the most recent. Unless you are aware of a specific problem with the latest kernel version, you should always use the most recent one.

We'll walk through a compile of the 2.4.23 kernel for a Debian Linux system running on a Dell laptop. Obviously, this only scratches the surface of kernel compilation. This book doesn't have the space to cover multiple versions of kernels, much less cover what it takes to compile on other specific systems. One good resource for information is the Kernel HOWTO listed earlier. Another is the linux-kernel mailing list, located at *http://www.tux.org/ lkml/.* This page has a very extensive questions section, where many common kernel answers are given.

Off to the races

Assuming that you have obtained the 2.4.23 kernel source from *www.kernel. org,* you'll want to uncompress the file and change into the working source directory (these instructions will work with later versions of the 2.4 kernel):

```
# tar xjvf linux-2.4.23.tar.bz2
# cd linux-2.4.23
```

If you want to save the original *.config* file from the source, you should back it up (if you obtained your kernel source from a tarball at kernel.org, this file won't exist):

```
# cp .config .config-original
```

If you have done anything in this directory other than the three commands listed previously, it's a good idea to run a couple of cleanup commands. These commands clean out all sorts of things that might have been compiled or configured in ways that you don't want:

```
# make clean
# make mrproper
```

At this point, you have four options for configuring your kernel before compilation.

Manual editing of the .config file

Not recommended unless you are a serious kernel hacker, and you know *exactly* what you're doing.

make config

This is a command-line interface that walks you through *every* possible config option, one at a time. It is very time consuming and very unfriendly. When you enter this command, you see something such as this on the screen:

```
rm -f include/asm
( cd include ; ln -sf asm-i386 asm)
/bin/sh scripts/Configure arch/i386/config.in
#
# Using defaults found in .config
#
*
* Code maturity level options
*
Prompt for development and/or incomplete code/drivers (CONFIG_
EXPERIMENTAL) [Y/n/?]
```

You must answer each and every question the script asks you in order to generate a valid *.config* file.

make menuconfig

This is a command-line menu interface that relies on the ncurses library to generate a menu-based configuration editor. It is a much more friendly interface than the preceding options. Here, instead of answering a question about each and every single possible kernel feature, you are presented with a hierarchical menu that breaks things down into sections. Figure 2-2 shows the main menu you obtain from running make menuconfig.

make xconfig

As the name implies, this is an X-Windows interface for the config process. You must be running some flavor of X-Windows to use this option. For most Linux users, this is Gnome or KDE. make xconfig produces a GUI window, as shown in Figure 2-3.

For most users, make menuconfig or make xconfig are going to be the most friendly. This book assumes that you have chosen one of these options. Every option in the following list that you pick is from a menu in make menuconfig or make xconfig.

The following list presents a number of options that you must choose to successfully compile your kernel for wireless connectivity. Note that there are many other options that must be selected to compile a kernel for your system, but they are not covered here. There are three options you can select: Y for yes, M for module, and N for no:

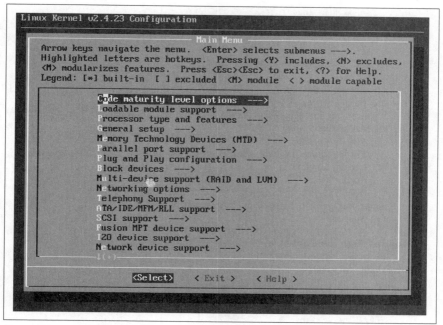

Figure 2-2. Initial menu from make menuconfig

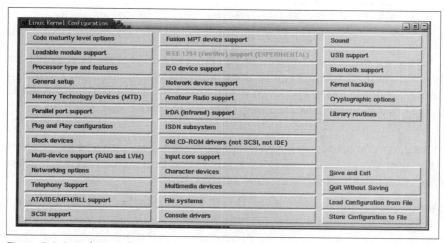

Figure 2-3. Initial menu from make xconfig

Code maturity level options
    Prompt for development and/or incomplete code/drivers: Y
Loadable Module Support
    Enable loadable module support: Y
    Set version information on all module symbols: Y

```
       Kernel module loader: Y
```
Processor type and features
```
    It is vitally important that you select your correct processor type
    in this option.  Otherwise your kernel will not be compiled properly
    and will definitely not boot.
```
General Setup
```
    Networking support: Y
    PCI Support (for PCI or CardBus wireless cards): Y
    Support for hot-pluggable devices (for PCMCIA, CardBus or USB support) Y
```
PCMCIA/CardBus support
```
        PCMCIA/CardBus support: Y
        CardBus support (if required for your setup): Y
```
PCI Hotplug Support
```
        Support for PCI Hotplug (required for madwifi driver): Y
        ACPI PCI Hotplug driver (required for madwifi driver): M
```
Power Management Support (required for ACPI): Y
ACPI Support
```
        ACPI Support (required for madwifi driver): Y
```
Plug and Play configuration
```
    Plug and Play support: Y
```
Networking options
```
    Packet socket: Y
    Socket filtering: Y
    Unix domain sockets: Y
    TCP/IP networking: Y
```
Network device support
```
    Network device support: Y
    Wireless LAN (non-hamradio): Y
        In this section you will want to choose a wireless
        driver for your card, if it is listed here.
```

Once you have selected these options (and any other options required for
your particular system), you're done with the config. You can choose to
Store Configuration to File if you would like to write this particular config to
a file other than the default .config. Otherwise, choose Save and Exit, which
writes your options to the .config file.

Your next step is to issue the make dep command. This runs a *Makefile* script
that compiles any dependencies required for your kernel. Depending on
your system, this likely takes a few minutes.

You're now ready to compile the kernel! This is done with the make bzImage
command. This takes quite some time.

Next, because you have selected the Loadable Modules section, you must
compile all of the modules by issuing the make modules command. On some
systems, depending on the number of modules you chose to build, this command may take more time than compiling the kernel.

Finally, you must install the modules you have just compiled. This is accomplished by the make modules_install command.

If you encounter errors during the compile process, note the specific error and the directory in which it occurred. Execute the make clean command. Go back into make xconfig and find the area corresponding to the directory where the compile failed. Examine the options you chose very carefully. Did you choose a kernel option or module that is not on your system? Did you choose an option that is labeled as EXPERIMENTAL? You may wish to alter your choices. While the menu makes choosing kernel options very easy, it does not give you advice on which options to choose. You may have to experiment with the settings until you get a successful compile.

Once you have compiled the bzImage and the modules, you are ready. Now, you must copy the *bzImage* file that was compiled to your */boot* directory. Many distributions use the filename of *vmlinuz* for this purpose, but you can call the file anything you want. The path below obviously varies depending on your system architecture. The following example is from kernel 2.4.23 compiled for i386:

```
# cp /usr/src/linux/arch/i386/boot/vmlinuz-2.4.23 /boot/
```

One last thing must be done: configure your boot loader program so that it recognizes your new kernel. The two most common boot loaders are GRUB and LILO. LILO is the older of the two, but it is still widely used. We assume that you are using LILO. For more information on configuring GRUB, see the GNU software pages at *http://www.gnu.org/software/grub*.

To configure LILO for your new kernel, edit the */etc/lilo.conf* file. A typical *lilo.conf* is shown here:

```
lba32
boot=/dev/hda
root=/dev/hda3
install=boot/boot-menu.b
map=/boot/map
delay=20
prompt
timeout=150
vga=normal
default=Linux
image=/boot/vmlinuz-2.4.23
    label=Linux
    read-only
image=/boot/vmlinuz-2.4.18
    label=Old Kernel
    read-only
```

The key pieces are at the end. This example uses default=Linux, the label associated with the image for kernel 2.4.23, which you have just built and copied to */boot*. Leave the old kernel image in the configuration file. This is very important, because it gives you a rescue option if your new kernel image does not boot or has errors.

To activate this *lilo.conf*, run LILO and specify the configuration file:

```
#lilo -C /etc/lilo.conf
Added Linux *
Added Old Kernel
```

You are now ready to reboot your system and boot into the new kernel that you just compiled.

Building and Configuring the pcmcia-cs Subsystem

As mentioned previously, you have two options for PCMCIA support. You can select PCMCIA/CardBus support when you compile your kernel, or you can build the pcmcia-cs subsystem from scratch.

The pcmcia-cs software package, available from *http://pcmcia-cs.sourceforge. net*, is the basis for the kernel PCMCIA support. Going forward into the 2.6 kernels, it appears that all new development will be on the kernel tree PCM-CIA. However, as of this writing and the 2.4.23 kernel, the pcmcia-cs version of 3.25 has newer utilities and drivers than the ones in the kernel PCMCIA. It is mainly for this reason that you will want to compile pcmcia-cs from source.

 If you compile your kernel with PCMCIA/CardBus support, you do not need to install the pcmcia-cs package from source. However, if you want the latest versions of the PCM-CIA utilities, you can install this package without interfering with kernel support for PCMCIA/CardBus. For more information, see "2.4 kernels and kernel tree PCMCIA" later in this chapter.

Once again, to compile kernel modules from source, you need the configured kernel source for your kernel. This generally means that you have configured and compiled your own Linux kernel. While it is certainly possible to compile kernel modules against Linux kernels provided by a stock distribution, it can be tricky. For more on compiling your own kernel, see the previous section "Configuring and Compiling Your Kernel."

There are a number of kernel options that may need to be enabled, depending on how you use the PCMCIA devices. Because many of these options pertain to wired network cards, SCSI and IDE adapters, we do not cover them here. However, if you do plan to use 16-bit PCMCIA (non-CardBus cards), you must enable CONFIG_ISA. This option can be found in the General Setup portion of make menuconfig or make xconfig as part of your kernel configuration.

To begin compiling the package, download the *pcmcia-cs.3.2.5.tar.gz* file into the */usr/src* directory. Unpack the *tar.gz* file and change into the top-level directory (if a later version is available, you should use that):

```
# tar xzvf pcmcia-cs.3.2.5.tgz
# cd pcmcia-cs.3.2.5
```

You must configure the package before compilation and make a few decisions on what kind of PCMCIA support you need. In most cases, you can accept the defaults on all of the config questions.

The kernel source directory defaults to */usr/src/linux*. If your kernel source is located in */usr/src/kernel-2.4.23*, you must enter that here:

```
# make config
Linux kernel source directory?
```

Next, you can choose whether to allow non-root users to modify PCMCIA card configurations. The default answer is no, which does not allow any non-root users to suspend, resume, or reset cards, or to change the PCMCIA configuration scheme. Answering yes allows non-root users all these privileges.

```
Build 'trusting' versions of card utilities?
```

In most cases, you want to enable CardBus support. Unless you plan only to use 16-bit 802.11 and 802.11b PCMCIA cards, CardBus is required for 802.11a and 802.11g PC Cards.

```
Include 32-bit (CardBus) card support?
```

This option inserts extra code into the PCMCIA subsystem, which allows it to check with a system's BIOS to obtain resource information on a motherboard's devices to help avoid resource conflicts. It can cause problems on some laptops, so this option is not enabled by default.

```
Include PnP BIOS resource checking?
```

Unless you are installing modules in an alternate directory for some reason, this should be the subdirectory of */lib/modules* that matches your kernel. In this case, the subdirectory is */lib/modules/2.4.23*.

```
Module install directory?
```

Once you've answered the questions and config has finished, you should run the following commands to build and then install the kernel modules and utility programs:

```
# make all
# make install
```

Once installed, the kernel modules will be located in */lib/modules/2.4.23/ pcmcia*, the binary PCMCIA control programs will be located in */sbin*, and all configuration files will be located in *letc/pcmcia*. A startup configuration file will also be installed, but this location varies with the Linux distribution in question. Debian locates the startup configuration in *letc/default/ pcmcia*. RedHat and several other distributions locate the startup configuration in *letc/sysconfig/pcmcia*.

The startup configuration file has several options that can be set. A sample file from a modified Debian system looks like this:

```
PCMCIA=yes
PCIC=i82365
PCIC_OPTS=
CORE_OPTS=
CARDMGR_OPTS=-f
```

If PCMCIA is set to anything other than "yes," the PCMCIA subsystem will not start at time of boot.

The only mandatory option in this file that must be set is PCIC=. There are three options: tcic, i82365, and yenta_socket. tcic is a driver for older PC Card controllers, and unless you're building on a 486 laptop, you won't use it. Most other systems will want to set this option as i82365, unless you have the kernel tree PCMCIA. If the kernel tree PCMCIA is configured in your kernel, you must set this option to yenta_socket. Finally, if your PCMCIA card is CardBus, you should set this to yenta_socket.

PCIC_OPTS are necessary only if your specific PC Card controller has options that need to be passed to it at boot time. For most modern controllers, this is not an issue.

CORE_OPTS are options for the kernel module pcmcia_core. `man pcmcia_ core` gives you a listing of all these options.

CARDMGR_OPTS are options for the cardmgr daemon. `man cardmgr` gives you a listing of these options. In this case, the `-f` option tells cardmgr to run in the foreground, rather than as a daemon, until any cards present are already configured.

There are quite a number of settings that are possible for various systems. If you have an unusual system or a desktop system with an add-on PCMCIA reader, you should completely read through the PCMCIA HOWTO:

http://pcmcia-cs.sourceforge.net/ftp/doc/PCMCIA-HOWTO.html

2.4 kernels and kernel tree PCMCIA

Note that if you have a 2.4 kernel and kernel tree PCMCIA configured in your kernel, the pcmcia-cs install process will install only the PCMCIA tools, cardmgr, and cardctl in the */sbin* directory. None of the kernel modules or client card drivers will be installed, because the pcmcia-cs installer will find existing modules from the kernel tree PCMCIA and by default will not overwrite them.

Included with the pcmcia-cs source is a README file on issues with the 2.4 kernel. (You can also find this file at *http://pcmcia-cs.sourceforge.net/ftp/ README-2.4.*) One of the questions in the Q&A section covers this issue. You cannot compile or install anything in the */usr/src/pcmcia-cs.3.2.5/modules* directory, as these modules would conflict with the PCMCIA subsystem in the kernel tree.

However, you can build client card drivers from the pcmcia-cs source code by executing make install in either the */usr/src/pcmcia-cs.3.2.5/clients* or */usr/src/pcmcia-cs.3.2.5/wireless* subdirectories after running make config.

You may need to build the drivers this way for a variety of reasons. For example, when we built and compiled the 2.4.23 kernel, pcmcia-cs, and associated wireless drivers, we discovered that the madwifi driver for Atheros chipsets required kernel tree PCMCIA. However, once the kernel was compiled and the Atheros card was successfully tested, we discovered that the Orinoco card would not initialize. The PCMCIA subsystem reported *orinoco_cs: CardServices release does not match!* In order to fix this, it was necessary to configure pcmcia-cs and run a make install in the *wireless* subdirectory, as described earlier.

Controlling the PCMCIA subsystem

To successfully initialize and configure a PCMCIA wireless card, there are a number of pieces that come into play. Three modules need to be loaded at boot time: ds, i82365 or yenta_socket, and pcmcia_core. If you have kernel tree PCMCIA enabled or have gone through the pcmcia-cs installation process, these modules load automatically.

The next important bit is the cardmgr daemon, which monitors the PCMCIA socket, loads client card drivers at startup, and runs user scripts when cards are inserted or removed. The two important files for cardmgr are located in */etc/pcmcia/config* and */etc/pcmcia/config.opts*. *config* contains information about all of the client card drivers, about how to identify various cards, and about which drivers to load for which card. This file shouldn't be modified unless you really know what you're doing and must load a driver for a card that is not described in the *config* file. Similarly, *config.opts* must be modified if you have special options that must be passed to the PCMCIA card from cardmgr, or if you are experiencing memory or address conflicts with a specific card.

To manage a given PCMCIA card, run a user-space program called cardctl. cardctl checks the status and configuration of a PCMCIA socket and allows you to modify the configuration, as well as insert, eject, and suspend PCMCIA cards. There are several commands that cardctl supports. Examples with sample output from the commands are shown next.

The config command shows low-level configuration for any PCMCIA card: the voltage type, interface type, IRQ in use, and I/O memory used. This is a very handy tool for troubleshooting if you are running into resource conflicts.

```
# cardctl config
Socket 0:
  Vcc 3.3V  Vpp1 0.0V  Vpp2 0.0V
  interface type is "memory and I/O"
  irq 12 [exclusive] [level]
  function 0:
    config base 0x03e0
      option 0x41
    io 0x0100-0x013f [16bit]
```

The ident command gives you the chipset identification strings for your PCMCIA card. In this example, you are looking at a Senao 802.11b card that uses the Intersil Prism II chipset. Note that one thing you don't see is the manufacturer name; rather, you see the chipset manufacturer name.

```
# cardctl ident
Socket 0:
  product info: "INTERSIL", "HFA384x/IEEE", "Version 01.02", ""
  manfid: 0x0156, 0x0002
  function: 6 (network)
```

The suspend and resume commands shut down a PCMCIA card without unloading the associated drivers, and then they allow you to resume normal card operation. reset reloads the card driver without shutting down power to the card or resetting the PCMCIA subsystem.

```
# cardctl suspend
# cardctl resume
# cardctl reset
```

The eject and insert commands are the software equivalent of physically ejecting and inserting a PCMCIA card, so the card drivers are loaded or unloaded, and the devices are configured or shut down. It's important to note that CardBus cards may not react well to physical ejection, and you should use the cardctl eject command before removing a CardBus card.

```
# cardctl eject
# cardctl insert
```

Schemes allow you to have multiple configurations for your PCMCIA card. With a wireless network card, multiple schemes provide you with the ability

---

to change ESSID and other wireless settings as well as TCP/IP configuration. Schemes are covered in more detail in the discussion of the PCMCIA configuration.

```
# cardctl scheme
```

To stop or start the entire PCMCIA subsystem, execute the *rc* script that is installed with pcmcia-cs or the kernel tree PCMCIA. Where this file is located varies depending on your Linux distribution. On most Linux distributions, these commands stop and start the PCMCIA subsystem:

```
# /etc/init.d/pcmcia stop
# /etc/init.d/pcmcia start
```

PCMCIA wireless card configuration

PCMCIA devices are grouped into classes that define how they are configured and managed. These classes include network, SCSI, CDROM, fixed disk, serial, and a couple of memory card classes. This chapter is really concerned with wireless network cards, so the only class that is discussed here is the network class.

When the Wireless Tools are installed (see "Installing the Wireless Tools" later in this chapter for more information), an additional class is added: wireless.

Classes are associated with device drivers in */etc/pcmcia/config*. Each class has two scripts located in */etc/pcmcia*: a main configuration script and an options script. For network cards, these scripts are */etc/pcmcia/network* and */etc/pcmcia/network.opts*. Similarly, the wireless class scripts are */etc/pcmcia/wireless* and */etc/pcmcia/wireless.opts*.

Both config scripts extract some information about the PCMCIA card from the PCMCIA subsystem and use this information to generate a device address. The first part of any PCMCIA device address is the current scheme.

While the PCMCIA scripts accept any number of parameters in the device address, the sample scripts use the following syntax:

```
case "$ADDRESS" in
*,0,*,*)
    # definitions for network card in socket 0
    ;;
*,1,*,*)
    # definitions for network card in socket 1
    ;;
esac
```

The comma-separated fields in this example are the scheme, the socket number, the device instance, and the card's hardware Ethernet address. The device instance is used only if the card has multiple network interfaces, so, in most cases, it is zero. In this example, the cards are configured based on their socket number, which is somewhat easier to manage than configuration based on hardware Ethernet address.

The *network.opts* file accepts a large number of parameters. For information on all that this file offers, read through the PCMCIA HOWTO:

http://pcmcia-cs.sourceforge.net/ftp/doc/PCMCIA-HOWTO.html

It is also beneficial to read through the default */etc/pcmcia/network.opts* file before making any changes. Back up the file before you start editing:

```
/etc/pcmcia# cp network.opts network.opts.orig
```

Here is a sample of a configured *network.opts* file that sets up a static IP address and related TCP/IP address information for the wireless network card in slot 0:

```
case "$ADDRESS" in
*,0,*,*)
    INFO="Sample network setup"
    IPADDR="10.42.7.2"
    NETMASK="255.255.255.192"
    NETWORK="10.42.7.0"
    BROADCAST="10.42.7.63"
    GATEWAY="10.42.7.1"
    ;;
esac
```

This configuration applies to any PCMCIA network card that happens to be placed in slot 0. To make the configuration adaptable to a laptop that needs to establish network configuration between home and work, set up the *network.opts* file:

```
case "$ADDRESS" in
yourjob,0,*,*)
    INFO="Work network setup"
    IPADDR="10.1.1.200"
    NETMASK="255.255.255.0"
    NETWORK="10.1.1.0"
    BROADCAST="10.1.1.255"
    GATEWAY="10.1.1.1"
    ;;
home,0,*,*)
    INFO="Home network settings"
    DHCP=Y
esac
```

With this setup, you can switch between the static IP address assigned by your employer and the DHCP address you receive at home from your ADSL or cable router. To switch to the home settings, run the following command:

```
# cardctl scheme home
```

The scheme is persistent after rebooting. This may be a problem if you shut down your system at home and bring it up at work, and you are still using your home network and wireless settings.

You can manually edit your *lilo.conf* so that the PCMCIA scheme is passed from LILO to the system init as a variable. Here is a *lilo.conf* that shows two different schemes:

```
root = /dev/hda1
read-only
image = /boot/vmlinuz-2.4.22
  label = home
  append = "SCHEME=home"
image = /boot/vmlinuz-2.4.22
  label = work
  append = "SCHEME=yourjob"
```

The */etc/pcmcia/wireless.opts* file can be handled in a similar manner as *network.opts*. Again, the *wireless.opts* file accepts a large number of parameters, and you should read through the Wireless HOWTO before starting:

> *http://www.hpl.hp.com/personal/Jean_Tourrilhes/Linux/#howto*

Also, read through the default */etc/pcmcia/wireless.opts* file before making any changes. Back up the file before you start editing:

```
/etc/pcmcia# cp wireless.opts wireless.opts.orig
```

Here is a sample of a configured *wireless.opts* file that sets an ESSID of home and a scheme of home:

```
case "$ADDRESS" in

home,0,*,*)
    INFO="Home wireless setup"
    ESSID="home"
    MODE="managed"
    RATE="auto"
    ;;
esac
```

 The fields of interest are the ESSID, the mode, the channel, and the rate. The ESSID can be set either to the correct case-sensitive ESSID from the needed access point or to any, which allows the card to associate with any wireless network it finds.

For most cards, the mode can be set to managed or to ad-hoc. Managed mode is the 802.11 infrastructure mode, which means your card is a client to an access point. Ad-hoc mode can be used to communicate directly between two computers. Many cards support a third "monitor" mode that can be used to monitor wireless traffic. This mode is covered in Chapter 3. Finally, if you have a Prism or Atheros-based card, a fourth "master" mode can be used to let your card act as an access point (see Chapter 6).

Setting the rate allows you to determine the network speed your wireless card uses. For 802.11b cards, the valid rates are 1MB, 2MB, 5.5MB, 11MB, and auto. Setting this to any of the numerical values locks your card into that rate, and it transmits and receives at no other rate. If you want the card to automatically choose a rate up to a particular limit, use the desired rate along with auto. For example, choosing "5.5MB auto" chooses automatically 1MB, 2MB, or 5.5MB, depending on the amount of available signal. You may want to force a rate (or range of rates) if you are operating in an area with marginal coverage. Locking in a lower rate can sometimes lead to better performance than auto if the card is continually renegotiating the data rate.

The channel setting is not always needed, particularly if you have ESSID="any". However, if you are in a noisy wireless environment with multiple access points, you may wish to set the ESSID and the channel to ensure that your card does not associate with other access points.

Building on the use of a scheme, here is an expanded *wireless.opts* that provides configuration for both home and work:

```
case "$ADDRESS" in

home,0,*,*)
    INFO="Home wireless setup"
    ESSID="home"
    MODE="managed"
    CHANNEL="11"
    RATE="auto"
    ;;
yourjob,0,*,*)
    INFO="Work wireless setup"
    ESSID="BigCorp"
    MODE="managed"
    CHANNEL="4"
    RATE="auto"
    KEY="s:bigsecret"
esac
```

Note that the work setup has another field: KEY="s:bigsecret". "bigsecret" is the Wired Equivalent Privacy (WEP) key, and it is used to encrypt traffic between the client network card and an access point. WEP, its uses, and its weaknesses are covered in Chapter 4.

Debian Network Device Configuration

Debian users have an alternate method of configuring their network devices, including any wireless PCMCIA devices. Rather than relying on the */etc/pcmcia/network.opts* and */etc/pcmcia/wireless.opts*, all options are set using */etc/network/interfaces*.

Any PCMCIA device you wish to configure with the */etc/network/interfaces* file should not be marked as "auto." Debian will try to configure these interfaces before PCMCIA support is started, and the network configuration will fail.

The *interfaces* file is responsible for setting TCP/IP settings for any network interfaces configured in Debian. A sample entry defining a static IP address would look like this:

```
iface wlan0 inet static
  address 192.168.1.2
  network 192.168.1.0
  netmask 255.255.255.0
  broadcast 192.168.1.255
  gateway 192.168.1.1
```

If you install the wireless-tools package via apt-get, rather than compiling from source, Debian adds hooks to the *interfaces* file to support new option statements. These options take the form of:

```
wireless_<function> <value>
```

When the interface is brought up during the boot process, these options result in the execution of the following Wireless Tools command:

```
iwconfig <interface> <function> <value>
```

Using this method, any command that is recognized by iwconfig, except for "Nickname," can be entered in */etc/network/interfaces* and passed to the wireless card when it is initialized. To expand on the previous sample entry, here is an expanded entry that sets various wireless parameters:

```
iface wlan0 inet static
  address 192.168.1.2
  network 192.168.1.0
  netmask 255.255.255.0
  broadcast 192.168.1.255
  gateway 192.168.1.1
  wireless_essid NoCat
  wireless_mode Managed
```

Installing the Wireless Tools

The Linux Wireless Tools and their companion API, the Wireless Extensions, are both the work of Jean Tourrilhes at Hewlett Packard, who maintains an excellent web page full of useful information for Linux and wireless LANs at *http://www.hpl.hp.com/personal/Jean_Tourrilhes/Linux/*.

While the Wireless Tools and Extensions are not the only methods of configuring and using wireless network cards under Linux, they are the most common and are discussed in this chapter.

Wireless Extensions

To use the Wireless Tools, you must have a kernel and drivers with the Wireless Extensions. Fortunately, most kernels since 2.2.14 have included the *wireless.h* that defines Wireless Extensions in the kernel. In order for the Wireless Extensions to be included in the kernel, you must make sure that the CONFIG_NET_RADIO option is enabled. If you built your kernel following the instructions earlier in the chapter, your kernel should be built properly with the Wireless Extensions.

Table 2-1 shows what version of the Wireless Extensions your kernel should support (see Jean Tourrilhes's web page for the most recent information).

Table 2-1. Wireless Extensions support in Linux kernels

Version	Kernel	Features
WE-9	2.2.14, 2.3.30	Basic 802.11b support
WE-10	2.2.19, 2.4.0	Add TxPower setting
WE-11	2.4.4	Driver version check, retry setting
WE-12	2.4.13	Additional statistics
WE-13	2.4.19, 2.5.3	New driver API
WE-14	2.4.20, 2.5.7	Wireless Scanning, Wireless Events
WE-15	2.4.21, 2.5.37	Enhanced iwpriv support
WE-16	2.4.23, 2.6	802.11a/802.11g fixes, Enhanced iwspy support

The Wireless Extensions Version 16 is used for all the examples that use the 2.4.23 kernel. While there are patches to upgrade older kernels to later versions of the Wireless Extensions, it is not recommended, as many of the changes in *wireless.h* are dependent on specific kernel features and were not tested in older kernel versions.

Compiling the Wireless Tools

Now that you know the version of the Wireless Extensions that your kernel includes, you should get the latest version of the Wireless Tools. At the time of this writing, the latest stable version is 26 and can be obtained from the pcmcia-cs web site:

http://pcmcia-cs.sourceforge.net/ftp/contrib/wireless_tools.26.tar.gz

If you don't want to compile from source, you can install a binary package. Debian users can install the Wireless Tools as a package using apt-get install wireless-tools. RedHat and Mandrake users can install the wireless-tools RPM from the installation CDs. Other distributions should have a similarly named package.

Your best option is to download the source code from the aforementioned link and build the Wireless Tools for your exact version of the Wireless Extensions in your kernel. If you install a package version, it may have been compiled against a different version of the Wireless Extensions. When this happens, every time you use one of the Wireless Tools, you will see this error message:

```
Warning: Driver for device wlan0 has been compiled
with version 14 of Wireless Extension, while this program is using version
15.  Some things may be broken...
```

As the error message states, if you are using a version of the Wireless Tools that has been compiled with a previous version of the Wireless Extensions, some features may not work. Looking at Table 2-1, you can see that if you use a version of the Wireless Tools that had been compiled against Version 13 of the Wireless Extensions, you would not be able to use the Wireless Scanning in Version 14, regardless of the version of the Wireless Extensions in your kernel.

To successfully compile the Wireless Tools, you should need only a working compiler environment and a kernel with CONFIG_NET_RADIO enabled. PCMCIA support is optional but obviously required if your wireless card is a PCMCIA card. To really use the tools, you definitely need a wireless driver that supports the Wireless Extensions. Most Linux drivers do. Consult Jean Tourrilhes's web page if you have questions about a specific driver. Of the drivers covered in this chapter, only the wlan-ng driver does not support the Wireless Extensions.

To begin compiling the package, download the *wireless_tools.26.tar.gz* file into the */usr/src* directory. Unpack the *tar.gz* file and change into the top-level directory:

```
# tar xzvf wireless_tools.26.tar.gz
# cd wireless_tools.26
```

There isn't any configuration to do. As Jean Tourrilhes says in the INSTALL text file, "in theory a 'make' should suffice to create the tools." You should be able to:

```
# make
# make install
```

One potential problem you may run into: there are compilation issues with certain kernel and libc combinations. If you receive the error "Your kernel/ libc combination is not supported," it means some code hacking is required. For your purposes, you are better off installing a packaged version from your distribution.

Using the Wireless Tools

You now have the Wireless Tools compiled and installed in *usr/local/sbin*. There are four binary executables included with the Wireless Tools. All four Wireless Tools pull information from */proc/net/wireless*, which is created only when your kernel is compiled with the Wireless Extensions.

iwconfig

This is the tool you use to configure the basic operating parameters of your wireless card. It is also the tool that is called during the boot process to configure your card based on settings in */etc/pcmcia/wireless.opts*.

Called without any arguments, iwconfig displays current wireless settings for any wireless cards in the system. A typical example would look something like this:

```
lo         no wireless extensions.
eth0       no wireless extensions.
wlan0      IEEE 802.11-b  ESSID:"NoCat-Grandview"  Nickname:"airhead"
           Mode:Managed Frequency:2.462GHz
           Access Point: 00:02:6F:04:78:7E
           Bit Rate:11Mb/s   Tx-Power=24 dBm   Sensitivity=1/3
           Retry min limit:8   RTS thr:off   Fragment thr:off
           Encryption key:off
           Power Management:off
           Link Quality:40/92  Signal level:-77 dBm
           Noise level:-100 dBm
           Rx invalid nwid:0  Rx invalid crypt:0  Rx invalid frag:0
           Tx excessive retries:5293  Invalid misc:86372
           Missed beacon:0
```

If you have multiple wireless network cards and you don't wish to see the "no wireless extensions" message each time you run iwconfig, make sure to specify the interface:

```
$ iwconfig wlan0
```

This only shows the configuration for the specified network card.

As you can see, there are quite a number of parameters that iwconfig can set. Not everything can be changed, however. Starting with Link Quality, the output is taken from */proc/net/wireless* and consists of read-only statistics.

All of these parameters, settings, and statistics are device- and driver- dependent. Each wireless driver is going to write different things to */proc/net/wireless*, and each driver supports commands from the Wireless Tools differently. For example, if you use an Orinoco card with the orinoco_cs wireless driver, your options for "Mode" are much more limited than if you use a Prism II–based card with the hostap_cs driver.

Let's step through the available iwconfig parameters. In the following examples, we use the eth1 interface, but it may be something different, such as wlan0 in the hostap_cs driver or ath0 in the madwifi driver:

essid <*name*>

Sets the network name or SSID to which the wireless card connects. A useful option is to set the name to any, which allows the card to connect to any available wireless network:

```
# iwconfig eth1 essid NoCat
# iwconfig eth1 essid any
```

freq *or* channel

Sets the operating frequency or channel of the wireless card. channel accepts a number in the range of 1–11 (U.S.) or 1–14 (E.U.). freq accepts the frequency in Hz. You should enter the exact frequency, such as 2.462 for channel 11. You can also enter the frequency with the suffix of G: 2.46G for channel 11:

```
# iwconfig eth1 channel 6
# iwconfig eth1 freq 2.437
# iwconfig eth1 freq 2.43G
```

mode

Sets the operating mode of the wireless card. There are different options depending on your wireless card and driver. Most cards and drivers under Linux support ad-hoc mode for communicating with another node, without any access points. The most common mode is managed, which allows the wireless card to connect as a client to an access point. One advanced mode is master, which is supported in the hostap and madwifi drivers, and makes the card into a software-controlled access point. Another advanced mode is monitor, which turns the wireless card into a passive receiver that can only receive packets:

```
# iwconfig eth1 mode managed
# iwconfig eth1 mode ad-hoc
```

ap

Enters a hardware address of a specific access point, which forces the card to associate with that access point. By default, if the connection quality degrades or is unusable, the card defaults back to automatic mode, where the card finds the best access point in range. You can defeat this by using the option off to disable automatic mode. any or auto enables automatic mode.

```
# iwconfig eth1 ap 00:02:2d:53:66:19
# iwconfig eth1 ap off
# iwconfig eth1 ap auto
```

sens

Sets the sensitivity threshold of the wireless card. The card does not receive any signal lower than this level. This avoids background noise. Positive values are assumed to be the raw value used by the hardware, or a percentage. Negative values are assumed to be dBm. Again, the settings are dependent on the hardware of the wireless card. Prism and Orinoco cards seem to treat only values of 1–3 as valid sensitivity settings. Depending on your hardware, this parameter may also control the defer threshold (the lowest signal level for which the channel is considered busy) and the handover threshold (the lowest signal level where the card stays associated with an access point).

```
# iwconfig eth1 sens -80
```

rate

Sets the bit-rate in bits/second. Once again the available options depend on your wireless card. The value of the option must be the exact bitrate number or should have M appended to the end of the number. auto is the default setting for most cards and falls back to lower bit-rates if there is noise.

```
# iwconfig eth1 rate auto
# iwconfig eth1 rate 11M    # (802.11b)
# iwconfig eth1 rate 54M    # (802.11a/g)
```

rts

RTS/CTS adds a handshake before each packet transmission to make sure that the channel is clear. This adds quite a bit of overhead and decreases the potential bandwidth. However, it can result in increased performance in the case of hidden nodes or large numbers of active nodes. Set a packet size that determines the minimum packet size threshold for enabling RTS/CTS, auto to have the driver automatically perform RTC/CTS, or off to disable:

```
# iwconfig eth1 rts 250
# iwconfig eth1 rts auto
# iwconfig eth1 rts off
```

frag

Sets the fragmentation threshold. This allows the card to split a packet into smaller packet fragments to transmit. As with rts, this adds overhead and reduces the available bandwidth, but in very noisy environments, it reduces the amount of errors and tries to send packets again.

As with rts, you set a packet size that determines the minimum packet size for determining when fragmentation should be enabled. You can also set auto to have the driver automatically perform fragmentation or off to disable fragmentation.

```
# iwconfig eth1 frag 512
# iwconfig eth1 frag auto
# iwconfig eth1 frag off
```

nick

Sets the nickname or station name of the wireless card. Most 802.11 devices define this parameter, but it is completely optional and doesn't affect performance or operation at all. Some diagnostic tools may use it.

```
# iwconfig eth1 nick "Network God"
```

key *or* enc

Sets the encryption mode and keys for the wireless card. on and off enable and disable encryption, respectively. Encryption keys can be entered as hex digits, with or without separation dashes, or ASCII strings can be entered in the format s:password. Generate an index of keys by appending an index number in brackets ([ ]) to the key when it is entered. Once you have multiple keys in the index, change keys by simply passing the index number as the option. Two modes are available: open and restricted. open accepts nonencrypted traffic, while restricted accepts only encrypted packets.

```
# iwconfig eth1 enc on
# iwconfig eth1 key 0a12fc132
# iwconfig eth1 key s:supersecret [2]
# iwconfig eth1 key [2] restricted
```

power

Sets power management modes and parameters. on and off enable and disable power management, respectively.

txpower

For cards that support multiple transmit powers, this sets the transmit power in dBm. on and off enable and disable radio transmissions entirely. auto enables automatic power selection if that feature is available. If the entry is followed by "mW," the value automatically is converted to dBm. Geeky math note: if W is the power in watts, the power (P) in dBm is $P = 30 + 10.\log(W)$.

```
# iwconfig eth1 txpower 30
# iwconfig eth1 txpower 200mw
# iwconfig eth1 txpower auto
# iwconfig eth1 txpower off
```

retry

> For cards that support MAC retransmissions, this allows you to change the parameters of the retry. You can set the maximum number of retries with limit and an absolute value. The maximum length of time the MAC should retry is set with lifetime, in seconds. You can append "m" or "u" to specify milliseconds or microseconds respectively. limit and lifetime can also be modified by the use of min or max, which allows you to set the upper and lower boundaries of limit and lifetime.

```
# iwconfig eth1 retry 16
# iwconfig eth1 retry lifetime 300m
# iwconfig eth1 retry min limit 8
# iwconfig eth1 retry max lifetime 500m
```

--version

> Displays the version of iwlist and the Wireless Extensions:

```
# iwconfig --version
iwconfig  Version 25
          Compatible with Wireless Extension v15 or earlier,
          Currently compiled with Wireless Extension v15.

wlan0     Recommend Wireless Extension v13 or later,
          Currently compiled with Wireless Extension v14.
```

To summarize: iwconfig allows you to change the configuration of your wireless network card on the fly. All of the options supported by iwconfig can be set in */etc/pcmcia/wireless.opts*, and when the PCMCIA subsystem is initialized, these options are executed as the card is configured.

iwlist

This is mainly used for showing lists of parameters that the current wireless card supports. However, it does have one very useful feature that is not a list of parameters.

If you would like to see a list of access points available for your wireless card, iwlist is your ticket. You won't have to install other network-scanning utilities like Kismet (covered in Chapter 3). Not all card drivers support this option. For instance, the orinoco_cs driver does not support scanning. To initiate scanning, this command must be run with root access:

```
# iwlist eth1 scan
```

Here is a sample of th output you might expect:

```
wlan0     Scan completed :
          Cell 01 - Address: 00:02:6F:04:78:7E
                    ESSID:"NoCat"
                    Mode:Managed
```

```
Frequency:2.462GHz
Quality:0/92  Signal level:-64 dBm  Noise level:-100 dBm
Encryption key:off
Bit Rate:1Mb/s
Bit Rate:2Mb/s
Bit Rate:5.5Mb/s
Bit Rate:11Mb/s
```

If you are in an area with multiple access points, you should see "Cell" entries for each access point, with specific information on signal and noise level. This is a very useful base tool for finding access points in an unfamiliar environment, or even for baselining your wireless network infrastructure.

Aside from this, iwlist serves as a query tool to determine what features your wireless card supports. Let's step through the available iwlist queries:

freq

Displays the list of available radio frequencies and the number of defined radio channels. It also displays the currently used radio channel. For a U.S. user, typical output from this command would be:

```
$ iwlist wlan0 freq

wlan0    14 channels in total; available frequencies :
         Channel 01 : 2.412 GHz
         Channel 02 : 2.417 GHz
         Channel 03 : 2.422 GHz
         Channel 04 : 2.427 GHz
         Channel 05 : 2.432 GHz
         Channel 06 : 2.437 GHz
         Channel 07 : 2.442 GHz
         Channel 08 : 2.447 GHz
         Channel 09 : 2.452 GHz
         Channel 10 : 2.457 GHz
         Channel 11 : 2.462 GHz
         Current Frequency:2.462GHz (channel 11)
```

ap *or* peers

This feature is deprecated in favor of the scan feature, previously mentioned. Most current drivers do not support this feature. However, some drivers may use this command to return a specific list of peers associated with the wireless card.

rate

Lists the bit-rates supported by the card and the current bit-rate in use:

```
$ iwlist wlan0 rate

wlan0    4 available bit-rates :
         1Mb/s
         2Mb/s
         5.5Mb/s
         11Mb/s
         Current Bit Rate:11Mb/s
```

key *or* enc
> Lists the encryption key size supported, the available keys in the wireless card, and the current key in use:
>
> ```
> $ iwlist wlan0 key
>
> wlan0     2 key sizes : 40, 104bits
>           4 keys available :
>                   [1]: off
>                   [2]: off
>                   [3]: off
>                   [4]: off
>           Current Transmit Key: [0]
> ```

txpower
> Lists the various transmit powers available on the wireless card. This feature appears to be broken, at least with respect to Wireless Extensions 15 and a Prism card using the hostap driver.

retry
> Lists the transmit retry limits and lifetime:
>
> ```
> $ iwlist wlan0 retry
>
> wlan0     Fixed limit    ;   min limit:0
>                               max limit:255
>           Current mode:on
>                     min limit:8 max limit:5
> ```

--version
> Displays the version of iwlist and the Wireless Extensions:
>
> ```
> $ iwlist --version
> iwlist    Version 25
>           Compatible with Wireless Extension v15 or earlier,
>           Currently compiled with Wireless Extension v15.
>
> wlan0     Recommend Wireless Extension v13 or later,
>           Currently compiled with Wireless Extension v14.
> ```

iwspy

This is a useful tool that shows you quality-of-link information for one or many nodes in a wireless network. The information is taken from */proc/net/wireless*, but when running iwspy, the statistics are updated each time a packet is received from the remote node. This does add some driver overhead, which means that local performance on the machine running iwspy is degraded. Note that different drivers may partially support iwspy or may not support it at all.

In the most basic mode, simply run iwspy interface:

```
$ iwspy wlan1
```

```
wlan1     Statistics collected:
    00:02:6F:03:FE:65 : Quality:42/92  Signal level:-90 dBm
    Noise level:-98 dBm
    00:02:2D:04:EB:15 : Quality:31/92  Signal level:-94 dBm
    Noise level:-98 dBm
```

As in the previous example, you should see a MAC address for every remote station, along with quality, signal level, and noise level statistics.

To start collecting statistics for a specific node, invoke iwspy with a DNS name, an IP, or hardware address:

```
$ iwspy wlan1 192.168.0.1
```

Then, when you invoke iwspy again for that interface, you see not only the current statistics for the remote node, but a set of averages as well:

```
$ iwspy wlan1
wlan1     Statistics collected:
    00:02:6F:01:6A:02 : Quality:18/92  Signal level:-82 dBm
    Noise level:-100 dBm (updated)
    typical/average   : Quality:36/92  Signal level:-62 dBm
    Noise level:-98 dBm
```

You can have iwspy monitor up to eight addresses simply by passing it multiple DNS names, IP, or hardware addresses on the command line:

```
$ iwspy wlan1 192.168.0.1 test.foobarus.com notebook.foobarus.com
```

Again, when you invoke iwspy for that interface, you see current statistics for each remote node plus an average across all three nodes.

If you are already monitoring three remote nodes and run iwspy again with a fourth IP address to monitor, iwspy will replace the monitoring of your existing three nodes with monitoring of the new IP address. To avoid this, use the + sign before the IP address on the command line:

```
$ iwspy wlan1 + 192.168.0.15
```

This appends the new address to your existing list of addresses that are already being monitored.

To disable any iwspy statistic collection you may have started, simply turn it off:

```
$ iwspy wlan1 off
```

Two more useful commands in iwspy let you set high and low signal strength thresholds for wireless events. setthr <low/high> sets the thresholds, and if an address monitored with iwspy goes higher or lower than the thresholds, a wireless event is generated:

```
$ iwspy wlan1 setthr 40 80
```

This means that you can monitor link status on multiple connections without having to continually run `iwspy`.

To show what the threshold has been set to, type the following:

```
$ iwspy wlan1 getthr
```

iwpriv

This tool allows you to configure private wireless options—in other words, options that are limited to a single wireless driver. This is different than `iwconfig`, which deals with generic settings that are applicable to all wireless cards.

Called without any arguments, `iwpriv` returns a list of available private commands. On a Prism II–based Senao 200 mW card, the following list is returned:

```
wlan0     Available private ioctl :
          monitor         (8BE4) : set   1 int    & get   0
          readmif         (8BE3) : set   1 byte   & get   1 byte
          writemif        (8BE2) : set   2 byte   & get   0
          reset           (8BE6) : set   1 int    & get   0
          inquire         (8BE8) : set   1 int    & get   0
          set_rid_word    (8BEE) : set   2 int    & get   0
          maccmd          (8BF0) : set   1 int    & get   0
          wds_add         (8BEA) : set  18 char   & get   0
          wds_del         (8BEC) : set  18 char   & get   0
          addmac          (8BF2) : set  18 char   & get   0
          delmac          (8BF4) : set  18 char   & get   0
          kickmac         (8BF6) : set  18 char   & get   0
          prism2_param    (8BE0) : set   2 int    & get   0
          getprism2_param (8BE1) : set   1 int    & get   1 int
```

This list shows that there are quite a few private options that can be set using `iwpriv` on a Prism II card. One option is WDS, the Wireless Distribution System, which is covered in Chapter 6. Most of the private commands are hardware- and driver-specific.

Many cards support some types of `iwpriv` reset command. The orinoco_cs driver includes `card_reset` and `force_reset` options for `iwpriv`.

Linux Wi-Fi Drivers in Depth

Most Linux distributions include a number of wireless drivers. In many cases, the driver that you need will be available. However, there are a number of situations where you must obtain the driver source and build it yourself. This is true for many newer Wi-Fi cards, particularly cards that support 802.11a, 802.11g, or both. The drivers for these cards are still under development and are not included with most Linux distributions.

A second reason to obtain the driver source and build it yourself is if you wish to build your own access point. (The details of Linux access points are covered in Chapter 6.) However, the drivers that enable you to have your own Linux AP all require that you obtain the source code and compile it.

 In addition to the drivers described in this chapter, there are two ways you can get Windows drivers to load on your Linux system. NdisWrapper (*http://ndiswrapper.sourceforge.net/*) is an open source project that loads Windows drivers, and Linuxant (*http://www.linuxant.com/*) is a proprietary product that also accomplishes this. We'll talk more about Linuxant in Chapter 4, where we discuss using Wireless Protected Access (WPA) with non-Prism cards.

orinoco_cs

There are two original drivers available for the Lucent WaveLan/Orinoco radio cards: wvlan_cs and wavelan2_cs. wvlan_cs was the first driver for Linux that supported the WaveLan IEEE (802.11 and 802.11b) radio cards. wavelan2_cs is a binary driver released by Lucent. The downside of the binary driver is that it's limited to i386 architecture, and the source is not available. With the sale of Orinoco to Proxim, development of the wavelan2_cs driver stopped. However, Agere continues to build the chipsets for the Orinoco radios, and has developed a driver called wlags49 based on the wavelan2_cs code. Details on wlags49 are found in Chapter 6.

The orinoco_cs driver was written by David Gibson, who was maintaining the wvlan_cs driver and was not satisfied with the code or the performance of the driver. orinoco_cs was written based on low-level parts of the wlan-ng driver and BSD drivers. The driver also supports Prism II radio cards, Symbol Spectrum 24, and Apple AirPort (but not AirPort Extreme) cards, with varying degrees of feature support. This driver is primarily written for support of the Lucent WaveLan IEEE cards, which are also known as Orinoco and are also sold by Agere and Avaya. Proxim is now selling cards branded "Orinoco" for 802.11a and 802.11g, which are based on the Atheros chipset.

The orinoco_cs driver can be obtained in several ways. Red Hat, Debian, and SuSE all have installation packages with names similar to *kernel-pcmcia-modules-2.4.x*. Choosing this package during installation or adding it later will install the orinoco_cs driver. The orinoco_cs driver has been merged into the kernel sources since kernel Version 2.4.3.

The pcmcia-cs software package, which comprises the PC Card Services for Linux, also includes the orinoco_cs driver. As with the kernel PCMCIA modules, pcmcia-cs can be installed as a package in most Linux distributions, or it can be installed from source. Both options are covered earlier in this chapter. pcmcia-cs is the only option for kernel Version 2.2 users.

Finally, you can download the most current beta version of the orinoco_cs driver from the download section of Jean Tourrilhes's web page: *http://www.hpl.hp.com/personal/Jean_Tourrilhes/Linux/Orinoco.html*. As of this writing, the most current version is 0.13e. The README on the download page does explain that unless you have a 2.2 kernel or you need some of the experimental features of the beta orinoco_cs driver, you would be better off using the kernel version.

In the download section, there is a list of patches to the orinoco_cs driver. Of note is the orinoco_usb driver, which is a separately maintained software package and supports Orinoco USB Wi-Fi adapters.

Also of note is the Shmoo Group's patch for the orinoco_cs driver that enables monitor mode for Versions 0.13e and earlier. If you need monitor mode with your Orinoco card, this is one option. The other option is to obtain the CVS code of the orinoco_cs driver, now in 0.14 alpha from *http://savannah.nongnu.org/cvs/?group=orinoco*.

To compile the orinoco_cs driver, download the latest *tar.gz* file from the aforementioned web site. You need the kernel source for whatever kernel version your Linux system is running. Major Linux vendors include the kernel source on their installation media as a package, and also as an optional package on their web or FTP sites. For example, on a Pentium 4 Debian system running the 2.4.18 kernel, use apt-get to install the package titled *kernel-source-2.4.18* from the installation CD. If you have upgraded your kernel, install *kernel-source-2.4.21* (or later) from one of the Debian update sites. It's worth noting that when you retrieve the kernel source files in this manner, apt does not uncompress them. You will have a *kernel-source-2.4. 21.tar.bz2* file located in */usr/src*, which you must extract. For information about using apt-get, consult the Debian web pages at *http://www.debian. org/doc/user-manuals#apt-howto*.

You can also download kernel sources from *http://www.kernel.org* or *ftp://ftp. kernel.org*. This is the primary archive site for all Linux kernel sources and is your best source for kernel code. For example, download the 2.4.21 kernel sources from *http://www.kernel.org/pub/linux/kernel/2.4/linux-2.4.21.tar.gz*.

Compilation of the orinoco_cs driver also assumes that the symbolic link of */lib/modules/<version>/build* points to the kernel source of your current kernel. For example, */lib/modules/2.4.21-5-686/build* should be a symbolic link that points to */usr/src/linux-2.4.21-5-686*. To create this link, execute the following command:

```
# ln -s /usr/src/linux-2.4.21-5-686 /lib/modules/2.4.21-5-686/build
```

To build the driver, unpack the *tar.gz* file and change into the top-level directory:

```
# tar xzvf orinoco-0.13e.tar.gz
# cd orinoco-0.13e
```

To compile and install the driver, run the following:

```
# make
# make install
```

If you try to load the driver and receive the error message "Card Services release does not match," the driver was compiled against the Kernel PCM-CIA drivers, but the system is actually using the drivers from the pcmcia-cs package. To fix this, you must edit the *Makefile* in the *orinoco-0.13e* directory and set the PCMCIA_CS variable to reflect your local source for the pcmcia-cs package.

Once the driver is installed, you can execute:

```
# modprobe orinoco_cs
```

to load the driver module.

hostap_cs

The HostAP driver is one of the drivers for Prism II radio cards. (wlan-ng is another widely used driver that is discussed in the following section.) The HostAP driver has a couple of noteworthy features not found in the wlan-ng driver. First, it supports access point mode on Prism II radio cards. wlan-ng supports only access point mode with a "tertiary firmware" loaded on the Prism II card. This firmware is not widely available. Second, the HostAP driver is well integrated with the Linux Wireless Tools. The wlan-ng driver provides its own set of tools.

The access point mode of a Prism II card does not provide a full 802.11b access point. What it does do is broadcast the beacon frames that advertise an access point. The HostAP driver, in this case, actually takes care of the 802.11 management. In a standalone access point, this function is usually in firmware. The tertiary firmware mentioned for Prism II cards turns a Prism II card into a full access point, which is what allows the wlan-ng driver to utilize this mode as an access point.

The author and maintainer of the HostAP driver is Jouni Malinen. His web site for HostAP is located at *http://hostap.epitest.fi*. In addition to the source for HostAP, the web site hosts a useful mailing list and anonymous CVS access to the source code.

The hostapd daemon is also available. When used in conjunction with the HostAP driver, it provides support for 802.1X, dynamic WEP rekeying, RADIUS Accounting, and minimal support for IAPP (802.11f). Use hostapd with a RADIUS server to provide authenticated access to 802.11b networks.

The hostap driver not only supports Prism II cards in a PCMCIA bus, but it also supports PCI cards (hostap_pci) and PLX cards; these cards look like they are a PCMCIA-to-PCI bridge adapter card, but actually, they are another beast altogether—hostap_plx.

Debian users can use apt-get to install a hostap source package from the stable package tree. To locate the hostap packages, use the apt-cache utility to search through the available package lists:

```
# apt-cache search hostap
hostap-source - Software access point driver for Prism2 based 802.11b cards
hostap-utils - Utilities and configurations for the hostap driver
hostapd - 802.11x access daemon for hostap driver
```

To install any of these packages, or all three, use the apt-get install command:

```
# apt-get install hostap-source hostap-utils hostapd
```

This example installs all three hostap packages and may require you to install additional packages as well. For more information on how to use apt-get and its associated utilities, consult the Debian web pages at *http://www.debian.org/doc/user-manuals#apt-howto*.

Note that HostAP is a kernel driver, so the aforementioned apt-get command installs the source only for HostAP. It does not install the actual binary kernel driver. The source is downloaded and placed in */usr/src/hostap-modules.tar.gz*. You must extract this file and follow the compilation instructions.

Mandrake users can find HostAP RPMs for HostAP at *http://www.rpmfind. net*. Kernel RPMs for Red Hat Versions 8 and 9 can be found at *http://www. cat.pdx.edu/~baera/redhat_hostap/*. The maintainer of this site has recompiled the production Red Hat kernels with the HostAP 0.0.3 kernel driver and made the RPMs available. As with the testing tree in Debian, you should use these RPMs at your own risk. You should note that these kernels are out of date since the latest stable release of HostAP is 0.1.2, and the development versions are 0.2.0 and higher.

The best option for most distributions is to compile the HostAP driver from source. As of this writing, the most current version is 0.1.3; the latest version can be downloaded from *http://hostap.epitest.fi/releases/* (see the HostaAP homepage for a link to the most recent stable and development releases). To compile kernel modules from source, you must have the configured kernel source for your kernel. This generally means that you have configured and compiled your own Linux kernel. While it is certainly possible to compile kernel modules against Linux kernels provided by a stock distribution, it can be tricky. For more on compiling your own kernel, see "Configuring and Compiling Your Kernel" earlier in this chapter.

The HostAP distribution includes three files, *hostap-driver-x.y.z.tar.gz*, *hostap-utils-x.y.z.tar.gz*, and *hostapd-x.y.z.tar.gz*. To build hostap-utils and hostapd, extract the tarball with `tar xzvf` *filename*, cd into the top-level directory, and run `make` and then `make install` as root.

To begin compiling the driver, unpack the *tar.gz* file and change into the top-level directory (the file and directory name will be different if you are using a more recent version):

```
# tar xzvf hostap-driver-0.1.3.tar.gz
# cd hostap-driver-0.1.3
```

How you proceed in the compilation at this stage depends on whether your system is using the kernel tree PCMCIA subsystem or the external pcmcia-cs subsystem.

If you are using the kernel tree PCMCIA, you must edit the *Makefile* in the *hostap-driver-x.y.z* directory. As with the orinoco_cs driver, you need the kernel source for the kernel that your Linux distribution is currently running. The KERNEL_PATH variable should be set to the location of your kernel source.

Once you have set the KERNEL_PATH variable, there are two commands to compile and install the hostap_cs driver:

```
# make pccard
# make install pccard
```

Once the driver is compiled and installed, you must restart the PCMCIA card services. On must Linux distributions, the *rc* file for this is located in */etc/init.d/pcmcia*, so you can execute:

```
# /etc/init.d/pcmcia restart
```

to restart the PCMCIA card services.

If you are using the external pcmcia-cs, you have two compilation options:

- You must set the KERNEL_PATH variable as in the previous example. You also must set the PCMCIA_PATH variable to point to the source for the pcmcia-cs. So, for example, if you download and extract the pcmcia-cs source code into */home/barfoo/pcmcia-cs-3.2.5*, you must set PCMCIA_PATH=*/home/barfoo/pcmcia-cs-3.2.5*.

  Once the PCMCIA_PATH variable is set, you should be able to run the make commands shown previously to compile the hostap_cs driver.

- Copy the entire contents of the *driver* subdirectory *except* for *driver/modules/Makefile* to the root of the pcmcia-cs source directory, so that *driver/modules/hostap.c* ends up in the *pcmcia-cs/modules* directory. The README for installing HostAP recommends doing the following:

```
# make sure that Makefile does not overwrite old Makefile in pcmcia-cs
mv driver/modules/Makefile driver/modules/Makefile-not-used
cp -a driver/* home/barfoo/pcmcia-cs-3.2.5
```

Once the copy is finished, compile and install pcmcia-cs with the hostap_cs driver included in the process using the commands:

```
# make config
# make all
# make install
```

This second method installs both pcmcia-cs and HostAP; therefore, complete the compilation and install, and you'll have successfully installed both the PCMCIA card services and HostAP. See "Building and Configuring the pcmcia-cs Subsystem" earlier in this chapter for information on compiling pcmcia-cs from source.

There are specific instructions in the README for installing the driver for use with PCI or PLX adapter cards. Consult the README if your card falls into one of these categories.

There are two excellent sources of information and assistance you can consult if you run into problems with the hostap driver. The first is the well-populated hostap mailing list. Subscribe at *http://lists.shmoo.com/mailman/listinfo/hostap*. The mailing list archives can be read at *http://sisyphus.iocaine.com/pipermail/hostap/*. Use Google to search through lists like hostap, because the archives do not have a search function. For example, if you want to search for the text "compile error," enter the following search parameters at Google: compile error site:lists.shmoo.com. Before posting to the mailing lists, it is advisable to read through both the FAQ and the README files, located on the main hostap page at *http://hostap.epitest.fi*.

wlan-ng

The wlan-ng driver is the other available driver for Prism II chipsets. The developer and maintainer of wlan-ng is AbsoluteValue Systems, which first released the linux-wlan driver supporting Prism I 802.11 chipsets in 1999, and followed that with linux-wlan-ng to support Prism II and later 802.11b in August of 2000. According to its web pages at *http://www.linux-wlan.com*, one of its cofounders was employed at Harris Semiconductor where the original Prism chipsets were developed, and three of its employees are voting members of the IEEE.

One thing that is mentioned on the front page of the wlan-ng web site is that AbsoluteValue Systems's approach to writing this driver is different from other available Linux wireless drivers because "everything is based on the IEEE 802.11 standard."

In a practical sense, this means that just about everything in the wlan-ng driver is different from most other Linux Wi-Fi drivers. For starters, wlan-ng does not support the Linux Wireless Tools (although certain Wireless Tools commands will work with this driver); instead, it has its own set of utilities. You don't configure wlan-ng in /etc/pcmcia like other drivers; it has its own configuration directory in /etc/wlan.

The driver does support PCMCIA, PCI, and PCMCIA cards in PLX adapters, and USB adapters, all using Prism II, 2.5, or 3 chipsets. By and large, most cards you find on the market are still based on Prism II. Prism 2.5 cards are integrated PCI cards, so you won't find a Prism 2.5 PCMCIA card. Prism 3 was announced in 2002 and has made its way into products from Linksys, among others.

There are several methods to install the wlan-ng driver. As with HostAP, there are packages available for Debian Linux in the testing and unstable trees. In order to do this, you must modify the /etc/apt/sources.list file, which defines where apt-get downloads package lists and the corresponding packages. To add the testing tree to apt, add the following line to sources.list:

```
deb http://ftp.us.debian.org/debian/testing main contrib non-free
```

Once you have added this line to sources.list, you must execute the following command:

```
# apt-get update
```

This command updates the lists of packages from the sources defined in sources.list. Because you have added the testing tree to your sources, you now have a list of packages that are in testing mode. A caveat: packages in the testing and unstable trees are just that - designed for testing and/or may be unstable. Use them at your own risk.

To locate the wlan-ng packages, use the apt-cache utility to search through the available package lists:

```
# apt-cache search wlan-ng
linux-wlan-ng - utilities for wireless prism2 cards
linux-wlan-ng-doc - documentation for wlan-ng
linux-wlan-ng-modules-2.4.20-3-386 - drivers for wireless prism2 cards
linux-wlan-ng-modules-2.4.20-3-586tsc - drivers for wireless prism2 cards
linux-wlan-ng-modules-2.4.20-3-686 - drivers for wireless prism2 cards
linux-wlan-ng-modules-2.4.20-3-686-smp - drivers for wireless prism2 cards
linux-wlan-ng-modules-2.4.20-3-k6 - drivers for wireless prism2 cards
linux-wlan-ng-modules-2.4.20-3-k7 - drivers for wireless prism2 cards
linux-wlan-ng-modules-2.4.20-3-k7-smp - drivers for wireless prism2 cards
```

At a minimum, you need the linux-wlan-ng package and the correct set of linux-wlan-ng-modules for your processor architecture. Note that these modules are compiled against kernel Version 2.4.20-3. apt-get checks dependencies for these packages, and if you do not have kernel Version 2.4.20-3 as your current kernel, it requires you to install 2.4.20-3 as part of the package install process. To install the necessary packages, use the following command:

```
# apt-get install linux-wlan-ng linux-wlan-ng-modules-2.4.20-3-686
```

This example installs the utilities and kernel drivers for a Pentium Pro/II/III/IV and may require you to install additional packages as well. For more information on how to use apt-get and its associated utilities, consult the Debian web pages at *http://www.debian.org/doc/user-manuals#apt-howto*.

The FAQ for wlan-ng, available at *ftp://ftp.linux-wlan.org/pub/linux-wlan-ng/ FAQ*, states:

> Q: Can I get Debian packages of linux-wlan-ng?
>
> A: Packages of linux-wlan-ng are available in the Debian unstable and testing trees now, and will eventually be shipped with a stable Debian release. The Debian packages include support for configuring linux-wlan-ng interfaces via /etc/network/interfaces, among other things. Complete details about the Debian-specific parts of these packages, including instructions for building a linux-wlan-ng modules package for your kernel can be found in the file /usr/share/doc/linux-wlang-ng/README.Debian.gz.

wlan-ng RPMs for Red Hat Linux can be found on the web at *http:// prism2.unixguru.raleigh.nc.us*. RPMs are available for RedHat 7.3, 8, and 9. The page is maintained by Tim Miller and is kept up to date. As with other independently maintained packages, use these at your own risk. You need three different RPM files to get all of the wlan-ng functionality installed under RedHat:

- *kernel-wlan-ng-<architecture>*: the base package
- *kernel-wlan-ng-<usb/pci/pcmcia-architecture>*: interface packages
- *kernel-wlan-ng-modules-<rh73/rh8/rh9-architecture>*:   kernel-specific module packages

For example, to install the RPM packages for Red Hat 9, kernel Version 2.4.20-20.9, i686 architecture, and a PCMCIA Prism II card, execute:

```
# rpm --install kernel-wlan-ng-0.2.0-7.i686.rpm
# rpm --install kernel-wlan-ng-pcmcia-0.2.0-7.i686.rpm
# rpm --install kernel-wlan-ng-modules-rh9.20-0.2.0-7.i686.rpm
```

Your other option, as always, is to compile the driver from source. It is available at *ftp://ftp.linux-wlan.org/pub/linux-wlan-ng/*. As of this writing, the most recent version is *linux-wlan-ng-0.2.1-pre12.tar.gz*.

To compile kernel modules from source, you need the configured kernel source for your kernel. This generally means that you have configured and compiled your own Linux kernel. While it is certainly possible to compile kernel modules against Linux kernels provided by a stock distribution, it can be tricky. For more on compiling your own kernel, see "Configuring and Compiling Your Kernel" earlier in this chapter.

If your Prism II card is a PCMCIA-based card, you also need the configured source code for pcmcia-cs to be available. Again, this means that you have configured and compiled pcmcia-cs from source, and you have that source available, usually located in */usr/src/pcmcia-cs-version*.

To begin compiling the driver, unpack the *tar.gz* file and change into the top-level directory (if you are using a more recent version, the filename and directory will differ):

```
# tar xzvf linux-wlan-ng-0.2.1-pre12.tar.gz
# cd linux-wlan-ng-0.2.1-pre12
# make config
```

You'll be asked a series of questions, including which type of interfaces you want the driver to support (pcmcia, pci, plx, usb) and where your kernel and pcmcia-cs sources are located. Once you've stepped through the config, compile and install the driver:

```
# make all
# make install
```

madwifi

The Atheros chipsets were eagerly awaited by the open source community, because Atheros was the first vendor to ship 802.11a equipment, and among the first to ship dual-mode and tri-mode radio chipsets.

The Atheros hardware is designed for use as a "software-defined radio," which means that the hardware itself is very basic, and on a Windows platform, the operating parameters of the card are all handled by the software driver. The development of a driver for the Atheros chipset was very difficult from an open source standpoint. Sam Leffler originally developed a BSD driver for the Atheros chipset with the help of Atheros. However, the driver did not enforce valid modes, so it violated FCC regulations by allowing the setting of invalid radio modes.

The solution to this was for Atheros to develop a Hardware Abstraction Layer (HAL), which is in binary form. It sits between the driver and the hardware to enforce valid FCC operating modes. As discussed earlier, the Atheros chipset design presents some problems for open source driver development.

The Multiband Atheros Driver for WiFi (madwifi) driver that is now available for BSD and Linux is currently the only working implementation of a driver for Atheros chipsets. There is a complete GPL driver implementation in the works. According to Jean Tourrilhes's page, some anonymous people and companies have worked to get documentation on the Atheros chipset made available, and are supporting the development of the GPL driver. This driver is known as "ar5k," and the web page for it is *http://team.vantronix.net/ar5k/*. As of this writing, the ar5k driver is not yet functional, and development seems to be stalled.

The FCC mandates that the manufacturers of software radios must prevent the software from being modified so that it can operate outside the FCC regulations. This mandate also makes it very difficult for maintainers of Linux distributions to include the madwifi driver as a package. The package cannot be redistributed under the GPL because the source is not freely available. As such, there are no Debian packages or RPMs of the madwifi driver available.

The following is from the README in the madwifi installation source:

> The ath_hal module contains the Atheros Hardware Access Layer (HAL). This code manages much of the chip-specific operation of the driver. The HAL is provided in a binary-only form in order to comply with FCC regulations. In particular, a radio transmitter can only be operated at power levels and on frequency channels for which it is approved. The FCC requires that a software-defined radio cannot be configured by a user to operate outside the approved power levels and frequency channels.

> This makes it difficult to open-source code that enforces limits on the power levels, frequency channels and other parameters of the radio transmitter. See *http://ftp.fcc.gov/Bureaus/Engineering_Technology/Orders/2001/fcc01264.pdf* for the specific FCC regulation. Because the module is provided in a binary-only form it is marked "Proprietary"; this means when you load it you will see messages that your system is now "tainted".

As of this writing, the most current version of the madwifi driver can be obtained from the SourceForge project page at *http://sourceforge.net/projects/ madwifi*. The driver supports both MiniPCI and Cardbus devices. The driver can be built as a module or linked into the kernel and depends on two other modules: *wlan.o* and *ath_hal.o*.

The madwifi driver has been written and tested with kernel Version 2.4.20 and the Linux Wireless Tools v25. As the README says, "expect some rough edges if you deviate from that combo," particularly with older kernel or Wireless Tools versions.

In order for the madwifi driver to compile and run successfully, make sure a number of things are compiled into your kernel:

- Kernel-tree PCMCIA (CONFIG_NET_RADIO)
- Wireless Tools (CONFIG_NET_WIRELESS)
- ACPI Support (CONFIG_ACPI)
- PCI Hotplug Support (CONFIG_HOTPLUG_PCI, CONFIG_HOTPLUG_PCI_ACPI)

Note that the ACPI and PCI Hotplug features are considered experimental in the 2.4 kernel tree.

To begin compiling the driver, unpack the *.tgz* file and change into the top-level directory (if you are using a more recent version, the filename and directory will differ):

```
# tar xzvf madwifi-20030802.tgz
# cd madwifi-20030802
```

The *Makefile.inc* should automatically determine the location of your running kernel and modules. If not, you may need to edit *Makefile.inc* manually and specify the KERNEL_PATH and MODULE_PATH variables.

On most Linux distributions, you should simply be able to execute these commands:

```
# make
# make install
```

make install copies the drivers to the appropriate location, i.e., */lib/modules/<kernel version>/<net>*. You can then run modprobe or insmod from inside the source directory to load the modules:

```
# insmod wlan/wlan.o
# insmod ath_hal/ath_hal.o
Warning: loading ath_hal/ath_hal.o will taint the kernel:
  non-GPL license - Proprietary
# insmod driver/ath_pci.o
```

Support for 802.11a and 802.11g cards in Linux is very new. The madwifi driver in particular is still being actively worked on. As such, there is every possibility that the last stable release of code will not work with your kernel or your hardware. Until development on madwifi settles down (keep your eye on the web site), we suggest that you check out the latest CVS code of the driver to get the most current updates.

CVS is a revision control system used by many open source project developers. Open source development sites like SourceForge (*http://www.sourceforge.net*) provide CVS access both for developers and for end users.

CVS is required to access a CVS repository. Most distributions install CVS by default, located in */usr/bin/cvs*. Debian users can install CVS by executing the commands apt-get update; apt-get install cvs. Red Hat users can find the CVS RPM on their installation CDROM or from a Red Hat source mirror. Many other distributions that use RPM can find CVS at *http://www.rpmfind.net*.

To obtain the latest CVS code for the madwifi driver, change to a directory where you want the code located and execute the following command:

```
cvs -z3 -d:pserver:anonymous@cvs.sourceforge.net:/cvsroot/madwifi \
    co madwifi
```

This will log in to the CVS server at sourceforge.net as an anonymous (read-only) user and check out (co) the madwifi source tree. It will place the source code in a directory titled *madwifi* in the directory you were in when the command was executed.

Once you have obtained the CVS code, you should be able to follow the compilation instructions described earlier. However, be aware that CVS code can change frequently, sometimes daily. CVS code is development code, which means it can have bugs. It may not compile on your system at all.

There are two excellent sources of information and assistance you can consult if you run into problems with the madwifi driver. The first is the excellent madwifi-users mailing list. Subscribe at *http://lists.sourceforge.net/lists/listinfo/madwifi-users*. The mailing list archives can be searched at *http://sourceforge.net/mailarchive/forum.php?forum=madwifi-users*. Second, a FAQ has been created by a volunteer member of the mailing list and has several tips for getting the CVS code to compile in various situations. The FAQ is located at *http://www.mattfoster.clara.co.uk/madwifi-faq.htm*.

## CHAPTER 3

Getting On the Network

Assuming that you didn't encounter any problems in Chapter 2, you should now have a functional wireless network adapter, and the knowledge to configure and use it under Linux. If you have a wireless network set up at home or at work, chances are you will use this network most of the time.

If, however, you have Linux installed on a notebook PC, chances are you're often in transit, and you probably want to find and use wireless networks in cities, airports, hotels, and conferences.

This chapter discusses tools and techniques that allow you to find available wireless networks, whether they are fee-based or free.

Hotspots

It would be pretty much impossible for any notebook user not to have heard the term *hotspot*. Wireless hotspots are popping up in many locations; coffee shops, airports, hotels, conferences, restaurants, city parks, and libraries are just a few places where you might find a hotspot.

You can easily build your own hotspot, and we cover this in detail in Chapter 6. A hotspot requires at least one access point, a good antenna that covers the needed area, a broadband Internet connection, and some form of access control (if you want to restrict access).

Most hotspots are built around these four basic pieces. Some use DSL as their broadband Internet connection, while many of the commercial hotspots use a T1 line or other dedicated circuit. However, many hotspots are simply in a house or apartment, particularly in dense urban areas, and these connections are DSL, cable, or even simply dial-up.

Before you leave for a trip, research online to find hotspots along the way to your destination. To find both fee-based and free hotspots, consult the following web sites:

WiFinder
   http://www.wifinder.com/search.php

HotSpotList
   http://www.hotspotlist.com

T-Mobile Hotspots
   http://www.t-mobile.com/hotspot

Wi-Fi Zone Finder
   http://www.wi-fizone.org/zoneLocator.asp

JiWire
   http://www.jiwire.com

Wireless Hotspot Providers

There are an increasing number of commercial hotspot providers, ranging from large companies, such as T-Mobile and WayPort, to small operations in local coffee shops, and wireless aggregators that allow you to access multiple networks from different hotspot providers.

Nearly all of these providers restrict access to their hotspots through a *captive portal*. This form of access control intercepts all TCP/IP traffic. To gain access through a captive portal, simply open a web browser and attempt to navigate to any web page, such as *http://www.oreilly.com*. Your browser traffic is intercepted and redirected to the login screen of the hotspot's portal software. Figure 3-1 shows a typical hotspot login screen.

With commercial hotspot providers, you have a number of payment choices for access. The large operators all offer monthly subscriptions in addition to pay-as-you-go pricing. This is convenient if you don't want to sign up with a specific provider or if you don't travel enough to justify the $20–40 per month that most monthly subscriptions cost.

If you travel frequently, you may want to sign up with one of the wireless hotspot providers. Deciding which one to use is tricky. It really depends on where you think you may spend the most time. T-Mobile provides access in nearly all Starbucks coffee shops, as well as Borders bookstores, Kinko's copy centers, and many airports. Surf and Sip has neatly taken up many of the non-Starbucks coffee shops in major cities. WayPort is a good choice if you need hotel or airport access.

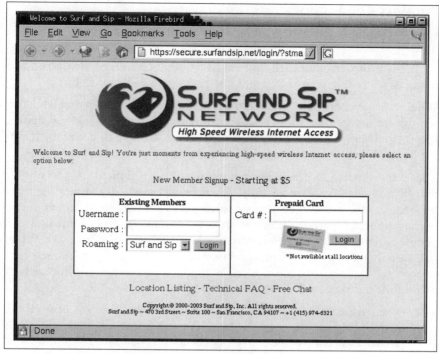

Figure 3-1. Typical hotspot login to a captive portal

Associating with a hotspot provider is easy. They all have easy-to-identify SSIDs. You can also locate their hotspots ahead of time using their web pages. Table 3-1 lists some major hotspot providers, their SSIDs, and their web pages for locating their hotspots.

Table 3-1. Hotspot providers, SSIDs, and location finders

Hotspot provider	SSID	Web location finder
Cometa	Cometa-Hotspot	http://www.cometa-hotspot.com/locations/
STSN	STSN	http://www.stsn.com/hotel_locator.php
Surf and Sip	SurfandSip	http://www.surfandsip.com
T-Mobile	tmobile	http://locations.hotspot.t-mobile.com/
Verizon Wireless	Verizon	http://www.verizonwireless.com/wifi/hot_spot/
WayPort	wayport	http://www.wayport.com/locations

Wireless Aggregators

With the rise in availability of commercial hotspot providers comes a conundrum: which hotspot provider do you sign up with? As you've seen, there are many providers, and each of them has different coverage. If you're a real road warrior, using several different hotspots could cost quite a bit.

Wireless aggregators have come into the market to address this problem. You sign up for an account with the aggregator, and through its revenue-sharing agreements with different hotspot providers, you are able to use many different hotspots while maintaining a single account with one company.

That's the theory. In practice, roaming is still very difficult, especially for non-Windows users. Boingo (*http://www.boingo.com*), the largest aggregator, requires the use of proprietary software on your notebook, and as of this writing, that software is Windows-only. There are reports of adventurous people running the Boingo software using a Windows emulator like Wine, but we're not going to attempt to cover that here. Unless the web-based captive portal offers a roaming option, roaming with Boingo and Linux isn't possible at this time.

Two other aggregators fall into the same category: Trustive (*http://www.trustive.com/*) provides only a Windows client software package, and iPass (*http://www.ipass.com*), while providing clients for Windows, Windows CE/Pocket PC, Mac OS X, and Mac OS, does not provide a Linux software client.

Fortunately, there is at least one roaming company that has gotten it right: FatPort. FatPort's roaming customers don't need any special software. Its locations and partner locations all use captive portal software that requires only a web browser.

Although FatPort is based primarily in Canada, it has a wide range of partner agreements with Surf and Sip, Boingo, and iPass. While not a complete coverage of all roaming sites, this is an excellent option for the Linux user who is constantly on the road. FatPort accounts range from hourly rates to yearly subscriptions. Check out *http://www.fatport.com* for more details.

Open Hotspots

Just as the software world is split into proprietary and open source, the hotspot world is populated with commercial hotspots (which we've covered) and open hotspots. These open wireless networks span a wide range of locations and philosophies:

- Businesses providing free wireless access as an incentive to customers. Hotels, coffee shops, restaurants, bookstores, and other businesses are all using free wireless access as a way to bring in customers and entice them to stay.

- Public places serving up hotspots as a public service. Libraries, city parks, town squares, city halls, and other publicly owned spaces view free wireless access as a way of promoting their city, county, or other locations, and attracting visitors.

- Community wireless groups working with businesses, governments, and private citizens placing hotspots in all sorts of locations, including apartment buildings, parks, downtown areas, and any place that would benefit from free wireless access. Many community groups view this as a way to better their neighborhoods.

Open hotspots are a mixed bag. You may simply be associating with a wireless router in someone's apartment, connected to his DSL line. On the other hand, it may be a custom-built Linux-based access point in a New York City park, installed by NYCWireless (*http://www.nycwireless.net*), with a T1 or DSL backhaul.

Access control is also going to vary. If you connect to someone's home network with an SSID of "default" or "linksys," chances are you won't find a captive portal or any other form of access control in place. Many community and business that open hotspots have some sort of access control in place, such as a web page that asks you to agree to a Terms of Service (ToS) agreement before you are allowed to use the network.

A good place to locate open hotspots is the Personal Telco Project in Portland, Oregon. Visit its Wireless Communities site at *http://www.personaltelco.net/ index.cgi/WirelessCommunities*. A second place to look for hotspots is WiFi-Maps at *http://www.wifimaps.com*. This site, while still in development, shows you hotspots all over the world.

Associating with Hotspots

To associate your Linux notebook with an open or commercial hotspot, you have a couple of options. If you know the SSID of the hotspot, simply set the SSID using `iwconfig`:

```
$ iwconfig eth1 ESSID SurfandSip
```

Once you've done this, fire up your favorite web browser, attempt to navigate to any web page, and you will be redirected to the hotspot captive portal login, as shown in Figure 3-1.

If you've settled in a coffee shop that has an unknown hotspot provider, the first thing you can try is:

```
$ iwconfig eth1 ESSID any
```

If there is a hotspot in range, your card should find and associate with it. This can be tricky, especially if you're in a densely populated urban area. For example, sitting in a coffee shop in San Francisco, we were able to associate with four different SSIDs. The signal strength from the coffee shop hotspot was not as strong as a neighboring open hotspot located in someone's apartment.

In these cases, you want to identify all of the access points in your immediate area before you decide which one to associate with. There are several methods of finding access points with Linux, and we cover each one in turn.

Wireless Network Discovery

If your network card supports it, the easiest method of locating available wireless networks is included with the Wireless Tools, which you installed in Chapter 2. The iwlist command supports a scanning parameter that lists any access points in range. It's worth noting, however, that some wireless card drivers do not support this feature. Chief among them is the orinoco_cs driver. If you're using this driver, you must use one of the alternative discovery methods next.

To determine if your card and driver support scanning, execute the iwlist command with no other parameters. If you see "scanning" listed in the output, you should be able to scan for available access points. Note that you must have root access to use this command.

```
# iwlist
Usage: iwlist [interface] frequency
              [interface] channel
              [interface] ap
              [interface] accesspoints
              [interface] bitrate
              [interface] rate
              [interface] encryption
              [interface] key
              [interface] power
              [interface] txpower
              [interface] retry
              [interface] scanning
```

Once you've determined that you can use the scanning parameter, execute the command. You must specify the network adapter that corresponds to your wireless card (eth1 in the following example). Again, you must have root access.

```
# iwlist eth1 scanning

eth1    Scan completed :
    Cell 01 - Address: 00:02:6F:01:76:31
            ESSID:"NoCat "
            Mode:Master
            Frequency: 2.462GHz
            Quality:0/92 Signal level:-50 dBm Noise level:-100 dBm
            Encryption key:off
            Bit Rate:1Mb/s
            Bit Rate:2Mb/s
            Bit Rate:5.5Mb/s
            Bit Rate:11Mb/s

    Cell 02 - Address: 00:30:65:03:E7:0A
            Essid:"SurfandSip "
            Mode:Master
            Frequency:2.422GHz
            Quality:0/92 Signal level:-66 dBm Noise level:-96 dBm
            Encryption key:off
            Bit Rate:1Mb/s
            Bit Rate:2Mb/s
            Bit Rate:5.5Mb/s
            Bit Rate:11Mb/s
```

Now that you've obtained a list of available networks, see what providers are in your area, and make a decision on the hotspot to use. scanning shows you relative signal strengths, so pay attention. You don't necessarily want to associate with the weakest hotspot in the area.

Note also that the scanning output gives you the frequency of each hotspot as well as whether encryption (WEP) is enabled.

Kismet

In contrast to the small bit of information you can glean by using iwlist scanning, Kismet is a seriously advanced wireless diagnostic tool. It is a passive network scanner, similar to commercial tools such as Network Associates' Sniffer Wireless and Airopeek. It is designed from the ground up specifically for scanning wireless networks, so it detects all 802.11 traffic from both access points and wireless clients. It can find "closed" networks (some access points allow you to disable the broadcast of the SSID) by monitoring traffic sent from clients, and it logs all raw 802.11 frames in standard *pcap(3)* format for later use with other specialized tools such as Ethereal, an open source network protocol analyzer.

To take advantage of Kismet's advanced features, you need a wireless card and driver capable of entering RF Monitor or promiscuous mode. Cards in this category include the Prism-based cards using the host_ap driver and the Cisco Aironet cards using the airo driver. Kismet also works well with Atheros-based 802.11a/g cards using the madwifi driver. However, if you need monitor mode in the madwifi driver, download the latest CVS driver code. Finally, you'll need a patched orinoco_cs driver or the latest CVS version of the orinoco_cs code to support monitor mode with Orinoco cards. We covered this in detail in Chapter 2.

Kismet is available as a package with most distributions. Debian users can install Kismet using apt-get:

```
apt-get install kismet
```

Red Hat and Fedora users can obtain RPM packages from *http://www. rpmfind.net*. Mandrake users can install Kismet using urpmi:

```
urpmi kismet
```

If you want to read Kismet's dump files in Ethereal, you must download the source code for Kismet from *http://www.kismetwireless.net*. Also, Ethereal must be installed from source, and the Ethereal source code tree must be available. Change into the Kismet source directory, and configure Kismet as follows:

```
# ./configure --with-ethereal=/your/ethereal/source/path/here
```

Once that is done, build Kismet with standard compile commands:

```
make
make dep
make install
```

Once Kismet is compiled or installed from source, you must edit */usr/local/ etc/kismet.conf* to suit your system. If you've installed from package, the file is probably located in */etc/kismet.conf*. At a minimum, you must edit the source= line to match your hardware. The format for this line is *driver,device,description*. For example, with a Prism card, edit the line to read:

```
source=hostap_cs,wlan0,Prism
```

See the comments in the *kismet.conf* file for more information on supported drivers.

If you want Kismet to play sound effects when it finds new SSIDs, it will. By default, it expects */usr/bin/play* to be installed, which is part of the Sox sound utilities, but any command-line audio player works. All of the audio and other display parameters are configured in */usr/local/etc/kismet_ui.conf*.

When Kismet is running, your wireless card will be in RF monitoring mode. Note that once in this mode, your card can no longer associate with wireless networks, so you may not have a network connection.

Now execute the kismet command using your normal user ID. You don't have to run the Kismet user interface as root. You should see the Kismet screen as shown in Figure 3-2.

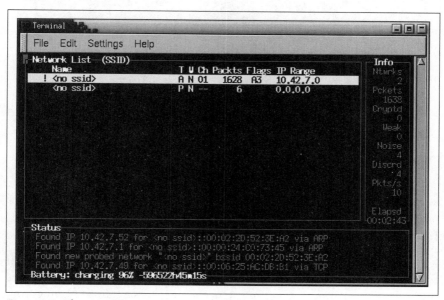

Figure 3-2. The main Kismet screen

Kismet incorporates a hopping algorithm to switch between radio channels in order to find all the networks in your locations. This makes your card hop between radio channels. The hop pattern is configurable to your needs. See the kismet_hopper manpage for details. Note that newer versions of Kismet call kismet_hopper automatically

By default, Kismet initially scans the network list based on the last time it saw traffic from each network. This list constantly changes, making it difficult, if not impossible, to select any one network for more detailed information.

To keep the list from constantly changing, manage the scanning sort order by hitting s at any time, followed by the desired sort order. For example, to sort by SSID, hit ss. Now use the arrow keys to select a network for further details. Press h at any time to see keystroke help and q to close any pop-up windows.

To get more information on a specific network, select it using the arrow keys and press i. You will see a more detailed screen as shown in Figure 3-3.

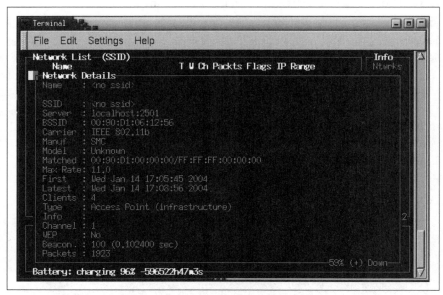

Figure 3-3. Kismet's detailed network information

Kismet finds closed networks (networks that do not broadcast their SSID). If there is no network traffic coming from a client of that network, Kismet lists the SSID with a name of *<no_ssid>*. Once Kismet sees a frame of traffic from a client, the SSID updates.

Note that your card is now out of monitor mode, but the original network settings are not returned. You can physically eject the card and reinsert or execute:

```
# cardctl reset
```

AP Radar

The previous methods are perfectly usable and provide you with all sorts of information regarding the available wireless networks near you. These are manual methods that don't approach the level of ease in wireless detection and configuration that is offered with other operating systems.

AP Radar is an attempt to make detection of and connecting to wireless networks easier and more manageable. It is both a graphical network discovery tool and a wireless profile manager. Using the Wireless Extensions, it has the ability to watch for wireless networks while staying associated to your existing network. It focuses on automating tasks, so that when you come in range of your home network, you are automatically connected.

AP Radar is the work of Don Park, and you can obtain it from the project's SourceForge development site at *http://apradar.sourceforge.net*. Currently, it is available as an RPM package or as a source file. In order to get the package running, you must have GNOME Version 2. You'll also need a 2.4.20 kernel or higher, or any 2.6 kernel.

To compile AP Radar from source, you must have the GTK+ header files and libraries, as well as the GTKmm header files and libraries. Users of Mandrake, RedHat, and other distributions that use RPM should see the AP Radar README file for a list of required RPMs.

Debian users should be able to install the same packages via apt-get; however, you must set up apt to obtain packages from the testing or unstable trees. See the sources.list manpage for details.

To build AP Radar from source, uncompress the source code file and change into the newly created directory. The commands to compile are standard, although the filename and top-level directory name will differ if you are using a newer version than we did:

```
$ tar xzvf apradar-0.50.tar.gz
$ cd apradar-0.50
$ ./configure
$ make
$ su -c "make install"
```

AP Radar works with a number of wireless cards and drivers. To determine whether AP Radar will run with your card and driver, execute iwlist scanning:

```
# iwlist wlan0 scanning
```

You should see some output like the following:

```
eth1   Scan completed :
       Cell 01 - Address: 00:02:6F:01:76:31
               ESSID:"NoCat "
               Mode:Master
               Frequency: 2.462GHz
               Quality:0/92 Signal level:-50 dBm Noise level:-100 dBm
               Encryption key:off
               Bit Rate:1Mb/s
               Bit Rate:2Mb/s
               Bit Rate:5.5Mb/s
               Bit Rate:11Mb/s
```

If you see anything else, chances are AP Radar will not function with your card. Some reasons for this include the use of the following drivers:

Orinoco_cs driver, wvlan, wavelan, and wavelan2 drivers

None of these drivers currently support wireless scanning. Patches are available for the orinoco_cs driver to enable scanning, and the CVS code for orinoco_cs also supports scanning. See Chapter 2 for more details.

host_ap driver

If you are using the newest host_ap code, Version 0.1.3 (as of this writing), you must execute the following command as root for AP Radar to function properly:

```
# iwpriv wlan0 host_roaming 1
```

Once you install AP Radar and determine that it will function with your wireless card/driver, simply start it as root:

```
# apradar
```

If you experience problems starting AP Radar, it may be due to oddities in your wireless card driver and how it writes status to */proc/net/wireless*. In order to avoid this problem, start AP Radar by specifying the interface name (ath0 in the following example):

```
# apradar -i ath0
```

The AP Radar main screen appears, as shown in Figure 3-4.

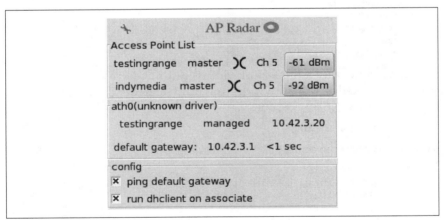

Figure 3-4. AP Radar main screen

AP Radar shows all access points that are in range. Almost every field on the screen is either clickable or provides you with information when you hover the mouse over it.

To associate with any of the access points shown under Access Point List, simply click on the name of the access point. By default, AP Radar not only associates your wireless card with the selected AP, but it runs dhclient to obtain an IP address via DHCP.

This and one other option can be set by clicking on the red symbol at the top of the AP Radar screen. You can set two options:

Ping default gateway
> This monitors the gateway that you receive from DHCP. When it does not receive a response from a ping after more than a second, AP Radar assumes that the gateway is out of range.

Run dhclient on associate
> This allows you to specify whether you want AP Radar to obtain a DHCP address for your PC after it associates with an access point. Turn this off if you need to use static addressing.

In addition to displaying the SSID, mode, and channel and signal strength for each access point, AP Radar also displays whether WEP is enabled by displaying the warchalking symbol for the network. See the later section "Warchalking."

Wardriving

Back in the good ol' days of hacking, *wardialing* was (and still is) the act of having a computer use a modem to dial phone numbers from a list or mathematically step through all possible numbers in a telephone exchange. Malicious hackers noted each line that had an answering modem and went back to those numbers to find systems that could be compromised.

With the proliferation of notebook computers, handheld computers, and wireless network cards, the term *wardriving* has been coined. When you wardrive, usually a two-man team takes off: one driving and the other handling the wireless scanning. In dense urban areas, a wardrive can locate hundreds if not thousands of active SSIDs.

With some added equipment such as external antennas and a GPS receiver, wardrivers can log each wireless network and place them on a physical map. *http://www.wifimaps.com* is just one example of a collaborative effort to place wardriving maps from all over the world in an online database. Kismet (discussed previously) makes an excellent tool for wardriving, and it interfaces with GPS systems. See Chapter 10 and the Kismet documentation for details.

People wardrive for different reasons. While many people do it simply for enjoyment or for the technical knowledge gained, there are also those who have more illicit purposes in mind. Some wardrivers are specifically out there looking for insecure networks that can be compromised for various purposes.

Wardriving may not be legal in your area. While it does not appear to be illegal in the United States, there are many countries where it is considered a crime.

Warflying

In the same vein, *warflying* is conducted by those lucky people who can afford to rent a plane for a few hours or who actually have their own plane. Warflyers generally need external antennas to pick up wireless networks below the plane.

If you think this practice sounds too far-fetched to be true, Google for the phrase "warflying". You'll be surprised at how many people do this.

Warchalking

During the Great Depression, many people in the United States were homeless because of economic conditions. Tramps and hobos traveled the country looking for work and food. Due to scarcity of work, hobos were not welcome in many places. Over time, hobos devised a set of logos that could be written in chalk or stone, or carved in trees near various houses, restaurants, and other places. These logos could communicate everything from "free food" to "you will be beaten."

You can visit the following web sites for more symbols used by the hobos:

- *http://www.slackaction.com/signroll.htm*
- *http://sedaliakatydepot.com/hobo.htm*

Matt Jones, an Internet product designer, operates a web site (*http://blackbeltjones.com*) that serves primarily as the Londoner's online resume and portfolio. In 2002, Jones combined the practice of using a sniffer tool to detect a wireless network with the hobos' set of logos to come up with the symbols for wireless networks (see Figure 3-5).

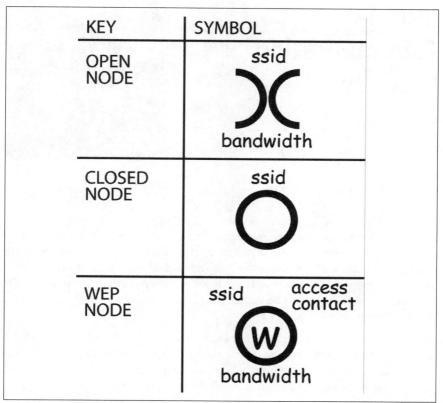

KEY	SYMBOL
OPEN NODE	ssid)(bandwidth
CLOSED NODE	ssid O
WEP NODE	ssid access contact (W) bandwidth

Figure 3-5. Warchalking symbols

Using these symbols, wireless users can discover if there is an available wireless network for their use. He was inspired by architecture students "chalking up the pavement" on his way to lunch. During a lunch, Jones and a friend, who had recently been discussing hobo signs, called their idea warchalking. You can learn more at *http://www.warchalking.org*.

## CHAPTER 4

Communicating Securely

In a wired network, physical security is complicated but manageable. You can restrict physical access to routers, switches, and network hardware. You can provide a complex authentication mechanism for proving that users are who they say they are. You can set up Virtual LANs or Virtual Private Networks for even more security. Even if an attacker were to plug into your wireless network, it would be difficult to penetrate further with these kinds of security measures in place.

The wireless network world is not nearly this secure. In fact, it's not secure at all. Disassembling your network packets and transmitting them wirelessly means that anyone within reach can see them. A wily attacker could join or passively monitor your network from a mile away with a high-gain antenna, and you would never see him.

The Pitfalls of WEP

The IEEE specifications for 802.11a/b/g all provide a form of encryption called Wired Equivalent Privacy (WEP). WEP operates at the Media Access Control (MAC) layer, or the Data Link layer, between the Physical Layer (radio waves) and the Network Layer (TCP). WEP encryption is based on the RC4 algorithm from RSA Data Security and employs a 40-bit encryption key.

Anyone who knows the secret key (unless you're the only user on the network, this key is shared, so it's not all that secret) can participate in a WEP network. Secret keys are generally either plaintext words or somewhat longer combinations of hexadecimal numbers.

There are two major problems with WEP:

- Encryption is handled at the Data Link layer, so if you connect to a WEP network with your notebook, the communication between your notebook and the access point is encrypted. All packets are decrypted at the access point and sent from there in the clear.

- Other computers that also have the secret key for this WEP network can read all packets sent to and from your computer. The secret key is a "shared" key, which means that all devices that encrypt packets must use the same key. Some access points use a passphrase to generate the WEP key, making the key even easier to deduce. Once you are connected to a WEP network, you can do all the packet sniffing you want with a tool like Ethereal.

A team of cryptographers from the University of California at Berkeley, as well as several other groups (see the references at the end of this section), have identified weaknesses in the way that WEP keys are generated and used, effectively making the number of bits in the key immaterial. Even though many manufacturers have added extra bits to the key length, up to 152 bits, the longer key length provides minimal protection, because WEP is not a well-designed cryptographic system.

With all of these problems, why is WEP still supported by wireless equipment manufacturers? Until recently, there had not been another standard for wireless encryption. You could have run a Virtual Private Network (VPN) on top of your wireless network, but this would have presented its own set of challenges, and it is not practical for home or even small-business users. The Wi-Fi Alliance announced a standard called Wireless Protected Access (WPA) in mid-2002. WPA is based on a draft of the IEEE 802.11i specification, which will probably be ratified in mid-2004. We cover WPA a bit later in the chapter.

So why would you want to use WEP on your wireless network at all? Consider it a first line of defense. While it is definitely possible to crack its keys and gain access to a WEP network, someone who is looking for free wireless access will choose an open network when given the choice. However, if you are worried about an attacker specifically targeting your network, you must take stronger measures.

Consider not using WEP at all. There are other alternatives that provide stronger encryption and authentication, and we cover those in this chapter. However, if you want an easy out-of-the-box setup, WEP is your ticket. To keep your WEP network as secure as possible, keep these guidelines in mind:

Make your secret key difficult to crack. Once a hacker has captured enough frames from your encrypted network, he needs to run a tool to guess your secret key. This is no different from a hacker running crack against a password database. The more complex your key, the less likely a standard dictionary attack will crack it. Choose a long, complex key that utilizes nonalphanumeric characters. If you can, use hexadecimal strings. Use the longest key that your hardware will support. If you have access points and clients that support 128-bit WEP, by all means use it. However, some implementations of WEP have weaknesses that allow attackers to recover the key even without mounting a dictionary attack.

Change your secret key often. WEP key attacks rely on two methods: a dictionary attack or the collection of large amounts of frames data in order to deduce the secret key. Obviously, you provide less of a chance for an attacker to break your key when you change it often. However, this option becomes more cumbersome with larger networks, giving you the classic key-distribution problem.

*Use **WEP** in combination with other security measures.* If your network uses equipment from a single manufacturer, you may be able to take advantage of nonstandard security features. Cisco and Proxim, for example, support rapid WEP key rotation and dynamic rekeying. If all of your clients can take advantage of these features, use them. You should also consider whether the various IP tunneling or VPN solutions will fit into your network infrastructure.

Several security measures that come standard with many access points are almost useless in protecting your wireless network:

Disabling SSID broadcast
> This creates a "hidden" network by causing the access point to suppress the broadcast of SSID information. In order to join a network with SSID broadcast disabled, the client must manually enter the SSID.
>
> Premise: if you don't know the SSID, you can't join the network.
>
> Reality: Kismet and other wireless network scanners can easily pick up the SSID by monitoring traffic from clients of the "hidden" network.

MAC address filtering
> Most access points allow you to set up a list of allowed network cards by entering their MAC address. If the access point sees a MAC address that is not on the list, it will not allow that device to associate.
>
> Premise: only authorized network cards can join the network.
>
> Reality: Kismet and other wireless scanners can easily pick up MAC addresses by monitoring client traffic on the wireless network. Spoofing a MAC address is very easy under Linux and other operating systems, allowing easy access to the network. Also, wireless network cards can easily be stolen. The MAC address filter only authenticates a device, so anyone can use it.

IP address filtering

Similar to MAC address filtering, this technique allows you to set up a list of allowed IP addresses that can send TCP/IP traffic on the network. Other machines may be allowed to associate with the access point, but they would not be able to participate in any TCP/IP network.

Premise: only known IP addresses are allowed to communicate on the network.

Reality: any network sniffer or analyzer, such as Ethereal or tcpdump, can easily find IP addresses in use on any given network. Spoofing IP addresses is even easier than spoofing MAC addresses.

References

As mentioned previously, several groups have identified weaknesses in the way that WEP keys are generated and used. To learn more, consult the following sources:

- Your 802.11 Wireless Network has No Clothes (*http://www.cs.umd.edu/ ~waa/wireless.pdf*) by Arbaugh, Shankar, and Wan. University of Maryland, March 30, 2001.
- Weaknesses in the Key Scheduling Algorithm of RC4 (*http://www. crypto.com/papers/others/rc4_ksaproc.ps*) by Fluhrer, Mantin, and Shamir. July 25, 2001.
- Using the Fluhrer, Mantin, and Shamir Attack to Break WEP (*http:// www.cs.rice.edu/~astubble/wep*). AT&T Labs Technical Report by Stubblefield, Ioannidis, and Rubin. August 21, 2001.
- Security of the WEP Algorithm (*http://www.isaac.cs.berkeley.edu/isaac/ wep-faq.html*) by Borisov, Goldberg, and Wagner, UC Berkeley. April 1, 2001.

WEP with Linux

Back in Chapter 2, we covered the use of *schemes* to set up multiple wireless networks on your PC with the ability to switch between them as needed. Here again is a sample */etc/pcmcia/wireless.opts* that contains schemes for two networks and includes the use of a WEP key:

```
case "$ADDRESS" in

home,0,*,*)
    INFO="Home wireless setup"
    ESSID="home"
    MODE="managed"
    CHANNEL="11"
```

```
        RATE="auto"
        ;;
yourjob,0,*,*)
        INFO="Work wireless setup"
        ESSID="BigCorp"
        MODE="managed"
        CHANNEL="4"
        RATE="auto"
        KEY="s:bigsecret"
esac
```

Use `cardctl yourjob` to switch to the WEP-enabled scheme.

The corresponding `iwconfig` command to configure a WEP key is `iwconfig enc` or `iwconfig key`. This command accepts several parameters:

`iwconfig eth1 key [on|off]`
    `on` and `off` enable and disable encryption, respectively.

`iwconfig eth1 key 0a12fc132`
    Secret keys can be entered as hex strings with or without separating dashes.

`iwconfig eth1 key s:supersecret`
    ASCII secret keys can be entered in the form of *s:secretkey*.

`iwconfig eth1 key s:supersecret [2]`
    An index of keys can be generated by appending an index number in brackets ([ ]) to the key when it is entered.

`iwconfig eth1 key [2]`
    You can change secret keys by passing the index number of the key as an option.

`iwconfig eth1 key [open|restricted]`
    Two operating modes are available: `open` accepts nonencrypted traffic, and `restricted` accepts only encrypted packets.

The Future Is 802.11i

The future solution from the IEEE to provide real wireless security and a strong cryptographic system is the proposed 802.11i standard. The IEEE Task Group responsible for this standard maintains a web page at *http://grouper.ieee.org/groups/802/11/Reports/tgi_update.htm*. As of December 2003, draft 7 of this proposal has been sent to a "sponsor ballot," and the results are not yet available. The word on the street is that 802.11i will become a ratified standard sometime in mid-2004.

Using NoCatAuth

If WPA isn't an option for you, you may want to consider setting up a captive portal (see "Wireless Hotspot Providers" in Chapter 3).

NoCatAuth, which ships with Pebble Linux (see Chapter 6), is a captive portal that offers two modes of operation: open and authenticated. Open mode intercepts a user's first web request with a simple splash page and a Click here to continue button. Authenticated mode relies on both the local NoCatAuth daemon and an authentication service on another machine. The daemon and authentication service communicate via an encrypted channel, so passwords are never sent in the clear.

NoCatAuth can be downloaded from *http://nocat.net*, and there is also a wiki and a fairly high volume development mailing list. Other captive portal systems are available for Linux, as well. You can find out more about them on the Personal Telco Project's portal software page at *http://www.personaltelco.net/index.cgi/PortalSoftware*.

The final standard of 802.11i will likely address the following:

Use of 802.1x for authentication
802.1x is a specification framework for mutual authentication between a client and an access point. 802.1x may also use a backend authentication server such as RADIUS and take advantage of one of the Extensible Authentication Protocol (EAP) variations. 802.1x uses a new key for each session, so it resolves the issue of a single static WEP key.

Use of the Temporal Key Integrity Protocol (TKIP)
TKIP uses 128-bit dynamic keys that are changed at random times. Because of the constantly changing keys, intruders would be hard pressed to collect enough radio frames to compromise the keys.

Use of the Advanced Encryption Standard (AES)
The full implementation of 802.11i will utilize AES encryption to make a very strong cryptographic system. However, using AES requires significant computational horsepower. Current models of access points will not be able to handle AES due to limited processors. Expect new models that are "802.11i ready" to arrive on the market in 2004.

WPA: a Subset of 802.11i

Work on 802.11i began in 2001 after the weaknesses in WEP were made public by several teams of researchers. However, as with any standards body, the IEEE does not always work as fast as some people would like.

In mid-2002, the Wi-Fi Alliance, an industry consortium, proposed a subset of 802.11i, based on draft 3 from the IEEE working group, and called it Wireless Protected Access (WPA). The upcoming full IEEE implementation is also being referred to as WPA v2.

WPA, as a subset of the 802.11i proposed standard, incorporates two major features:

- Use of 802.1x for authentication
- Use of the Temporal Key Integrity Protocol (TKIP)

Chipsets supporting WPA began to become available in 2003. As of this writing, many access points either support WPA out of the box or have firmware updates available that include WPA.

WPA is not only an encryption mechanism but also includes 802.1x authentication, so support is required on the client for the authentication mechanism. As of this writing, your options are very limited regarding WPA support in Linux.

A few vendors have released updated firmware for older radio cards with WPA support; Apple AirPort cards, the Linksys WPC-11, and the Dell True-Mobile 1150 all have updates available.

WPA Support in Access Points

WPA and 802.1x are starting to become available in new access points, and earlier models are getting firmware updates that support WPA. The Linksys WRT54G and D-Link 900AP+ can both support WPA after a firmware upgrade. Newer Linksys and D-Link models are packaged with this support already enabled. Enterprise-level access points from Cisco, Proxim, and others also support WPA and are starting to advertise themselves as "802.11i-ready."

The Dell 1150 card is a rebranded Orinoco card; Agere has drivers on its web site listed "for evaluation only" that include this same update. However, Proxim, the new owner of the Orinoco brand, has nothing on its web site about WPA for older cards.

All of this is interesting but not immediately useful, however, because you can't use any of these cards under Linux and take advantage of the WPA code in the cards. Why? Because their associated Linux drivers do not support WPA. As of early 2004, you have two options if you want to use WPA under Linux, which we discuss below. In order to take advantage of these methods, you should understand how 802.1x works.

802.1x Authentication

802.1x was originally designed for wired Ethernet networks. It is a port-based authentication mechanism; when a client is authenticated, traffic is allowed to flow from the Ethernet port of the client through the authenticating device and out into the secured network.

In a wireless network, the principle is the same. Your notebook client is required to authenticate to the access point. If authentication does not occur, wireless frames are not allowed to be sent through the access point to the wired network.

802.1x authenticates users via a four-part process:

1. The Supplicant (the client that wants to access a network resource) connects to the Authenticator (whose resource is needed).
2. The Authenticator asks for credentials from the Supplicant and passes the credentials to the Authenticating Server.
3. The Authenticating Server authenticates the Supplicant on behalf of the Authenticator.
4. If the Supplicant is authenticated, access is then granted.

Note that before the authentication is performed, all the communications go through an uncontrolled port. After authentication, the controlled port is used.

For the Authenticating Server to authenticate the Supplicant, the Extensible Authentication Protocol (EAP) is used. EAP supports multiple authentication mechanisms and was originally developed for PPP.

There are many variants of EAP. Here are some that you may come across in wireless security literature:

EAP-MD5

 EAP-MD5 uses the challenge/response method to allow a server to authenticate a user by requesting a username and password. EAP-MD5 does not provide mutual authentication and is vulnerable to an offline dictionary attack.

EAP-Transport Layer Security (EAP-TLS)

EAP-TLS is based on X.509 (an ITU standard specifying the contents of a digital certificate) certificates. It is currently the most commonly used EAP type for securing wireless networks. However, EAP-TLS requires the use of Public Key Infrastructure (PKI), which is not feasible to be implemented on small networks.

Protected EAP (PEAP)

To counter the complexity of using EAP-TLS, PEAP was proposed as an alternative. PEAP uses a server-side certificate to allow the authentication of the server. It creates an EAP-TLS tunnel and then uses other authentication methods over the tunnel. EAP methods such as MD5, MS-CHAP, and MS-CHAP v2 are supported. PEAP was proposed as an IETF standard by Microsoft, Cisco, and RSA.

EAP Tunneled TLS (EAP-TTLS)

EAP-TTLS is similar to PEAP. It creates a tunnel between the user and the RADIUS server. It supports EAP methods such as MD5, MS-CHAP, and MS-CHAP v2.

Lightweight EAP (LEAP)

LEAP is Cisco's proprietary version of EAP, which works mostly with Cisco's wireless cards, RADIUS servers, and access points.

Microsoft Challenge-Handshake Authentication Protocol Version 2 (MS-CHAP v2)

Originally designed by Microsoft as a PPP authentication protocol, MSCHAP v2 is a password-based, challenge-response, mutual authentication protocol that uses the Message Digest 4 (MD4) and Data Encryption Standard (DES) algorithms to encrypt responses. MS-CHAP v2 is now an EAP type in Windows XP.

In the wireless world, suppose a notebook PC needs to connect to an access point. The notebook PC is the Supplicant, and the access point is the Authenticator. The access point, as the Authenticator, maintains a list of users and passwords and acts as the Authenticating Server. For small networks, this is not an issue; for large networks, however, this is an additional overhead in maintenance and a potential security risk, because it means that users must have another account and password.

In this case, the access point is told to refer to an external RADIUS server. RADIUS was developed by Livingston (now part of Lucent) for use in large dial-up modem pools, and is widely used by ISPs as the authentication mechanism for PPP and PPPoE users. The protocol is now defined by RFCs 2058, 2138, and 2139.

A RADIUS server maintains the user and password list, and performs authentication on behalf of the access point. The RADIUS server in this scenario is the Authenticating Server. Frequently, a RADIUS server is merely a method to transform authentication from some other source—for example, NIS, LDAP, or Kerberos authentication from a corporate network, which is then used by the RADIUS server to authenticate clients.

WPA on Linux

As of this writing, if you want to use WPA and/or 802.1x as a client on Linux, you have two options:

- Obtain the WLAN Driver Loader from Linuxant. This is a compatibility wrapper that allows you to use the standard Windows NDIS drivers that ship with wireless network cards. The advantage to this is that you can use a wide array of WiFi cards that currently do not have open source drivers available.

- Use a Prism-based Wi-Fi card with the latest HostAP CVS code. The newest versions of HostAP contain a WPA Supplicant in software that allows you to connect to WPA-protected networks.

If you want to use your Linux box as a WPA Authenticator, you're currently out of luck. The HostAP development team is working towards a full implementation of a WPA Authenticator. Right now, however, the *hostapd* daemon acts as an 802.1x Authenticator and authenticates against a RADIUS database.

Windows XP and Mac OS X both include support for 802.1x Supplicants. There is an open source implementation available for Linux called Xsupplicant, which is located at *http://www.open1x.org*.

A last option is to use your Linux box as the RADIUS server (Authenticating Server), and use an inexpensive access point as the WPA Authenticator. You can then use any WPA Supplicant to connect to the access points, and the backend authentication is handled by Linux/RADIUS.

WLAN Driver Loader

The Linuxant WLAN Driver Loader is a compatibility wrapper that allows the use of Windows NDIS wireless network drivers under Linux. Open source purists have issues with this software, because parts of it are released only in binary form, and after 30 days you must pay $20 for a permanent license. If you're completely opposed to anything Windows-related, keep in mind that this solution requires you to run Windows binary drivers, so this option may not be for you.

However, at this point in time, Linuxant is the only game in town if you need access to WPA-protected networks from a Linux box and you don't have a Prism-based wireless card. More to the point, the WLAN Driver Loader software allows you to use WiFi cards that do not have any open source drivers, including cards with chipsets from Broadcom and Texas Instruments. For many of the popular 802.11g cards, this may be your only option in Linux.

 A completely open source project to provide NDIS driver loading for Linux is located at *http://ndiswrapper.sourceforge. net*. As of this writing, support for radio chipsets is limited and there is no support for WPA.

You can obtain the software from the Linuxant web site at *http://www. linuxant.com/driverloader/wlan/full/downloads.php*. Linuxant provides RPM packages for Fedora, Red Hat, Mandrake, SuSE, and Turbolinux, and has built them for various architectures. Debian users can download a *driverloader.deb* package for installation with dpkg. For other systems, or if you wish to compile the driver, the source code can be downloaded as well.

In order to use the WLAN Driver Loader with WPA-PSK (personal) authentication, Linuxant provides a wpa_supplicant daemon that is also available in its downloads section. If you need to have WPA-EAP authentication, the Xsupplicant from *open1x.org* is required in addition to the wpa_supplicant from Linuxant. We cover installation of both supplicants next.

To compile the Driver Loader software from source, extract the package and change into the newly created directory. A single make command compiles and installs:

```
$ tar -xzf driverloader-version.tar.gz
$ cd driverloader-version
$ make install
```

By default, WLAN Driver Loader starts up a localhost web-based configuration tool on port 18020. You can access it by pointing a web browser to *http:// 127.0.0.1:18020* and logging in as root. You can also configure the software from a shell by executing the dldrconfig command.

If you wish to disable the web configurator for security reasons, use dldrconfig --webconf=off. To reenable it, use dldrconfig --webconf=127.0. 0.1:18020. Note that this command enables you to choose an alternate port for web-based configuration.

The `dldrconfig` command can also be used to change certain configuration options or recompile (generic packages only) the kernel modules after installation or kernel upgrades. Run `dldrconfig --help` for usage information.

If necessary, the device drivers can be unloaded using the `dldrstop` command.

Figure 4-1 shows the screen that you will see when you point a web browser at the localhost address created by the WLAN Driver Loader installation.

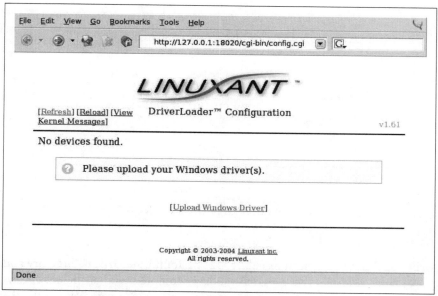

Figure 4-1. DriverLoader initial configuration

As shown, the first thing you must do is provide the DriverLoader with Windows NDIS drivers for the device you want to use. Click on the Upload Windows Driver link, and you will be presented with another screen, shown in Figure 4-2, that allows you to browse the local filesystem for an *.INF* or *.NTF* file that comes in the Windows driver package for your wireless card.

In our example, we used a Linksys WPC55AG PC Card. We downloaded the latest driver in ZIP format from the Linksys web site at *http://www.linksys.com/ download*. The file we obtained was *wpc55ag_driver_utility_v1.2.zip*, which we extracted using the `unzip` command. This created three subdirectories: *Drivers*, *image*, and *utility*. In the *Drivers* subdirectory, we found two *ar5211.sys* files and a *net5211.inf* file, which are exactly what we needed to continue. Obviously, this procedure will vary for each different wireless card. Linuxant maintains a list of wireless cards known to work with WLAN Driver Loader and links to downloads of the associated Windows drivers. This list can be found at *http://www.linuxant.com/driverloader/drivers.php*.

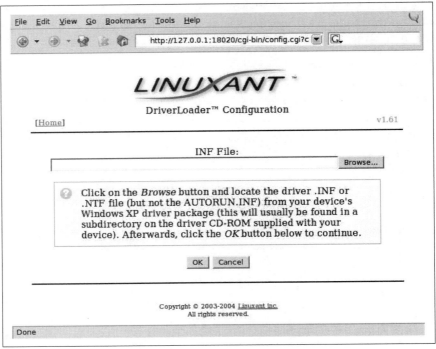

Figure 4-2. Browse for Windows driver files

Using the browse function in Figure 4-2, we found the *Drivers* directory and selected *net5211.inf*. The program quickly prompted us that the *ar5211.sys* file would be required and asked us to locate it. Once we clicked OK, the driver file loaded, and we were presented with the screen in Figure 4-3.

As we mentioned, the Linuxant software is proprietary. Permanent licenses can be purchased from Linuxant, and you can also obtain a 30-day license for trial purposes from the Linuxant web site at *http://www.linuxant.com/ store*. In order to get a license, you must fill out a registration form, wait for an email from Linuxant with a verification code, and enter that code. Once entered, you can generate a license. In order to do this, Linuxant requires the MAC address from your wireless card. You can obtain this either from the web interface or by running:

```
# dldrconfig -info
Linuxant DriverLoader for Wireless LAN devices, version 1.61

Web configurator: listening on 127.0.0.1:18020

Wireless interface name: eth1
        MAC address    : 00:0C:41:0A:24:F8
```

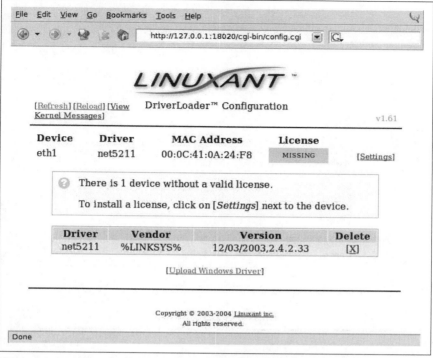

Figure 4-3. DriverLoader shows a missing license for the newly installed driver

```
Device instance: PCI-0000:05:00.0-168c:0013-1737:0017
Device driver    : net5211
License owner    : unknown
License key      : none
License status   : MISSING
```

Enter the MAC address into the form on the Linuxant web site, and after a few seconds, you will be presented with a 30-day-trial license key, a 12-character hexadecimal string that needs to be entered either in the web configurator or by executing dldrconfig --license. You'll be asked to enter the email address you used to register with Linuxant along with the license key, as shown in Figure 4-4.

Once you've entered the license information, you'll be returned to the main web screen, but this time it should show that your driver is loaded. You can perform additional configuration on the card by clicking on Settings and then selecting Advanced. Here you'll see the license information and any other configuration options that are supported by the NDIS driver for your card. A sample screen is shown in Figure 4-5.

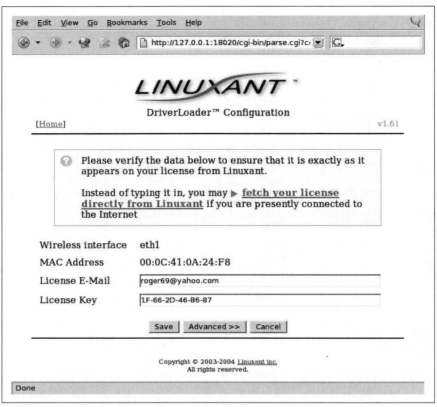

Figure 4-4. Entering the Linuxant license information

After having made any changes in the Advanced configuration, exit the web-based configuration. Your wireless card should now be active. In this example, you can see that our Linksys WPC55AG wireless card has been assigned to *eth1*:

```
# iwconfig
lo        no wireless extensions.

eth0      no wireless extensions.

eth1      IEEE 802.11g  ESSID:"whitecottage-wpa"  Nickname:"unknown"
          Mode:Managed  Frequency:2.447GHz  Access Point: 00:0C:41:D4:71:AB
          Bit Rate=54Mb/s   Tx-Power=8 dBm
          RTS thr:off   Fragment thr:off
          Encryption key:off
          Power Management:off
          Link Quality:1/1  Signal level:-38 dBm  Noise level:-83 dBm
          Rx invalid nwid:0  Rx invalid crypt:0  Rx invalid frag:0
          Tx excessive retries:0  Invalid misc:0   Missed beacon:0
```

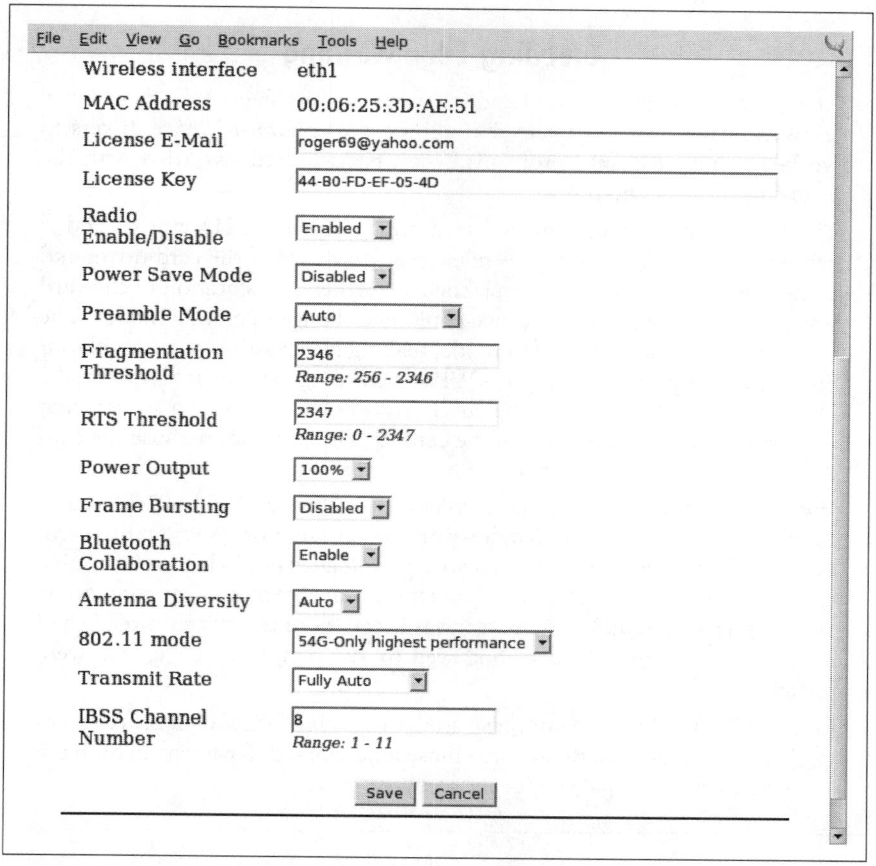

Figure 4-5. Advanced configuration under WLAN Driver Loader

As you can see from the ESSID, we are connected to a WPA-protected network. To authenticate, see "Authenticating with wpa_supplicant" later in this chapter. The next section describes how to connect to a WPA network with a Prism-based card and the HostAP driver without using the WLAN Driver Loader.

HostAP

Jouni Malinen, the developer behind the HostAP project, has developed a package called wpa_supplicant. In this section, we discuss how you can use a Prism-based wireless card, the HostAP driver, and the wpa_supplicant to connect your Linux box to a WPA-protected network.

Bleeding-Edge Warning

The Linuxant WLAN Driver Loader software is very new. As with any new software, particularly software that allows cross-platform device drivers to work, you may run into problems. The first two cards we tried with the Linuxant software did not work.

The Linksys WPC55AG card is based on the Atheros 5211 chipset and is compatible with 802.11a/b/g. While it was easy to load the card driver and make it work with WLAN Driver Loader, further configuration of the card was prohibited by the fact that we could not change operating modes. The card remained stuck in 802.11a mode, making it impossible to test with our 802.11g access point that supports WPA. According to Linuxant Support, the INF file included with the WPC55AG driver doesn't contain a section that deals with changing the mode of the card; this is a bit odd, because the card does support this function in Windows.

We then attempted to load the drivers for an Orinoco Gold 802.11b card. Agere has recently released Windows drivers that support WPA on this card, available from *http://www.agere.com/support/downloads*. While we were able to load the drivers, WLAN Driver Loader was not able to find any compatible devices on the system. We suspect this is because our test system already had the orinoco_cs driver loaded, but even by disabling orinoco_cs, we were unsuccessful.

Our last, and only, successful test used a Linksys WPC54G 802.11G radio card. This is based on a Broadcom chipset and worked flawlessly, in both the setup and with the wpa_supplicant software.

In order to use the wpa_supplicant in conjunction with HostAP, you must have a Prism-based Wi-Fi card with station firmware Version 1.7 or later. The latest version of firmware as of this writing is 1.8.0, although Version 1.7.4 is more widely available and works as well. The most complete collection of Prism firmware is located at *http://www.red-bean.com/~proski/firmware*

To update your Prism card firmware, refer to the excellent tutorial at *http://linux.junsun.net/intersil-prism*. If you have questions or problems with the firmware update process, we recommend that you check there first. However, we do go over the basics of updating your firmware later in this section. To determine whether you need to update the firmware.

1. Build and install the *hostap* utilities (see "Building the hostap tools" later in this chapter).

2. Use the `hostap_diag wlan0` command to determine the current version of your Prism firmware. Alternatively, use `dmesg | grep wlan0`. *hostap_diag* returns output similar to the following:

```
NICID: id=0x8013 v1.0.0 (PRISM II (2.5) Mini-PCI (SST parallel flash))
PRIID: id=0x0015 v1.1.0
STAID: id=0x001f v1.4.9 (station firmware)
```

3. You should be concerned with the Station Firmware version, which must be at least Version 1.7.0. Chances are that your card is below that version, and you will need to upgrade the firmware. Take note of the NICID in the output of *dmesg* or *hostap_diag*. This is the ID of your Prism card and there are many different IDs. Some IDs have only certain firmware versions available. To determine the software that is required for your card, consult the tutorial at *http://linux.junsun.net/intersil-prism*.

Once you've determined which firmware you need, you can build *hostap* and its utilities, and then update the firmware, as described in the following sections.

Building hostap from CVS

While you don't necessarily need the CVS version of the HostAP code to update your Prism firmware, you will need it to use the wpa_supplicant features and to obtain the wpa_supplicant code.

You can obtain the CVS development snapshot from the HostAP web pages at *http://hostap.epitest.fi*. Select the link for *development branch* in the section titled "CVS snapshot of the driver source code." You must have the development branch of the code to get the WPA features.

Once you've downloaded the compressed file, extract it and change to the newly created directory:

```
# tar xzvf hostap.tar.gz
# cd hostap
```

You must edit the file *drivers/modules/hostap_config.h* and make sure these two items are uncommented: #define `PRISM2_DOWNLOAD_SUPPORT` and #define `PRISM2_NON_VOLATILE_DOWNLOAD`. In the CVS version, the first #define statement is already uncommented.

Once you have edited this file, go back to the *hostap* directory and build the software:

```
# make
# make install
```

To load the new HostAP drivers, stop and restart the PCMCIA services:

```
# /etc/init.d/pcmcia restart
```

Building the hostap tools

In the *hostap* source directory is a subfolder containing the *hostap* utilities. Building them is easy:

```
# cd utils
# make
```

There is no make install command, so if you want the tools installed outside of the *utils* directory, you must move them yourself. Our examples merely run the utilities out of the directory where they are compiled.

Updating the firmware

Copy the version of firmware files that you need for your prism card into the *utils* directory. The utility that manages the firmware upgrade is prism2_srec. This utility not only updates the *station firmware* of your card, but also the *primary firmware*. Updating the primary firmware is beyond the scope of your needs, so focus simply on updating the station firmware.

Station firmware is always provided in the format s[*platform*][*version*].hex. The tutorial web pages at *http://linux.junsun.net/intersil-prism* give you information on determining your platform. Make sure that you are using the station firmware file and no other file. You could render your card useless if you were to update it with the wrong firmware (the faint of heart may want to consider updating their card using a Windows-based updater from the manufacturer, which is likely to be the only supported technique).

First, do a test run in verbose mode:

```
# ./prism2_srec -v wlan0 s1010701.hex
```

The *-v* argument specifies verbose mode, and because we have not called the tool with any other options, it simply tests the firmware against the card. If at the end of the output you see OK, you can proceed to the next step. If you see anything else at the end of the output, do not proceed. You will know that the firmware is not compatible with your card if you see output like:

```
NICID was not found from the list of supported platforms. Incompatible
update data
```

Assuming that your test run returned an OK, you can proceed to the next step, and write the firmware to the flash on the Prism card. First, if you use a laptop, make sure it has a fully charged battery and is plugged into the wall outlet. If your computer is a desktop, be sure that it is plugged into a UPS. (If the power fails during this step, your Wi-Fi card will be useless.)

```
# ./prism2_srec -v -f wlan0 s1010701.hex
```

The process takes about 30 seconds, and you should make sure that the card is not removed during the update. Once finished, you should see output that shows the new firmware versions on the card and that should be returned to a shell prompt:

```
Components after download:
   NICID: 0x8003 v1.0.0
   PRIID: 0x0015 v0.3.0
   STAID: 0x001f v1.7.1
#
```

The card driver is unloaded after the firmware update, so you should remove the card and reinsert it to reload the driver.

Authenticating with wpa_supplicant

The supplicant software is included in the CVS releases of HostAP 0.2.x source, so you have already downloaded it when you installed the CVS version of HostAP in the previous section. Linuxant also provides the source for wpa_supplicant in the downloads section of its web site, but as of this writing, the version included with HostAP 0.2.x source is more current. We recommend obtaining the HostAP source to build wpa_supplicant even if you plan on using it with the WLAN Driver Loader.

Operating wpa_supplicant with either HostAP or the WLAN Driver Loader doesn't require a different setup. You must make sure that the wireless card that you intend to use with WLAN Driver Loader supports WPA in both the card firmware and the Windows NDIS driver. See the sidebar "Bleeding-Edge Warning" for details on how some WPA-enabled cards may not work.

The only difference between running wpa_supplicant with HostAP and WLAN Driver Loader is what interface you call from the shell. HostAP interfaces are always *wlanX*, typically *wlan0*. For all of the cards we tried with WLAN Driver Loader, the interface came up as *eth1*.

In the *hostap* source directory is a subfolder that contains the wpa_supplicant. Building it from source is easy:

```
# cd wpa_supplicant
# make
```

Again, there is no make install, so you must copy the generated executables to where you want them: wpa_supplicant and wpa_passphrase, and the configuration file *wpa_supplicant.conf*.

According to the README file included with the source, wpa_supplicant is designed to run as a background daemon. A frontend program that provides a user interface is planned but is not yet available.

On currently available access points, there are two possible operating modes for WPA:

WPA-PSK (pre-shared key)
Also called "WPA-Personal" by the Wi-Fi Alliance; this somewhat resembles WEP in that it allows you to use an identical key (a pre-shared key) on both the access point and the client. The access point, acting as the WPA Authenticator, uses this pre-shared key to generate a master session key.

WPA-EAP
Also called "WPA-Enterprise" by the Wi-Fi Alliance; this relies on an external authentication server, most likely RADIUS, and the EAP used by 802.1x. The master session key is generated by the Authentication Server and then passed to the access point, which authenticates the client with that key.

In both cases, WPA implements a 4-Way Key Handshake and Group Key Handshake, which generates and exchanges data encryption keys between the Authenticator (access point) and Supplicant (client). The only difference between the two methods is where the master session key is generated.

You want to start wpa_supplicant as a daemon, give it the path to the configuration file, and specify the wireless interface. In most cases, you can use the line shown in Example 4-1.

Example 4-1. Launching wpa_supplicant

```
# /path/to/wpa_supplicant -Bw -c/path/to/wpa_supplicant.conf -iwlan0
```

This makes the process fork into the background and wait for the *wlan0* interface, so you can insert this command into an appropriate place in your startup environment. WPA handshakes must be complete before data frames can be exchanged, so wpa_supplicant must be started before a DHCP client, for instance.

wpa_supplicant must be running when using a WPA-protected wireless network, so it should be started from system startup scripts using the command shown in Example 4-1, or it can be called from the pcmcia-cs scripts if you are using a PC card.

To enable WPA support using the pcmcia-cs scripts, add these lines to */etc/pcmcia/wireless.opts*:

```
MODE="Managed"
WPA="y"
```

Add the following code to the end of the start action handler in */etc/pcmcia/wireless*:

```
if [ $WPA = "y" -a -x /usr/local/bin/wpa_supplicant ]; then
    /usr/local/bin/wpa_supplicant -Bw -c/etc/wpa_supplicant.conf \
        -i$DEVICE
fi
```

Finally, add the following code to the end of the stop action handler in */etc/pcmcia/wireless*:

```
if [ $WPA = "y" -a -x /usr/local/bin/wpa_supplicant ]; then
    killall wpa_supplicant
fi
```

The combined effect of these changes make cardmgr start up wpa_supplicant when the card is plugged in. wpa_supplicant waits until the interface is set up, and then negotiates keys with the access point.

The example *wpa_supplicant.conf* file can be used to generate a configuration for your environment. The file needs at least two mandatory parameters, and it has several options depending on how your network is configured. The general file format should be as in the example below. Empty lines and lines starting with # are ignored.

```
network={
        ssid="locked-down"
        psk="s00pers3cr3t"
        key_mgmt=WPA-PSK
        pairwise=CCMP TKIP
        group=CCMP TKIP
}
```

Here is a list of the possible fields in the configuration file:

ssid=
> A mandatory field that can be either an ASCII string in quotes or a hex string.

bssid=
> Optional, only needed if your network uses a BSSID.

key_mgmt=
> A list of accepted key management protocols. Options are WPA-PSK, WPA-EAP, and NONE. If not set, this defaults to WPA-PSK WPA-EAP.

pairwise=
> A list of accepted pairwise (unicast) ciphers for WPA. Options are CCMP (AES encryption), TKIP, or NONE. If not set, this defaults to CCMP TKIP.

group=
> A list of accepted group (broadcast/multicast) ciphers for WPA. Options are CCMP, TKIP, WEP104, and WEP40. If not set, this defaults to CCMP TKIP WEP104 WEP40.

`psk=`
>
> A mandatory field when using WPA-PSK. This field can be entered as 64 hex digits or as an ASCII passphrase. The ASCII passphrase must be at least 8 characters in length and can be a maximum of 63 characters.

In our example configuration, we are connecting to a WPA-PSK network, and we have chosen to put the ASCII passphrase in the text configuration file. If you want more protection, the included tool wpa_passphrase can be used to generate 256-bit keys from an ASCII passphrase. This tool uses a fair amount of CPU time, so it should be used only when the passphrase has actually changed.

If you don't have WPA set up on your access point, see the section "Example WPA setup on a Linksys access point," which provides information on setting up a Linksys access point for WPA.

wpa_supplicant has an experimental interface for integrating with Xsupplicant. This allows you to connect to a WPA-EAP network by having Xsupplicant manage the 802.1x and EAP authentication. In order for this to work properly, Xsupplicant must be modified to send the master session key to wpa_supplicant after successful EAP authentication.

The latest wpa_supplicant code includes an *xsupplicant.patch* that can be used to patch the source code for Xsupplicant. However, this patch has been merged into the Xupplicant CVS code, so we recommend you check out CVS code instead of dealing with the separate patch.

Xsupplicant

The folks at the Open1x project build the Xsupplicant software, available at *http://www.open1x.org*. The latest stable release is Version 0.8b. However, for our purposes, we need the CVS code, which you can check out from the SourceForge CVS server using the following commands (press Enter when prompted for a password):

```
# cvs -d:pserver:anonymous@cvs.sourceforge.net:/cvsroot/open1x login
# cvs -d:pserver:anonymous@cvs.sourceforge.net:/cvsroot/open1x co \
    xsupplicant
```

These commands check out the CVS code and deposit it in a newly created *xsupplicant* directory.

Xsupplicant requires that Openssl 0.9.7 or greater be installed. Mandrake, Fedora, and Red Hat users can install the *openssl* package, Debian users can run apt-get install openssl, and the source can be downloaded from *http://www.openssl.org*. Most distributions already have this package installed by default, but you may need to upgrade it to ensure that you have the version required.

In order to get the CVS code running, you must install the *automake1.7* and *autoconf2.5* packages (or more recent compatible versions). Once these are installed, compiling from source is straightforward:

```
# cd xsupplicant
# ./configure
# make
# make install
```

This installs *xsupplicant* and some related tools in */usr/local/bin*. However, the CVS make install does not install a *config* file, so you must copy the sample *etc/xsupplicant.conf* to */etc/1x/1x.conf* (this is the default location of the *conf* file).

Edit the *1x.conf* file. Many of the defaults can be left in place, but you must change a few particulars starting with the identity, then moving on to the EAP type. Although the sample configuration file gives you a starting point for each type of EAP, we'll use EAP-MD5 because it's easy to implement and doesn't require us to generate a certificate. After that, you need to configure the phase2 authentication type and chap:

identity =
> What Xsupplicant responds with when presented with an EAP ID Request. This is typically the username, and because this can be an arbitrary string, you should enclose it with a <BEGIN ID> and <END ID>.

eap-md5
> In this section, you must enter a username and password.

phase2_type
> Here you must specify the type of phase2 authentication. The default is chap, which we use for our example.

chap
> In this section, you must enter a username and password.

If you're uncomfortable entering confidential information into clear text files, Xsupplicant can be called from the command line with switches that allow you to enter your username and password with the -u and -p options. However, these options allow anyone who can execute a ps command on your system to see your password.

Xsupplicant can be used both to authenticate your Linux machine to an 802.1x server as well as in combination with wpa_supplicant to connect to WPA networks.

In either case, Xsupplicant must be activated after the interface is brought up so it can transmit authentication information; Xsupplicant is unlike wpa_supplicant, which must complete the WPA handshakes before any data can be transmitted.

After you have entered all of the correct information into the *1x.conf file*, call Xsupplicant from the command line:

```
# xsupplicant -i wlan0 -D
```

This command line puts Xsupplicant into daemon mode after it receives the password. Put the *1x.conf* file in the default location so you don't need to specify the location of the *conf* file. This command allows you to authenticate against any 802.11x server.

To use Xsupplicant in combination with wpa_supplicant to connect to a WPA-EAP network, you must change a few things:

1. First, you must edit the *wpa_supplicant.conf* file and change the key_mgmt entry to WPA-EAP.

2. Now you can start Xsupplicant, but it must be started with an extra command line switch:

```
# xsupplicant -I wlan0 -D -W
```

The -W switch tells Xsupplicant that it must communicate the master session key that it obtains from the 802.11X/EAP server back to wpa_supplicant.

Xsupplicant also comes with some example ifup and ifdown scripts in the *tools* directory of the source tarball. We suggest that you use these scripts instead of the normal distribution scripts when you wish to bring up or down an interface that uses 802.1x authentication.

Example WPA setup on a Linksys access point

All of our testing with WPA-PSK and WPA-EAP was done using a Linksys WRT54G Wireless Router. With Version 2.0 and above of firmware, the WRT54G is capable of both WPA methods as well as TKIP and AES encryption.

Figure 4-6 shows the configuration necessary for a WPA-PSK setup.

Figure 4-7 shows configuration for a WPA RADIUS setup.

WPA RADIUS setup details

In order to make this work, we set up a Mandrake 9.2 system as a dedicated RADIUS server. For a RADIUS server, we installed the *freeradius* packages and their dependencies with urpmi freeradius. RedHat, Fedora, and Debian users should be able to install the *freeradius* packages similarly on their systems. We did not attempt to compile the source code for our testing, but it can be downloaded from *http://www.freeradius.org*.

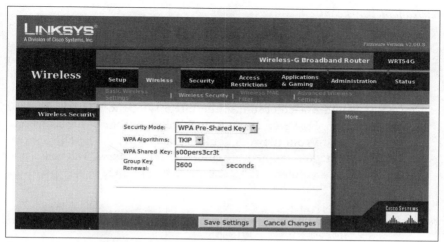

Figure 4-6. WPA-PSK setup for a Linksys WRT54G

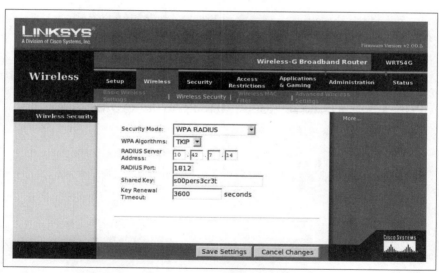

Figure 4-7. WPA RADIUS setup for a Linksys WRT54G

FreeRadius supports a wide variety of database backends, including LDAP, MySQL, and others. This was major overkill for our purposes. In order to run FreeRadius, we had to edit two files:

/etc/raddb/users

We didn't use any backend database for users, so we simply added several test users to this file. A sample user entry is shown here:

```
"roger"      Auth-Type := Local, User-Password == "useless"
             Reply-Message = "Hello, %u"
```

/etc/raddb/clients.conf

For each client of the RADIUS server, you can define an entry with a shared secret. This isn't particularly secure, because RADIUS shared secrets are sent in the open with no encryption (for this reason, you should use a wired link on a physically secured network between the RADIUS server and access point). If this shared secret were compromised, it would not compromise the integrity of the 802.1x-protected communication. However, an attacker with knowledge of the secret and physical access to your network could replace either the RADIUS server or access point. We defined an entry for our Linksys WRT54G and made sure that we entered the same shared secret here as we did in the Linksys setup:

```
client 10.42.7.14 {
        secret          = s00pers3cr3t
        shortname       = wrt54g
        nastype         = other
}
```

Once we edited these files, we started FreeRadius manually with debugging enabled so we could watch for any problems:

```
# /usr/sbin/radiusd -x
```

At this point, we were able to use the combination of Xsupplicant and wpa_supplicant described earlier in the chapter to establish a WPA link with the WRT54G, and authenticate through to the RADIUS server.

## CHAPTER 5

Configuring Access Points with Linux

So you've purchased an access point. You brought it home from the store, broke open the packaging, discarded all of the extraneous bits of fluff, and you're likely left with an access point, a power supply, an Ethernet cable and a CD that says "Windows Software Installation."

This chapter explains how to avoid this scenario. While there are vendors of wireless equipment that still expect you to configure their gear from a Windows PC, there are many alternatives for the Linux user.

Many of the early access points from vendors, such as WaveLAN/Lucent/ Orinoco, Linksys, and others, required an external setup program. With few exceptions, these setup and configuration programs ran only under Windows. However, as the price of wireless equipment continued to drop and access points began to be marketed to home users, a number of vendors chose to make their equipment configurable with a web browser.

There are also several manufacturers that allow Telnet access for configuration of their access points. One thing you're unlikely to find, however, is SSH-enabled access. As of this writing, there are no commercial access points capable of SSH. However, at least one company is producing wireless routers that operate using a Linux kernel. Several organizations have built custom firmware for these boxes that include SSH daemons. See Chapter 6 for details.

Linux-Friendly Wireless Vendors

While it is impossible to provide a complete and up-to-date list of all wireless vendors, Table 5-1 shows a list of many of the major manufacturers, the types of equipment they sell, and how their equipment is configured.

Table 5-1. Linux-friendly wireless vendors

Vendor	Equipment types	Configuration methods
Linksys[a] *www.linksys.com*	Access points, bridges, routers	Web-based
Netgear *www.netgear.com*	Access points, bridges, routers	Web-based
D-Link *www.dlink.com*	Access points, bridges, routers	Web-based
Cisco *www.cisco.com*	Access points, bridges	Web-based, Telnet, SNMP
SMC *www.smc.com*	Access points, bridges, routers	Web-based
EnGenius *www.engeniustech.com*	Access points, bridges, routers	Web-based, Telnet, SNMP
Belkin *www.belkin.com*	Access points, bridges, routers	Web-based
US Robotics *www.usr.com*	Access points, routers	Web-based
Microsoft *www.microsoft.com*	Access points	Web-based
ActionTec *www.actiontec.com*	Access points, routers	Web-based

[a] Linksys was acquired by Cisco in June 2003.

Alternatively, Table 5-2 shows a list of vendors that are not configurable from Linux out of the box. However, with some of this equipment, there are alternative methods of configuration, and even the ability to reflash the firmware to run Linux or make the device act like a different model.

Table 5-2. Linux-less-than-friendly wireless vendors

Vendor	Equipment types	Configuration methods
Proxim Orinoco *www.proxim.com*	Access points	Windows GUI[a]
Apple *www.apple.com*	Access points	Apple GUI
Tranzeo	Access points, bridges	Windows GUI, limited telnet
SmartBridges *www.smartbridges.com*	Access points, bridges	Windows GUI

[a] Proxim makes available the Orinoco CLI Proxy, which is covered later in this chapter.

Commercial Wireless Equipment Overview

With the explosion in Wi-Fi popularity, a corresponding plethora of vendors and equipment choices have surfaced. There are an amazing number of access points, but there are also wireless routers, wireless bridges, wireless-to-Ethernet bridges, and some Linux-powered equipment as well.

Access Points

In Chapter 1, we covered the basics of 802.11 and the two modes of operation it supports. Infrastructure Mode, the most common mode, requires the use of a wireless access point.

Most access points on the market share a common number of connectors: at least one external antenna, one Ethernet port, status LEDs, and an external power supply or wall wart. Other features you might find on some models include connectors for attaching external antennas, a reset button to return the unit to factory settings, multiple Ethernet ports, and support for *Power Over Ethernet* (POE).

Once you get past the outside connectors, the internal features of access points begin to vary widely. There are all sorts of devices on the market, ranging from simple home-use devices to enterprise-class units designed for large deployments. The following list describes various manufacturers and some of their equipment:

Apple AirPort

This was one of the first access points available. Apple brought this access point and the AirPort client cards to market before the 802.11b standard was finalized. The internals of the unit are built by Lucent/Orinoco and are identical to the Orinoco RG-1100. Note that this applies only to the original AirPort model. The second model (Snow) and the subsequent AirPort Extreme are based on a different processor.

Chapter 6 covers some utilities that can be used to reflash the firmware on these units, allowing you to swap personalities and even to run Linux on them. As shown in Table 5-2, the AirPort and the RG-1100 are not configurable out of the box from Linux. This is easily remedied. Also, early versions of the AirPort had problems with non-Apple wireless cards. Many of these cards would not associate with the access point. This has since been fixed through firmware updates.

Power over Ethernet

If you're familiar with network cabling, you know that Ethernet uses only two pairs of the wire inside a standard Category 5 cable. Pairs 1–2 and 3–6 are used, leaving 4–5 and 7–8 available.

POE sends DC power over these unused pairs, enabling the placement of access points or other network hardware away from power sources. This is especially useful if you need to mount your access point on a pole, on the ceiling, or in other inaccessible places. Run CAT5 wire rather than going to the trouble of running electrical conduit. You can now supply both Ethernet and power to the unit.

In June 2003, the IEEE released its specification for POE, 802.3af. More information on this standard can be obtained from the IEEE web site at *http://www.ieee802.org/3/af/*.

The IEEE standard is only a few months old as of this writing, so most POE equipment available for purchase will not meet the standard. There are excellent documents from community wireless organizations available on building POE equipment. A few good examples are the Bay Area Wireless Users Group (BAWUG) page at *http://www.bawug.org/howto/hacks/PoE/* and the NYCWireless page at *http://www.nycwireless.net/poe/*.

In order to make POE work, you need a power injector, which is referred to in the 802.3af standard as the Power Sourcing Equipment (PSE), and a corresponding unit on the other end. The standard refers to the end device as a PD.

If your equipment is designed to support POE out of the box, you need only a PSE. This unit typically has three jacks: DC power, Ethernet IN, and Ethernet/power OUT. Connect power, Ethernet from your network, and then connect Ethernet/power OUT to the Cat 5 cable running to your Powered Device.

On the other end, if your equipment does not natively support POE, what you need is a splitter, a reverse of the PSE. It also has three jacks: Ethernet/power IN, Ethernet OUT, and DC power OUT. This device takes your incoming Ethernet/power and splits it again for connection to your device.

WARNING: unless you have electrical and LAN wiring experience, making your own POE equipment can be dangerous or fatal to you and your equipment.

Orinoco AP-series

This series includes some of the most popular enterprise-class access points. The AP-500 has a single radio inside, an Orinoco PC Card. The AP-1000 was the first access point to feature two radios, again both in PC Card format. Orinoco access points have a wide array of features:

MAC address filtering, network protocol filtering to enforce such policies as preventing IPX from traversing your wireless network, support for RADIUS authentication, and custom power over Ethernet adapters. Orinoco calls these units "Active Ethernet," and they are available in 1-, 6-, and 12-port models, so that you can power up to 12 access points using the same POE adapter.

More recent models include the AP-2000, the successor model to the AP-1000 (which features upgradeability to 802.11a or 802.11g, or both), giving you a tri-mode access point with all of the Orinoco features, and the AP-2500, which is a "hotspot-in-a-box" model that includes a captive portal and many other features necessary for setting up a wireless hotspot.

Linksys

Linksys made a huge splash with its WAP-11 access point when it was first introduced. It had a good feature set and external antenna adapters, and was priced for the home market. Unfortunately, it is mainly configurable through a Linksys-specific setup program, which runs on Windows. There is an SNMP utility for Windows, and Linksys did publish an SNMP Management Information Base (MIB) for Linux/Unix users. (An MIB is one or more text files that allow Linux's SNMP tools to generate human-readable statistics from SNMP management strings.)

Later Linksys models still continue to ship with Windows-only setup programs. However, they now offer web-based configuration that is easily accessible from Linux web browsers.

Much of the other consumer-level wireless gear can be placed in the same area as Linksys. D-Link, SMC, and Netgear all offer models with nearly identical features and price points.

EnGenius/Senao

Early in 2002, rumors surfaced of a 200 mW radio card. While one manufacturer, Zcomax, had made these available, they were hard to find and were expensive.

At that point, with a few exceptions, most radio cards and access points were powered by 30 mW radios. You can imagine how excited the wireless users were at the thought of being able to expand their range.

Today, EnGenius/Senao offers several access points for indoor and outdoor use, all with 200 mW radios. Along with Cisco, it is one of the few vendors to support Telnet access for configuration. Figure 5-1 shows a sample web-based configuration screen from an EnGenius access point.

Tranzeo

Tranzeo is one of a number of vendors focused on supplying wireless Internet service providers. Tranzeo's equipment is designed to work outdoors and comes in many models, some of which include an integrated directional panel antenna. Its access points are accessible via Telnet as well as a Windows-based GUI. Many of its models offer some routing features (see "Wireless Routers" later in this chapter).

Cisco

The 800-pound gorilla of networking, Cisco, entered the 802.11 market when it acquired Aironet in late 1999. Aironet was already a manufacturer of 802.11 first-generation equipment, and Cisco bought Aironet at precisely the right time to take advantage of the 802.11b introduction.

Cisco's access points, as expected, integrate extremely well into a Cisco network. They have a wide feature set and compare well with the products from Orinoco in the enterprise space. Also, as expected, the Cisco units all support Telnet as well as web-based configuration. Figure 5-2 shows the main Telnet screen from a Cisco AP.

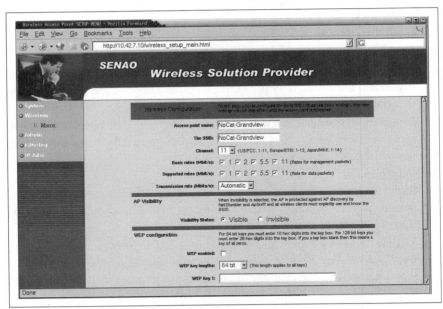

Figure 5-1. Web-based configuration for an EnGenius/Senao access point

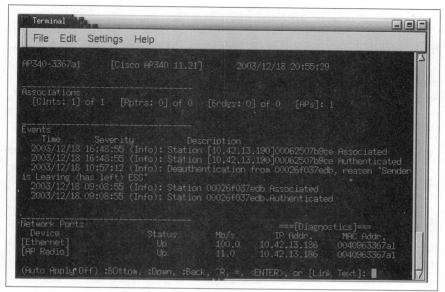

Figure 5-2. Cisco Telnet configuration window

Wireless Routers

The line between an access point and a wireless router is very blurry. Many devices sold as access points include routing features. For example, the Apple AirPort models offer Network Address Translation and a DHCP server. Wireless routers are basically a combination of home ADSL/cable routers and a wireless access point.

There are some key differences, however, between most of the wireless routers now available and standard access points. You can expect to find at least some of these features on a wireless router:

Routing protocol support
   RIP or RIPv2 on many models

Network services
   DHCP, DNS, and others

Encryption support
   Client or router support for IPSec and PPTP VPNs

Limited firewalls
   IP masquerading and some packet filtering

Port forwarding
   Sending certain TCP or UDP ports to a specific machine

These units are really designed for home or small-office use. You'll find that the larger network vendors such as Cisco don't manufacture this type of hardware, because they want you to purchase one of their full-fledged routers.

Security in many models of these routers is also questionable. The bugtraq mailing list at *http://www.securityfocus.com/archive* shows you that the number of vulnerabilities in this type of consumer hardware is fairly high. While these units increase security compared to a standalone PC connected to a DSL modem, they are not the end-all be-all for network security.

Wireless routers are available from almost any manufacturer that also makes access points. An alternative to commercial wireless routers is to build your own using Linux. Chapter 6 covers this topic in detail.

Wireless Bridges

Perhaps the most well-known wireless bridge is the Linksys WET-11. A wireless bridge takes in an Ethernet signal and repeats it out to a wireless network, and vice versa.

A wireless bridge is not an access point, however. The bridge is only capable of acting as an infrastructure client to a distant access point. The practical uses of these devices abound. If you want to connect your Ethernet-enabled PC to your wireless network, attach it to a bridge. Wireless ISPs can install a wireless bridge as their customer premises equipment (CPE), allowing the customer to have a wired Ethernet network in her home, bridged wirelessly to a remote access point. Any device with an Ethernet port can be added to a wireless network using a wireless bridge.

As with wireless routers, most of the companies that manufacture access points have at least one model of wireless bridge available. If you want an outdoor wireless bridge with an integrated antenna, excellent models are available from Tranzeo at *http://www.tranzeo.com*. Models for home or office use can be found from Linksys, D-Link, SMC, and all the other usual suspects.

Configuring Access Points

While many of the manufacturers we've covered allow their wireless equipment to be configured through a web or telnet interface, this is not an option for Orinoco or Apple access points. However, there are two options for configuring Orinoco access points under Linux and at least one option for Apple AirPort configuration.

Orinoco CLI Proxy

Orinoco provides a program it calls the CLI Proxy. It's available at *http://www.proxim.com/support/all/orinoco/software/dl2002_orinoco_apcli_117_linux.html*. If you look at the accompanying *README* file, there appears to be support from Orinoco for this product.

The release notes and program are from 2002 and have not been updated in a while. The system requirements state that the program runs under Red Hat Linux 6.1 or similar systems. We were able to successfully install and run the package on both Red Hat 9 and Debian Woody distributions.

To install the CLI Proxy, download the *.tgz* file from the Orinoco web site. The help notes suggest unpacking it in the */opt* directory, but that's not necessary. The package can be unpacked in any location that makes sense for your filesystem. For our purposes, we'll assume you're using */opt*. You'll need 1.5 MB of disk space for installation.

To unpack, execute the following command as root:

```
tar xzvf clili117.tar.gz
```

The package is a compiled binary with no source, so at this point all you can do is execute the program with the command /opt/cliproxy/cliproxy. You'll see this prompt:

```
[CLI]>
```

First, read through the HTML documentation that is installed with the program in the */opt/cliproxy/Help* directory.

The program works by downloading a configuration from an Orinoco access point on your local subnet. The program makes use of broadcast traffic, so your Linux box must be on the same physical network as the access point for it to work. You can also open a local configuration file. This is done through the use of the configure command. Saving the file is accomplished by writing the file to disk or writing it to the access point, and is done by issuing the command write.

The interface is very similar to Cisco IOS, along with tab-completion of commands and the use of the ? key to find context sensitive help. For example, show ? gives you all of the options to the show command.

Once you have opened a configuration for editing, you can modify any of the access point features available, from the wireless interface to TCP/IP options to setting up bridging. The Orinoco access points have a pretty broad set of features.

The software ships with default configuration files for the Orinoco AP-1000 and AP-500, which you can open and modify to fit your needs.

Airport/RG-1000 Configurator

Jon Sevy of Drexel University has built a Java-based configuration program for the Apple AirPort and the Orinoco RG-1000 access point. He also has versions of this program for the newer AirPort models with two Ethernet ports and the AirPort Extreme 802.11g model. The software can be downloaded from *http://edge.mcs.drexel.edu/GICL/people/sevy/airport/#Configurator*.

There are versions for Unix as well as MacOS 9, Mac OS X, and Windows. You need a Java 1.2–compliant runtime engine (JRE). The latest versions of Java for many platforms can be downloaded from Sun Microsystems at *http://java.sun.com/j2se/1.4*.

Once you've downloaded the Configurator, unpack it in a directory of your choice and run the program using this command line:

```
java -jar AirportConfigurator.jar
```

When Java starts, it executes the Java Archive (JAR) code, which will result in Figure 5-3.

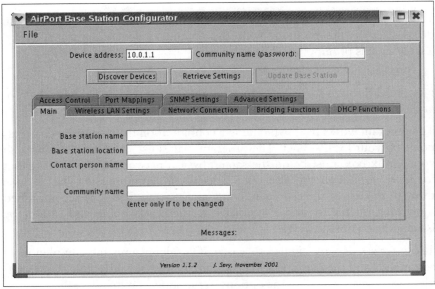

Figure 5-3. Java AirPort/RG-1000 Configurator main screen

If you're familiar with either the Orinoco configuration programs available for Windows or the FreeBase configuration software written to configure an Apple AirPort from Windows, this screen is very familiar.

As you can see, you have the option to discover compatible devices on your network or to specify the IP address of a device you wish to configure. Configuration is handled through a series of tabs, giving you options for wireless and wired network settings, bridging, DHCP, and a whole host of advanced settings.

Flashing Your Access Point

One feature that is not immediately apparent in the Java Configurator is located in the drop-down File menu: *Upload New Base Station Firmware*. This feature is also available in the Orinoco configuration software for Windows and in the Apple AirPort software for Mac OS X, as well as in the Free-Base software mentioned earlier.

However, a neat hack that the Java configurator and FreeBase allow is the uploading of firmware to a device that does not explicitly match the firmware in question.

For example, the original Apple AirPort and the Orinoco RG-1000 are identical hardware, so you can flash either unit with the firmware image of the other. You can also flash both of these models and the Orinoco RG-1100 with the Orinoco AP-500 or AP-1000 firmware (which is quite a feature upgrade because it supports bridging, protocol filtering, RADIUS, and many other advanced configuration options).

To flash the firmware, you need the firmware images. The Orinoco CLI proxy software comes with binary (*.bin*) firmware images for the AP-500 and AP-1000. The Orinoco AP Manager software for Windows comes with these images, as well as the RG-1000 and RG-1100 images. It is available from *http://www.proxim.com/support/all/orinoco/software/dl2002_orinoco_ap_75.html*.

Apple has built its firmware updates into the executables for its AirPort updater software. If you're a Mac-head, you can use ResEdit to remove the binary firmware from the executable. However, we won't go into that here. There is a non-Apple web page available that provides binary firmware images for the various AirPort versions: *http://www.icir.org/fenner/airport*. Use these images at your own risk. For more information on creative ways to flash an access point, see Chapter 6.

CHAPTER 6

Building Your Own Access Point

Wi-Fi access points are inexpensive, because they are now accepted as commodity hardware. You can buy them at discount stores, warehouse clubs, and probably your local gas station. Models with many features and support for 802.11g can now be purchased for well under $100.

Why then would you want to build your own access point? Aside from the usual geek reason ("because you can," a.k.a. "why even ask?"), there are many practical reasons:

Make use of old or surplus PC hardware. An effective access point can be built with a 486/33 and 16 MB of RAM. Many commercial access points are not any more powerful inside. Don't know what to do with that old Pentium? Stick a radio card in it and unwire your house.

Take advantage of a complete Linux installation. Run an iptables firewall to protect your network, build a web caching server, and set up intrusion detection. If you build a Linux-based access point, you can do almost anything with it.

Run a customized Linux kernel on off-the-shelf hardware. Wireless access point/routers from Linksys and other manufacturers are actually running Linux kernels inside. Several groups of people have put out alternative firmware for these units. You can build your own custom firmware if you want.

These are only a few good reasons to build your own access point. In order to get started, you need some hardware, a Linux distribution, and some configuration basics. We cover each in turn.

Hardware

As we mentioned, building an access point can be a useful way to resurrect old PC hardware you may have sitting around. Depending on where you want to install it, you can leave it in that old bulky case or dress it up with a spiffy waterproof case and install it outside.

One of the wireless routing nodes we built for the NoCat network (*http://nocat.net*) in Sonoma County, California, is a beige Macintosh G3/266 desktop machine. It runs Yellow Dog Linux and has two PCI-PCMCIA converters and two Agere Orinoco Silver 802.11b radio cards. An odd choice, you might think—but we had the hardware and it has already functioned as a wireless router for over a year as of this writing.

There are a few things you'll want to keep in mind when deciding whether any given hardware is right for building an access point:

Processor speed

> While it might seem nostalgic to consider using a 386 or a non-PowerPC Mac for your access point project, these machines are so slow and old that it can be painful running Linux on them. Once you do, they don't have the horsepower to do many neat Linux tricks such as firewalling. Anything faster than a 486/33 is able to act as an access point with little trouble.

Support

> Older PCs can certainly be made into access points. Bear in mind, though, that you must dig up such ancient artifacts as ISA network cards and SIMM memory. If you need to build on the cheap, this can be the way to go, but all hardware ages and fails sooner or later. If you want reliability, you might want to think about newer hardware. There's also the issue of relying on a PC with a spinning hard disk inside—they *will* fail, often when you really need them.

Standardization

> You might be expanding a larger network rather than just installing an access point in your closet. If you build more than one access point for whatever reason, you've just crossed over into the zone of network administration. In this world, standard hardware is the norm, because you can keep single types of replacement hardware on hand, and if you're in a multisite network, it means that everyone who's responsible is familiar with the same hardware.

Power

> Depending on where you want to locate your access point, you must consider power requirements. Do you really want a noisy old 486-power

supply fan blowing in your closet? One alternative is to consider DC-powered devices, which range from a dedicated embedded PC to an off-the-shelf access point.

Ports

In a nutshell, does the hardware you're considering have all the right ports? Does it have onboard Ethernet, or do you need to add a network card? If you add that network card, do you have room for a radio card? Are there enough memory slots? Does it have a serial interface for a console? Do you need a console?

Recycled Hardware

The first thing you should consider is whether you have any old PC hardware sitting around that can be dusted off, turned on, and made into a Linux-powered access point. If you're on a budget, this may be one of the cheapest solutions, but this depends on what hardware you have, and what you want to use it for.

At a minimum, your hardware should be able to accommodate a Wi-Fi card and an Ethernet card. As we've discussed already, you should not consider using anything slower than a 486/33 processor. Additionally, if you have old Macintosh hardware available, you can easily run Linux on systems such as a PowerMac 8500/120. It's also possible to run Linux on the first generation of PowerMacs, but their motherboard are expandable only with NuBus interface cards, so you're not going to find a radio for these models.

How much memory you need depends on what distribution you decide to run. If you choose to boot your system in read-only mode from a CD or Compact Flash (CF) RAM, and use one of the custom distributions designed specifically to be small, 16–32 MB of RAM will suffice. More RAM is always better, of course, and if you plan on doing anything memory-intensive, such as web caching or intrusion detection, you'll want at least 128 MB.

The beauty of using your own or buying used hardware is that you need very few components to build a working system:

- Motherboard
- Memory
- Processor
- Power supply
- Bootable media drive: hard disk, CD, CF
- Ethernet card
- Radio card

All the other components you'd usually find on a regular PC are optional. A case is nice to keep dust off, but a box or a large Rubbermaid container works just as well. You need a video card, keyboard, monitor, and (optionally) a mouse for installation, but once the access point is operational, you can boot without them. If your hardware is *really* old, it may not support booting without a keyboard. Check the options in your BIOS to see if it will ignore a missing keyboard on boot.

All of the extraneous items that are in any old PCs can probably be removed: floppy drives, sound cards, modems, and anything else not on the list above should all be taken out. You don't need them.

Another option that you should consider is an old laptop PC. The key concern here is PCMCIA slots. You want at least two of them, unless the laptop has a built-in Ethernet port, which you probably won't find in older laptops. The beauty of a used laptop is that they are inexpensive, especially if the LCD screen is dead (which you don't need!). As long as it has an external video adapter or even a serial port that can be used as a console, you should be set.

Fujitsu Stylistic

These units definitely fall under the category of recycled hardware, because they have been out of production for years. They are not laptops, but rather the predecessor of the Tablet PC. The Stylistic 1000 models are regularly available on Ebay for under $100. Fujitsu still manufactures PCs in the Stylistic series, but all of its new models are Tablet PCs and cost as much as a new laptop.

The 1000 series have three PCMCIA slots, one of which is the boot device. The Stylistics shipped with internal type III PCMCIA hard disks, but you can also boot the unit from a CF using a CF-PCMCIA adapter.

The 1000 models are powered by a 486 DX4/100 processor and expandable to 40 MB of RAM, and they feature an integrated LCD display with cordless pen input and a 4-hour battery. The 1200 models are identical except that they are powered by a 120 MHz Pentium processor.

We have successfully used Stylistic 1000 units for access points and wireless routers on the NoCat and Seattle Wireless networks. A single Stylistic 1000 served as the primary Internet gateway for our Internet coop (*http://www.wscicc.org*) for over a year.

Small Board and Embedded PCs

So you don't have any used hardware sitting around that is suitable for building an access point, or you want to build a small unit that might be placed in a location where using a full-size PC is impractical, such as mounting it in a waterproof enclosure or installing it on your roof with a directional antenna.

However, an outdoor enclosure is only one reason you might want to think small. Power consumption, noise levels, and available space are all good reasons to consider a small board or embedded computer system for building your access point. Be warned, however: building one of these systems from the ground up may cost you at least $400.

Your options in this arena range from custom-designed embedded PCs specifically built for communications and networking to tiny PC motherboards that use the Mini-ITX form factor and measure only 17×17 centimeters. Some of the more popular options include:

Soekris (http://www.soekris.com)
> Packaged in a green metal case that is improbably the color of a refrigerator from the early 1970s, the Soekris motherboards are a popular choice with do-it-yourself networkers. Soren Kristensen has designed and built several custom motherboards based on the x86 architecture, and as of this writing, he has four different models available for single purchase or bulk quantities. All of the Soekris units are DC-powered and wired to support Power Over Ethernet. In addition, all units have a serial console port.
>
> The net4801 is the newest addition to the Soekris line. It is powered by a 266 MHz GEODE Pentium-class processor. It sports *three* 10/100 Ethernet ports, a CF slot, both MiniPCI and PCI slots, and up to 256 MB of RAM soldered on board. See Figure 6-1 for a detailed picture. As of this writing, in single quantities a board and case will cost you $265.
>
> If you need PCMCIA support, you'll want to look at the net4521. It's a different form factor, because the PCMCIA slots are positioned side-by-side rather than over-under as in most laptops. The net4521 has a 133 MHz AMD ELAN processor, which is equivalent inside to a 486. It has *two* 10/100 Ethernet ports, a CF slot, a MiniPCI slot, and up to 64 MB of RAM soldered on board. See Figure 6-2. A board and case will cost you $235.

Figure 6-1. The Soekris net4801 embedded PC

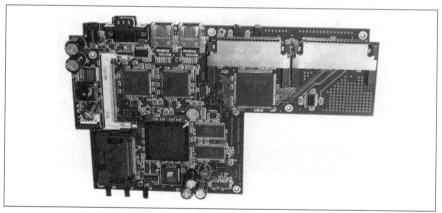

Figure 6-2. The Soekris net4521 embedded PC

BARWN outdoor routers

BARWN is the Bay Area Research Wireless Network. Tim Pozar and Matt Peterson have created BARWN, which has some interesting research projects, including an easy-to-build outdoor wireless router.

At the time this idea was conceived, few commercial products were available that fit the needs of an outdoor weatherproof design. To this date, not many products are available that also allow you to run a Linux or BSD operating system on the wireless router, and have it mounted outside.

The BARWN guys put together a white paper based on Matt Peterson's initial prototype of an outdoor router, and that white paper is available at *http://www.barwn.org*.

One fine, sunny day in May 2003, several interested groups of people converged at Tim Pozar's house in San Francisco to assemble 30 or so of these outdoor routers. It was a messy job, because three holes had to be drilled in each box, and those holes then had to be filed and sanded so that barrel connectors and RJ-45 twist-lock connectors could be inserted.

Figure 6-3 shows a completed installation with the Soekris net4521 mounted inside a weatherproof box.

Figure 6-4 shows one of these boxes in action on San Bruno Mountain south of San Francisco, as part of the BARWN network.

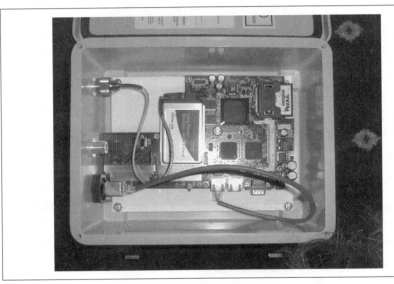

Figure 6-3. Completed BARWN Outdoor Router

OpenBrick (http://www.openbrick.org)

The OpenBrick is a hybrid, a cross between a custom-designed embedded PC and one of the Mini-ITX motherboards. It's designed to be a very small server or act as a workstation, so it has onboard video, keyboard and mouse connectors, serial ports, USB ports, onboard sound, and a Small Form Factor (SFF) IDE connector for a 2.5-inch laptop hard drive.

Figure 6-4. A BARWN Outdoor Router in action

However, it does run on DC power, and it features a single PCMCIA slot, onboard 10/100 Ethernet and a CF slot. It comes standard with 128 MB of RAM and is powered by a 300 MHz fanless Geode processor. Figure 6-5 shows the back of an OpenBrick. As of this writing, an OpenBrick will set you back a cool $360.

A newer model, the OpenBrick/E, is powered by a Via C3 533 MHz processor and features three Ethernet ports, but has no PCMCIA or PCI bus slots, which makes it less useful for building an access point.

Figure 6-5. The OpenBrick

Via Mini-ITX PCs (http://www.viavpsd.com)

Via developed the Mini-ITX format, which defines a motherboard of 17×17 centimeters. It offers a range of motherboards in the EPIA line, with processor speeds from 500 MHz to 1 GHz. They are intended to be general-purpose PC workstations, so they come with a wide array of features: onboard Ethernet, video, sound, USB, FireWire, IDE interface, and a single PCI slot.

The Via motherboards can all be powered by an external DC adapter if you wish, but their power requirements are such that adapting them for use with Power Over Ethernet is not advised. You can simply boot from a standard IDE hard disk, or if you are using a CF-to-IDE adapter, boot a Via (or any PC) from a CF card. (See "Bootable Media" later in this chapter.)

If you want a silent unit, make sure that the EPIA motherboard you buy is powered by the Eden ESP processor. This is a low-power processor that requires cooling only from a heatsink instead of a processor fan. The Via C3 processors are available at higher clock speeds, but they require a fan.

Older models of the EPIA M motherboards are widely available, and you can find them with 500 MHz Eden processors. If you buy them on eBay, these motherboards can be purchased for as little as $50. If you buy them new, they are pretty easy to find for $100.

Via's newest EPIA motherboard is the EPIA MII, which seems to be designed specifically for our purposes. Not only does it have a fanless Eden processor, it features a PCI slot, a CardBus slot, *and* a CF slot. All you need to build an access point with this motherboard is a power supply, memory, radio card, and CF card. As of this writing, the MII can be purchased at *http://www.mini-itx.com* for $218. Figure 6-6 shows the MII motherboard in detail.

There are many other embedded PC designs on the market. One example is the PC-104 motherboard standard, which is commonly used for industrial applications. However, obtaining PC-104 boards in small quantities is very expensive. The motherboards offer low performance compared to the other options we've already discussed, and the cost alone is prohibitive.

Bootable Media

Your new custom access point will run a general-purpose operating system rather than a custom operating system designed for embedded processors, so you will need a bootable media device.

Figure 6-6. The Via EPIA MII motherboard

There's nothing wrong with using a hard disk. After all, they are inexpensive and reliable, and if you're using recycled hardware, you probably already have one. Hard disks have their own set of problems, however. They are mechanical devices, with limits to the temperature and humidity that they can withstand. They generate noise, draw a fair amount of power, and are fragile. Mechanical devices, no matter how well-designed, are going to fail eventually. If your access point needs to be small and quiet, or needs to run on Power Over Ethernet or be installed outside, you should consider other bootable media options.

A CD drive shares some of the same caveats as a hard disk. It's a mechanical device, it isn't suited to run at high temperatures, and it is fragile. The cost for generic CD drives is very low; they can be purchased new for less than $30. Again, if you have recycled hardware, you may already have a spare unit.

Using a CD as bootable media is advantageous because the device is read-only. This makes it rather resistant to malicious hackers, because system files cannot be changed without physical access to the machine. This is also a disadvantage, because making configuration changes is rather difficult, and any configuration you do change won't be saved if you need to reboot. There are several Linux distributions specifically built to boot from a CD, and we discuss them in the "Software" section of this chapter.

A third option is to skip using bootable media altogether and boot your device from the network. Several of the small board PCs support Preboot eXecution Environment (PXE), which is a technology developed by Intel. You can find out more on PXE at the following link: *http://www.intel.com/labs/manage/wfm/wfmspecs.htm*. Most PCs sold since 1999 support PXE booting in their BIOS.

PXE allows you to tell a device that it will obtain booting information from another device attached to a network. In practice, this works only on a wired network, because PXE is designed for Ethernet cards. A PXE boot over a wireless network would require wireless drivers to be built into a device BIOS. You would then have to set up a PXE boot server, which answers requests from PXE boot clients and feeds them the code necessary to start up. This is a pretty advanced setup. You can get tutorials on how to set up PXE here: *http://www.kegel.com/linux/pxe.html*.

Your last option, and one that we recommend, is to use flash RAM as the boot device. While PCMCIA flash cards are available, they tend to be expensive and are not as widely available as the CF cards. CF cards are now available in sizes up to 1 GB of storage. Several of the motherboards that we discussed earlier have CF slots included. 128 MB cards can be found for less than $40, and 256 MB cards can be found for under $50.

Compact Flash cards have many advantages. While they aren't nearly as cost-effective as a hard disk, they are tiny, lightweight, consume almost no power, can operate in high-temperature conditions, and can be dropped with no consequence. They can be rewritten many thousands of times. However, CF cards can eventually be written too many times, but you can avoid this by using a Linux distribution that mounts the CF as read-only. We cover how to do this later in the chapter.

It's even possible to use CF cards on any system that has IDE connectors on the motherboard by utilizing a CF-IDE adapter card. These devices have a slot for the CF card, an IDE connector, and a power connector. You attach the adapter to the IDE bus on your PC with a standard IDE cable. The CF card should appear to your PCs BIOS as a standard IDE device.

A great source for CF-IDE adapters is Mesa Electronics. You can find a whole range of adapters on its web page, including adapters for Smart Media cards and Memory Sticks, and other small flash cards that are widely available. Check out *http://www.mesanet.com/diskcardinfo.html* for more details on the cards it offers. Figure 6-7 shows the model CFADPT1, which has both IDE and SFF-IDE connectors.

Figure 6-7. CF-IDE adapter

The CF-IDE adapters from Mesa are something to consider if you want to build an access point from an old laptop. Suppose you have a Pentium-based laptop with two PCMCIA slots. You will need one slot for a radio card and the other for an Ethernet card. Mesa's adapters have an SFF-IDE connector for the small-form IDE cable that laptops use, so you can boot your laptop from CF. Mesa also sells the SFF IDE cables, which can be hard to find in retail outlets.

Radio Cards

In Chapter 2, we covered all the steps you would need to get a number of different wireless cards working with various Linux distributions. We showed you how to use the Wireless Tools to change operating modes of your radio card.

Most 802.11 Linux card drivers support at least two modes: client (Infrastructure) Mode, also called managed mode by the Wireless Tools, and ad-hoc mode. Some cards and their drivers support a third monitor mode, which we discussed in Chapter 3. There is a fourth mode, master mode, that is of prime importance when building your own access point.

Master mode

A commercial access point has multiple functions. Not only does it have an 802.11 radio of some kind, but it also functions as the Master of any client radio that connects to it in Infrastructure mode. The access point broadcasts beacon frames, which advertise the SSID of the access point to clients. Once a client associates with an access point, the access point manages all radio communication. When multiple clients associate with an access point, the access point follows a set of algorithms to control radio traffic.

These access points usually have a separate onboard chipset that provides the additional functionality besides the 802.11 radio, or the radio card inside the access point is loaded with *tertiary* firmware, which gives the card access point capability.

In our case, we can't rely on custom chipsets to provide access point functionality to our radio cards. Depending on your particular radio card, the tertiary firmware may be an option. We discuss the ins and outs of flashing tertiary firmware to your radio card in the "Software" section of the chapter.

So where does that leave us? There are at least two types of chipsets and associated drivers that allow the use of master mode in the driver:

- Prism 2/2.5/3–based radio cards with the HostAP driver
- Atheros–based radio cards with the Madwifi driver

When set to master mode, these cards do not actually provide a full 802.11 access point. They only broadcast the beacon frames that advertise an access point to clients. The HostAP and Madwifi drivers actually take care of the 802.11 management functionality that would otherwise require a separate chipset or tertiary firmware.

In addition, if you have a Lucent WaveLAN IEEE/Orinoco/Agere 802.11b radio card, there are a couple of options you can use to have your card act as an access point. The HermesAP project is a modified version of the orinoco_cs driver that allows use of the tertiary firmware for Orinoco cards. While the driver does not include the tertiary firmware, it does provide instructions on where to obtain the firmware.

The second option is an updated driver from Agere. This driver is not available from any of the other Orinoco manufacturers, including Proxim. This driver is an updated version of the wavelan2_cs driver and has been renamed wlags49_cs. The driver includes support for master mode. We set up these drivers in the "Software" section of the chapter.

Software

There are a number of ways you can set up Linux on any of the hardware we discussed in the previous section, ranging from custom-built distributions specifically designed for a particular motherboard to simply installing a full Linux distribution on the hard disk of your recycled PC. We discuss several of the most common distributions that you may want to consider.

What all of these distributions share in common is, at least, the wireless drivers you need. As mentioned in "Master mode," there are currently two drivers that support the use of master mode: the HostAP and Madwifi drivers. In addition, there are two driver options you can use with a Hermes I (Lucent WaveLAN IEEE/Orinoco/Agere 802.11b) or Hermes II (Agere/Proxim 802.11g) radio card to run in master mode. We cover all four of these driver options in detail.

Linux Distributions

There are several available versions of Linux that are specifically geared toward building your own Linux-powered access point. Most of them have been under development for quite some time and are very stable. Wireless ISPs and community network organizations use these distributions to power their access points.

Running Linux off a CF card

One thing you will need for many of these installations is a Linux system that can read a CF card. Don't panic! You don't need a custom-built motherboard such as the Soekris or the Via MII. You need a CF adapter, and you can find it in three flavors:

1. CF-to-PC Card adapter sleeves
2. USB CF reader
3. CF-to-IDE adapter

Any of these types of units will work fine for our purposes. The USB reader will obviously require that your Linux system be configured properly for USB, and we don't have the space to go into those details here. However, most USB card readers, once recognized, will use a device name of */dev/sd<x>* where *x=a–z*. If you have other SCSI devices in your system, the CF may not be recognized as */dev/sda*.

The CF-to-PC Card adapter sleeve is your best option if you are working with a laptop system. You simply fit the CF card into the end of the adapter, then insert the adapter like a regular PC Card. In order for this to work in

Linux, you must have pcmcia-cs installed or kernel tree PCMCIA configured in your kernel. We covered both of these in detail in Chapter 2.

If you have a desktop system, the CF-to-IDE adapter is your other option if you don't have a USB reader. (We discussed these adapters in the "Bootable Media" section earlier in this chapter.) We suggest using this type of adapter only if you don't need any special drivers loaded. As long as your system recognizes an IDE device, you're set. Insert the CF into the adapter when your system is powered off, and on boot, your Linux distribution should recognize the CF as an IDE device.

Almost all CF cards sold on the market come preformatted with the Microsoft FAT16 filesystem. Why? Because this has become the de facto filesystem that most digital cameras read. Digital cameras are the primary users of CF cards, so it makes sense for the CF manufacturers to have their media ready to play.

We have encountered problems off and on with getting some makes of CF cards to reformat properly in Linux. After you fdisk the CF card and run mkfs to make a new filesystem, everything appears to run smoothly. However, when you attempt to mount the new filesystem, you receive an error similar to "FAT filesystem not supported."

On some Red Hat 8 and 9 systems, we were not able to resolve this problem. On other distributions, we were able to use the cfdisk graphical partitioning utility instead of fdisk, and that resolved the issue. One other workaround was to fdisk the CF card in a Sharp Zaurus PDA.

Pebble

This distribution was developed by Terry Schmidt of NYCWireless. Terry has worked very hard on this distribution, and it shows. Pebble is designed specifically with the Soekris hardware in mind, but it also runs quite nicely on the Stylistic and Via hardware.

The NoCat lab runs Pebble on various Pentium-era systems down to a Pentium 75 with an ISA 3Com Ethernet card and an ISA PCMCIA adapter for an Orinoco wireless card. According to the README, Pebble has also been known to run on 1U servers, IBM ThinkPads, and a robot at the Defcon hacking conference.

Terry developed this distribution specifically for the Soekris, so it was built from the ground up to be run from a 128 MB CF memory card. While you could strip out some functionality by removing Perl, NoCatAuth, djbdns, and a few other utilities, and get the distro to fit on a 32 MB CF card, it's barely worth the effort because you can find 128 MB CF cards for $30.

To prevent excessive writes to the CF card, Pebble is designed to boot read-only, and it creates a RAM disk for any temporary files that need to be written in the course of regular system operation. This means that once the system is configured, the flash is never written to, which will extend the life of your CF card. The other great advantage of a read-only mounted operating system is that you can lose power at any time, and you won't corrupt any data.

Pebble is based on the Debian GNU/Linux 3.0r1 release, so customizing the installed software is easily done with the included apt utilities. For example, the Pebble boxes on the NoCat network are customized from the standard pebble release, so run apt-get install sudo ntp-simple bind9 bind9-host and apt-get remove djbdns ppp pppoe nano before you deploy a new Pebble machine. This approach is much more flexible than some of the other small distributions we discuss later in the chapter. While the apt databases do take up some space, the flexibility they offer is worth it.

Pebble is freely available at *http://www.nycwireless.net/pebble*. As of this writing, the latest version is *pebble.v39.tar.bz2*. This release includes:

- Linux Kernel 2.4.22 with Crypto modules
- HostAP 0.1.2 and utils and hostapd
- MadWiFi CVS version from 11/17/03
- bridge-tools
- djbdns caching dns server
- elvis (tiny vi)
- gnupg
- iptables 1.2.6a
- lilo
- NoCatAuth, running as non-root user, post 0.81 nightly
- ntpdate
- openSSH server 3.4p1-1.woody.2 patched
- openSSL 0.9.6c patched with security fixes backported by Debian
- pcmcia-cs (kernel module pcmcia)
- Perl 5.6.1
- ISC dhcpd and dhclient
- zebra 0.92a-5 (BGP, OSPF, RIP Routing Daemon)

Pebble has wireless card driver support for many but not all wireless cards. There are drivers for Orinoco, Cisco, Atheros (madwifi), and Prism (HostAP). It supports a fairly wide variety of Ethernet drivers, including

3Com, Intel, National Semiconductor (Soekris), and Via-Rhine (Via motherboards), as well as the Tulip driver, which supports a wide range of Ethernet cards.

We assume for the purposes of this section that you will install Pebble on a CF card for use in a Soekris or other machine that can boot from a CF. This shouldn't keep you from loading it on other media. It works well from a hard disk, and you can simply substitute a mounted IDE hard disk for the CF card in the following instructions.

As Terry mentions in the README, there are many types of CF cards. He has had problems with Kingston flash cards and recommends SanDisk CF cards. We concur, having had a few flash cards ourselves that simply would not boot properly. Pebble fits nicely on a 128 MB flash. We don't recommend anything smaller unless you plan to trim packages, and we don't cover that here. See "Running Linux off a Compact Flash Card," earlier in this section.

Once the CF card is in your system and is successfully recognized, there are several steps to obtaining a working Pebble distribution on the CF. Terry has greatly improved this process over time, and the latest versions of Pebble have an installation script that takes care of most of the heavy lifting for you.

Here's what you must do as root. These examples assume that your CF card is recognized as */dev/hde*. This is the case on a typical system with a single IDE hard disk and an IDE CD-ROM. Consult dmesg to make sure you know which device your CF card is using.

1. Use fdisk to create one large partition. You don't need swap, because Pebble mounts read-only and writes everything entirely to RAM.

   ```
   # fdisk /dev/hde
   ```

2. Next, use mkfs.ext2 to create an ext2 filesystem. You don't need or want a journaling filesystem such as ext3 or jfs. Again, Pebble mounts read-only, so the journal uses up space that you could use:

   ```
   # mkfs.ext2 /dev/hde1
   ```

3. Create a mount point for the CF card (you don't need to mount it, because the *pebble.update* script, which you'll run later, takes care of this for you):

   ```
   # mkdir /mnt/cf
   ```

4. Make a directory to untar the Pebble distro so the install script can work:

   ```
   # mkdir /mnt/pebble
   # cd /mnt/pebble
   ```

5. Uncompress and untar the Pebble distro to the directory that you have just created (the actual version number may be different):

   ```
   # tar jxvf /path/to/pebble.v39.tar.bz2
   ```

If you want to do manual configuration of your Pebble install before invoking the installation scrip, there is an opportunity here for editing filest. For instance, if you want to configure dhcpd or any of the other daemons that run at startup, this is a good time to do so. In particular, you should consider editing *etc/network/interfaces* to define TCP/IP for *eth0*, and also editing *etc/pcmcia/network.opts* and *etc/pcmcia/wireless.opts* to configure your radio cards. This way, you can bring up a working system from the get-go.

We also recommend editing *etc/inittab*. Terry runs the NoCatAuth captive portal from *inittab* to make sure that it always respawns if it dies unexpectedly. This is fine, but until you have a completely configured Pebble system with all of its network interfaces active, you will receive garbage on the console while NoCatAuth tries to start, fails, and respawns. The last line of *etc/inittab* reads:

```
NC:23:respawn:start-stop-daemon -S -c nocat -exec /usr/local/nocat/bin/
    gateway -- -F
```

Comment this line out by placing a # at the beginning of the line. Then you can run:

```
# ./pebble.update
```

This is the installation script. It's interactive, so you must answer a few questions before it can start.

```
Where is the pebble installer (this) directory? default=/mnt/pebble:
Which device accesses the compact flash? default=/dev/hde:
Which directory should I mount the FlashCard to? devfault=/mnt/cf:
Which module? Enter 1 for pcmcia, 2 for net4501, or 3 for net4521/net4511 \
    default=net4501
```

You should know the answers to the first three questions, because we've discussed them in the previous steps. The last question is critical, because the answer affects which modules load in the Pebble installation you create, as well as other startup operations.

If you're setting up a Soekris system, the answers are obvious for any other system that uses a PC Card radio, you must choose option #1. If you have a PCI or a MiniPCI radio card, none of these options will completely suit you. Choose #1 and make some configuration changes later.

Once you have the questions answered, the installer script goes to work, making changes to the configuration files depending on how you answered the last question. Once done, it copies the modified distribution from */mnt/pebble* to the mounted CF card at */mnt/cf*.

After copying, it performs ssh key generation for the sshd keys, so that there are no duplicate Pebble ssh keys running in the world, and finally, it makes you change the root password. Once done, it unmounts the CF card, and you are ready to insert the CF card into your chosen access point hardware.

If you have a Soekris system, this is the point where you'll want to hook up a serial cable to a PC and run some terminal software at 9600 8-N-1, so you can see the console as Pebble boots. If you made configuration changes prior to running the installation script, this is doubly important so you can make sure things start like you expect. If you're on a PC system with video output, hook up a monitor.

At this point, you should have a working Pebble access point. If you happen to have a Prism-based card in your system, it should come up in master mode and appear as an access point with an SSID of "Freenetworks." Later in this section, we cover some specifics on configuration of the HostAP driver that makes this setup possible.

There are two places to get help with Pebble. First, read completely through the README, available at *http://www.nycwireless.net/pebble/pebble.README*. If you can't resolve your issue with the help of the README, subscribe to the Pebble mailing list at *http://freenetworks.org/mailman/listinfo/pebble-linux*. The list is active and full of knowledgeable readers who should be able to provide you assistance.

LEAF/WISP-Dist

LEAF stands for the Linux Embedded Appliance Firewall. Rather than being a single distribution, LEAF has actually become a clearinghouse of sorts for a number of related distributions, all of which are available from the LEAF pages: *http://leaf.sourceforge.net*.

Most of the LEAF distributions are children of the Linux Router Project (LRP), which was designed as a single-floppy bootable Linux-based router. As the project matured, spin-offs developed that included newer kernel support, among other things. LEAF is now the parent organization for six active distributions and some inactive ones.

At one time, Wireless ISP Distribution (WISP-Dist) was an independent distribution, but recently it has moved under the support of LEAF. For the purposes of building a custom access point, WISP-Dist is the only LEAF distribution we cover.

WISP-Dist is a modular embedded Linux distribution for wireless routers but can be used for other purposes as well. The entire system fits in 8 MB flash/16 MB RAM, making it much smaller than Pebble. The stated goal of the project is "to create an open, customizable, and easy to use embedded router for ISP needs."

As of this writing, the current version of WISP-Dist is 2624, but it is referred to in the documentation as WISP-2003, because it was the only release in that year. Current features include:

- Linux kernel 2.4
- Simple to use menu-based configuration system for basic functionality
- Command-line access for advanced configuration
- The ability upgrade remotely via automatic script
- Modularity: you can add/remove packages
- Local access via console or serial port
- Remote access via sshd
- Statistics available via SNMP, including wireless statistics
- Layer 3 bridging support based on proxy ARP
- OSPF, RIPv2 dynamic routing support integrated with Zebra routing engine
- NAT (with H.323, PPTP pass-through support)
- Bandwidth shaping
- PPP
- PPPoE client
- VTUN for encrypted PtP
- VLAN trunking
- Access point support for Prism2/2.5/3/Atheros
- MAC filter support for access point
- Advanced network diagnostics: NTOP, tcpdump, bmon, etc.
- The ability to log all system events to remote system with syslog
- checkping: system reboots if some of the specified hosts are unreachable (useful when radios get stuck)
- The ability to store all files, which makes it easy to service on standard FAT partition.

While WISP-Dist is very small, it runs on pretty much any x86-compatible CPU. The developers recommend at least a 100 MHz processor in addition to the minimum of 8 MB of disk space and 16 MB of RAM. WISP-Dist has been tested on the Soekris hardware as well as several single-board computers designed for the ISP market. It includes drivers for Cisco, Orinoco, Atheros, and Prism-based cards. There are two types of wireless cards that it does not support: cards based on the Texas Instruments chipset (such as the D-Link DWL-520/650+) and USB wireless adapters.

As with Pebble, WISP-Dist is designed to be installed on a CF card. The size requirements are much smaller, however—you can run WISP-Dist on as little as 8 MB of flash. You do need a system that can read CF cards. See "Running Linux off a CF card," earlier in this section.

The WISP-Dist installation is nowhere near the simplicity of the Pebble installation script. The distribution is provided in two different types:

Partitionless installation from a .bin or .img file

Once you have downloaded the *wisp-dist_2624_img_wdist.bin* file (or a newer version) and have a CF card inserted in your reader, you must use the dd command to copy the image to the CF card. dd makes a block-by-block copy of the image, so you don't need to partition the CF. This invocation assumes your CF card is on */dev/hde*:

```
$ dd if=wisp-dist_2624_img_wdist.bin of=/dev/hde
```

Partition-based installation from package distribution .zip file

You must manually partition the CF card using the fdisk command. The first partition that you create should be at least 6800 Kb in size, and you should set this partition to Active. You should also specify the partition type as FAT. The second partition should be at least 1,300 Kb in size. If you have more than 16 MB RAM in your system, you can skip the creation of the second partition, as WISP-Dist will create a RAMdisk on boot to use instead of a second partition, similar to Pebble's operation.

Next, create the filesystem on the first partition:

```
# mkfs.msdos /dev/hde1
```

Now obtain the SYSLINUX bootloader from *http://syslinux.zytor.com*, and install it on the first partition. SYSLINUX can also be installed in Debian using apt-get. Mandrake and Red Hat/Fedora users can install an RPM. SYSLINUX is designed to boot Linux from a FAT filesystem. Once you have the SYSLINUX binary on your system, execute this command:

```
# syslinux /dev/hde1
```

This creates a boot sector on the disk and copies a file named *LDLINUX.SYS* into the root directory.

Next, you should mount the CF card, unzip the *wisp-dist_2624_pkg_wdist.zip* file (or a newer version that matches the version of the *.bin* file) into a temporary directory, and copy files from the temporary directory to the root of the CF card:

```
# mount -t vfat /dev/hde1 /mnt/cf
# cd wisp-dist
# cp -a * /mnt/cf
```

Lastly, edit the *syslinux.cfg* file. If you did create the second partition in the first step, you must add the statement *rwfs=/dev/hda2*. This assumes that on your target system, the CF card is the IDE primary master */dev/ hda*. If your system is booting from a different device, you must also change any occurrence of *boot=/dev/hdaX* in the *syslinux.cfg* file to the appropriate device.

At this point, you should be able to unmount */dev/<hde>* (or whatever device your CF is on) from your system, eject the CF card, and place it in the system that will be running WISP-Dist. As with Pebble, it's a good idea to connect a serial console or monitor to the system to watch the initial boot.

WISP-Dist should appear with a default configuration that has no root password, the *eth0* Ethernet interface at 192.168.1.1 with a 255.255.255.0 netmask, and a serial console on ttyS0 at 9600 8N1. When you log in as root, you are immediately presented with a menu, as shown in Figure 6-8.

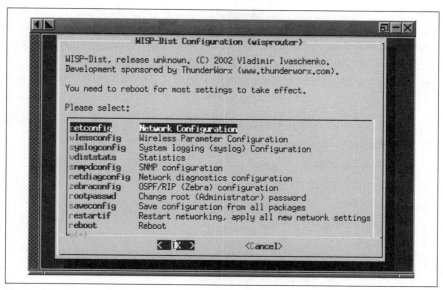

Figure 6-8. WISP-Dist Configuration menu

The WISP-Dist configuration system is straightforward and easy to set up. If you want a command line for advanced configuration, you can choose Quit from the menu and you will be presented with the root command line.

If you need help with WISP-Dist, you should first read through the User Guide, which is located at *http://leaf.sourceforge.net/devel/hzdrus/doc/html*. For some reason, there is no WISP-Dist topic in the LEAF FAQs at Source-Forge, so the next place you should check is the leaf-user mailing list. You

can search the archives at *http://www.mail-archive.com/leaf-user%40lists.*
sourceforge.net or subscribe to the list at *http://lists.sourceforge.net/lists/*
listinfo/leaf-user.

LinuxAP

The LinuxAP distribution began life as an upgrade to the OpenAP code,
which was developed to run on certain access point hardware. See the section titled "Running Linux on Non-Linux Devices" later in this chapter for
details.

As of this writing, the current version of LinuxAP is based on the 2.4.20 kernel, and it supports both the Eumitcom WL11000 motherboards that power
some access points, as well as the Soekris hardware platform. The LinuxAP
web pages are at *http://linuxap.ksmith.com*, and as of this writing, the most
current version of the LinuxAP source is *linuxAP-2003-09-13.tar.bz2*.

Installation and compilation of LinuxAP is somewhat modular in that you
can choose up front which daemons and utilities you want to include with
your compiled kernel. In addition to the LinuxAP source, you can download additional compressed files from the LinuxAP web site, including:

- Kernel 2.4.20
- Bridge utilities
- BusyBox shell/network utilities
- C-Kermit
- CRAMFS filesystem utilities
- CIPE tunnel driver and utilities
- HostAP driver
- IP tables firewall
- pcmcia-cs
- Tiny login
- Uclibc compact C library
- uDHCP client/server
- UMSDOS enhanced FAT filesystem
- Wireless tools

As with the previous two distributions, in order to get LinuxAP loaded on a
CF card for use in a Soekris unit, you need a CF card reader. See "Running
Linux off a CF card" earlier in this section.

1. First, uncompress the LinuxAP distribution. The developer recommends that you place the compressed file in */usr/src* so that your code tree resides in */usr/src/linuxAP*. You must replace *2004-09-13* with whatever version of LinuxAP you downloaded:

```
# cd /usr/src
# tar xjvf linuxAP-2004-09-13-tar.bz2
# cd linuxAP
```

2. Next, make a directory for the utilities that you selected and downloaded:

```
# mkdir tarfiles
```

3. Uncompress each source file for the utilities, but leave the *.tar* file intact, and copy the *.tar* files into the newly created directory:

```
# cd /usr/src
# bunzip2 linux-2.4.20.tar.bz2
# cp linux-2.4.20.tar linuxAP/tarfiles
```

4. Now, run make, which allows you to select the type of hardware, Eumitcom or Soekris, and also the utilities you want to include:

```
# cd linuxAP
# make
```

5. Once the compile is completed, in the *linuxAP* directory you will have two created files: *kernel* and *ramdisk*. At this point, prepare your target disk and install SYSLINUX. (See the "LEAF/WISP-Dist" section earlier in the chapter for details on where to obtain SYSLINUX.) Set up the first partition as 8 MB, set it as Active, and make it a FAT16 partition. Make a new MSDOS partition, and then install SYSLINUX. If your CF card is on a different device, replace */dev/hde* with the appropriate device.

```
# fdisk /dev/hde
# mkfs.msdos /dev/hde1
# syslinux /dev/hde1
```

6. The last step is to mount your newly formatted CF card and copy the compiled *kernel*, *ramdisk*, and the *syslinux.cfg* files over:

```
# mount -t vfat /dev/hde1 /mnt/cf
# cd /usr/src/linuxAP
# cp syslinux.cfg ramdisk /mnt/cf
# cp kernel /mnt/cf/linux
# umount /mnt/cf
```

7. Once again, you can now remove the CF card, insert it in your Soekris hardware, and boot it up with a serial cable attached to observe the initial boot.

For help with LinuxAP, refer to the LinuxAP-dev mailing list, hosted at *http://linuxap.ksmith.com/mailman/listinfo/linuxap-dev*. There is an active development and user community who should be able to provide you with advanced assistance.

Other distributions

As of this writing, Pebble and WISP-Dist are the two most full-featured distributions specifically aimed to make a small-board computer into an access point. There are some other distributions you may want to investigate:

Sydney Wireless HostAP CD

> The wireless folks down under have produced this ISO CDROM image of a Linux bootable CDROM installer. This is *not* just a bootable CDROM; it will fdisk and format a hard disk or device that you choose and install a custom version of Debian Linux. The distribution features support for PCI and PCMCIA Prism cards using the HostAP driver, has support for a wide variety of Ethernet cards, does advanced routing with the Zebra routing engine, and has IPv6 capabilities.
>
> The installed distribution takes up approximately 43 MB, so you can consider this as another alternative operating system to try on your CF card. The CD can be downloaded from *http://www.sydneywireless.org/ ?Projects*.

LocustWorld MeshAP

> MeshAP is a unique distribution in many respects. Jon Anderson, in the UK, created MeshAP and has added some interesting features. First, MeshAP is designed from the ground up to actually build mesh networks using the Ad-hoc On-demand Distance Vector (AODV) routing protocol. AODV builds routes between nodes on demand, as desired by those nodes. You can get detailed information on AODV at *http:// moment.cs.ucsb.edu/AODV/aodv.html*.
>
> Second, as part of the MeshAP project, Jon created the Wireless Internet Assigned Numbers Authority (WIANA), found at *http://www.wiana.org*. This is slightly controversial, as WIANA will assign you a 1.x.x.x IPv4 address for the wireless mesh portion of your MeshAP. WIANA certainly is not the first organization to assign unused IPv4 address space to wireless networks; the folks at *http://freenetworks.org* have done the same with the 10.x.x.x address space. Both of these assignments are really hacks on the existing infrastructure, until IPv6 is actually implemented on a larger basis.
>
> MeshAP is provided in a similar format to the Sydney Wireless CD, in that you download an ISO CDROM image, burn that image to CD, and boot from the CD. The installation process lets you select a device for installation, and it then partitions and formats the destination device and installs a MeshAP distribution. Once you have MeshAP installed, you must register at *http://www.wiana.org* to receive a 1.x.x.x address for your Mesh.

You can get documentation for MeshAP from the LocustWorld Wiki at *http://www.locustworld.com/tracker/wiki?p=WikiIndex*. There is also a MeshAP User mailing list. To subscribe, send an empty email message to *meshapuser-subscribe@lists.locust.net*.

HostAP

In Chapter 2, we covered in detail the compilation and installation of the HostAP driver, so all the examples from this point on assume that you have compiled and installed HostAP (if necessary—some distributions include it), and then configured the HostAP driver for your Prism-based radio card. Also, we assume that the driver works with your card in managed mode.

As we've explained previously, the HostAP driver performs the 802.11 management functions that would normally be performed in an access point by either tertiary firmware in a radio card or dedicated additional hardware.

Setting up HostAP to function this way is a simple matter of changing the card to master mode. You can do this through the iwconfig tool (replace **MyAP** with the name you want to use for your access point):

```
# iwconfig wlan0 essid myAP mode master
```

To bring up the HostAP driver in master mode during startup, modify */etc/pcmcia/wireless.opts*. Here is an example (you can change the ESSID and CHANNEL settings):

```
# wireless.opts

case "$ADDRESS" in

*,*,*,*)
  INFO="Prism card in Master mode"
  ESSID="myAP"
  MODE="Master"
  CHANNEL="11"
  RATE="Auto"
  ;;

esac
```

Chapter 2 also discussed the address-matching syntax used in the *wireless.opts* and *network.opts* files. This syntax is:

```
scheme, socket, instance, MAC address
```

You can use this syntax in many different ways. *Schemes* are mostly useful for client-based laptops, where you need to switch between different wireless settings for home and work. instance is supposed to be used for network cards that have multiple interfaces. We've never found a wireless card that uses this parameter.

However, for an access point, it can be extremely useful to specify which slot should only hold the access point radio card:

```
*,0,*.*)
```

This syntax would ensure that only a card in PCMCIA socket 0 would be given the *master* mode configuration. It would even be more useful to add a wildcard MAC address match:

```
*,0,*,00:02:6F:*)
```

Now, any card that is inserted in slot 0 and is a Senao/EnGenius Prism-based card is given the *master* mode configuration, and allowed to act as the access point card. If you're spending a lot of time futzing around with your radio card configuration, this is one way to make sure that you know what to expect when you plug in a certain card.

 Some machines, including the Stylistic and Soekris, have problems loading the HostAP driver with high-power 100 mW and 200 mW Prism-based radio cards. The card is detected on insert but fails to initialize, and it reports an obscure error: "GetNextTuple: No more items." If you have this problem, add this line to */etc/pcmcia/hostap_cs.conf*:

```
module "hostap_cs" opts "ignore_cis_vcc=1"
```

The driver attempts to verify that one entry on the card's acceptable voltage table matches the voltage reported by your PC Card slot. In some cases, this voltage can be reported incorrectly, causing the driver to fail. This option causes the driver to ignore the reported voltage and load anyway.

If you have a PCI or MiniPCI Prism card, configuration is not handled via the pcmcia-cs configuration scripts, but is handled like any other Ethernet interface. On Debian systems, you can add an up `iwconfig` line to the TCP/IP definition for the radio card in */etc/network/interfaces*:

```
iface wlan0 inet static
     address 192.168.1.1
     netmask 255.255.255.0
     broadcast 192.168.1.255
     up iwconfig wlan0 essid myAP mode master channel 11 rate auto
```

On Mandrake, RedHat, and Fedora systems, you can add radio configuration for PC Card, PCI, and MiniPCI Wi-Fi adapters in */etc/sysconfig/network-scripts*. This is a sample *ifcfg-wlan0* script:

```
DEVICE=wlan0
BOOTPROTO=static
ADDRESS=192.168.1.1
NETMASK=255.255.255.0
BROADCAST=192.168.1.255
```

```
ONBOOT=yes
MODE=Master
ESSID=myAP
CHANNEL=11
RATE=AUTO
```

Once you have your card configured for *master* mode, you can now treat
wlan0 as any other Ethernet interface. Assign IP addresses, set up routing,
and bind processes to the interface as needed. HostAP takes care of all the
details of managing wireless clients attached to your access point.

Bridging

In the previous examples, your Prism card on *wlan0* has its own IP address.
This requires you to set up routing on your Linux system. While this really
isn't a problem, there may be situations where you don't want routing, but
rather want to bridge all wireless traffic across to your wired Ethernet port.

Later in this chapter, we discuss setting up Wireless Distribution System
(WDS), which bridges HostAP and a Linksys access point. In order to set up
bridging or WDS, we needed to install the *bridge-utils* package. On our
Mandrake 9.2 system, this was installed using the command urpmi bridge-
utils; Red Hat and Fedora users should be able to similarly use the rpm
installation, and Debian users can do apt-get install bridge-utils. You
can also obtain the source code from *http://bridge.sourceforge.net*. You must
also make sure that your kernel has support for 802.1d Ethernet bridging.
On the factory kernels from Mandrake and Fedora, this was enabled by
default, but for RedHat and Debian systems, we needed to compile this
option into the kernel ourselves.

To bridge your Prism card running in *master* mode with your first Ethernet
card, use the following, preferably from the console of your access point (if
you try to mess with networking while you are connected via ssh, things will
probably become weird):

```
ifconfig eth0 0.0.0.0
ifconfig wlan0 0.0.0.0
brctl addbr br0
brctl addif br0 eth0
brctl addif br0 wlan0
ifconfig br0 192.168.1.2
route add default gw 192.168.1.1
```

As we report in the WDS section later in this chapter, it can take up to 30
seconds for the bridge to come up and began passing TCP/IP traffic. Don't
be alarmed if you can't ping across the bridge from your client immediately
after pressing Enter on the last command.

If you have only one bridge on your network, you can safely turn off the Spanning Tree protocol with:

```
brctl stp br0 off
```

This prevents the bridging code from needlessly sending 802.1d traffic to other nonexistent bridges. You can see the configuration of your bridge at any time by using `brctl show`:

```
# brctl show
bridge name    bridge id              STP enabled    interfaces
br0            8000.00026f15423F      no             eth0
                                                     wlan0
```

Bridges tend to be "set and forget" devices (although you must run the commands shown in this section after each reboot, so you may want to put them in a startup script). Once configured, your bridge maintains itself, barring a huge amount of traffic. Be sure to read the documentation available at *http://bridge.sourceforge.net* as well as the documents listed at the end of this section.

Keep in mind that although a bridge is simple to configure, it isn't very secure. You don't have any control over the packets that flow across your bridge. To use a bit of cliché, you may want to consider enacting a toll on your bridge by implementing some firewalling. Unfortunately, standard iptables firewall commands don't work with bridging in the 2.4 kernels. Rob Flickenger has detailed how to bridge with a firewall in his excellent book, *Wireless Hacks* (O'Reilly).

For more information, please consult the following sources:

- The Linux Bridge STP HOWTO (*http://www.linux.org/docs/ldp/howto/BRIDGE-STP-HOWTO*)
- The Linux Bridge and Firewall mini HOWTO (*http://www.tldp.org/HOWTO/mini/Bridge+Firewall.html*)
- *Wireless Hacks*, by Rob Flickenger (O'Reilly)

MAC address filtering

We touched briefly on this subject in Chapter 4. MAC filtering does not offer much security, because a person running Kismet can easily sit in range of your access point, capture a number of frames, and quickly deduce at least one MAC address that is allowed to associate with your access point. It is pretty trivial under Linux to spoof a MAC address, allowing an attacker to join your wireless network. You should combine MAC filtering with WEP and implement a captive portal with authentication to provide a reasonable measure of security.

While the filtering of MAC addresses is certainly not the best security measure for your wireless network, it does at least provide the first layer of defense. Filtering MAC addresses not only blocks traffic that is not destined for your network, but also attempts to prevent other users from associating with your access point.

When using MAC filtering, make a list of wireless devices that you wish to allow, and then deny all others. With the HostAP driver, this is done using the iwpriv command:

```
# iwpriv wlan0 addmac 00:01:02:03:04:05
# iwpriv wlan0 addmac 05:06:07:08:AA:BB
```

This adds MAC addresses to an internal table maintained by HostAP. You can add as many addresses to the table as you like, one on each line, and then tell HostAP what to do with the table you've built:

```
# iwpriv wlan0 maccmd 1
# iwpriv wlan0 maccmd 4
```

The maccmd 1 tells HostAP to use the table as an *allowed* list and deny all other MAC addresses from associating. The maccmd 4 disconnects all associated clients, forcing them to reassociate. At this point, only clients in the table are allowed to reassociate with your access point.

Sometimes, you may only need to ban a troublemaker or two, rather than set up a list of permitted devices. Again, you would use the iwpriv command:

```
# iwpriv wlan0 addmac 01:10:20:02:30:03
# iwpriv wlan0 maccmd 2
# iwpriv wlan0 kickmac 01:10:20:02:30:03
```

As before, you can use addmac to add as many addresses to the table as you need. The maccmd 2 sets the policy for the new table to deny, and kickmac boots the specific MAC immediately from the access point. This is nicer than booting everybody and making them reassociate.

To disable MAC filtering, enter this command:

```
# iwpriv wlan0 maccmd 0
```

If you make a mistake typing in a MAC address, you can use the delmac command just as you would addmac. Should you ever need to flush the current MAC table entirely but keep a defined policy in place, issue:

```
# iwpriv wlan0 maccmd 3
```

Finally, you can view the current MAC table in */proc*:

```
# cat /proc/net/hostap/wlan0/ap_control
```

While iwpriv manipulates the running HostAP driver, it doesn't preserve settings across reboots. Once you're happy with your MAC filtering tables and policies, make sure you put the necessary commands in an *rc* script to run at boot.

Madwifi

Unfortunately, the Madwifi driver does not have nearly all of the bells and whistles of HostAP. However, if you want a Linux-based 802.11a or 802.11g access point, this driver is really your only working option as of this writing.

Again, we covered the installation and compilation of the Madwifi driver in Chapter 2. We assume that you are able to use the driver in *managed* mode.

The Madwifi driver, like HostAP, performs the 802.11 management functions that normally are performed in an access point by either tertiary firmware in a radio card or dedicated additional hardware.

Setting up Madwifi to function this way is a simple matter of changing the card to *master* mode. You can do this through the iwconfig tool (you can change *myAP* to whatever you prefer for the SSID):

```
# iwconfig ath0 essid myAP mode master
```

To bring up the Madwifi driver in *master* mode during startup, you can modify */etc/pcmcia/wireless.opts*. Here is an example (you can replace *ESSID* and *CHANNEL* with your own settings):

```
# wireless.opts

case "$ADDRESS" in

*,*,*,*)
  INFO="Atheros card in Master mode"
  ESSID="myAP"
  MODE="Master"
  CHANNEL="11"
  RATE="Auto"
  ;;

esac
```

The Atheros cards are all CardBus adapters, so they are treated as hotplug devices, and configuration can also be handled like any other Ethernet interface. On Debian systems, you can add an up iwconfig line to the TCP/IP definition for the radio card in */etc/network/interfaces*:

```
iface ath0 inet static
    address 192.168.1.1
    netmask 255.255.255.0
    broadcast 192.168.1.255
    up iwconfig wlan0 essid myAP mode master channel 11 rate auto
```

On Mandrake, RedHat, and Fedora systems, you can add radio configuration for PC Card, PCI, and MiniPCI Wi-Fi adapters in */etc/sysconfig/network-scripts*. This is a sample *ifcfg-ath0* script:

```
DEVICE=ath0
BOOTPROTO=static
ADDRESS=192.168.1.1
NETMASK=255.255.255.0
BROADCAST=192.168.1.255
ONBOOT=yes
MODE=Master
ESSID=myAP
CHANNEL=11
RATE=AUTO
```

Once you have your card configured for *master* mode, you can treat *ath0* as any other Ethernet interface. Assign IP addresses, set up routing, and bind processes to the interface as needed. Madwifi takes care of all the details of managing wireless clients attached to your access point.

The Madwifi driver at this time does not support MAC address filtering, but you can set up bridging using an Atheros card. (See the "Bridging" section previously in this chapter where we discussed setting up a bridge with HostAP and a Prism card.) To set up a bridge with your Atheros card, simply substitute *ath0* for *wlan0* in the bridge setup.

Hermes AP

Hermes-based radio cards (the tremendously popular but confusingly named Lucent/Orinoco/Avaya/Proxim silver and gold cards) are notoriously difficult to operate as an access point. By design, the cards themselves are actually not able to provide 802.11 BSS master services on their own. You might find this surprising, because they are the radio cards embedded in the original AirPort AP, as well as the RG1000, RG1100, AP1000, and many others.

Before these cards can operate as a BSS master, they need additional firmware uploaded to the card. Orinoco and many other cards originally based on the Prism designs can actually host three firmware images: primary or operating firmware; station or client firmware; and tertiary firmware. This *tertiary firmware* is uploaded to the card's RAM and lost if the card loses power. To make matters even more difficult, the firmware in question is licensed software and can't legally be distributed by anyone but the manufacturer.

The ingenious Hermes AP project (*http://hunz.org/hermesap.html*) addresses both of these tricky issues. It consists of a set of modified drivers, a utility for uploading the tertiary firmware, and a simple script that downloads the firmware from Proxim's public FTP server. Running Hermes AP successfully is not trivial, but it can be the perfect piece of software if you absolutely need a host-based Orinoco AP.

To get Hermes AP running, you need a kernel with Dev FS enabled. This allows the kernel to manage the /dev directory, dynamically creating device files for every physical device that the kernel supports. Run a make menuconfig or make xconfig, and select Code maturity level options → Prompt for development and/or incomplete code/drivers. Now go back to the main menu, and under File systems enable /dev file system support, as well as Automatically mount at boot. When running Dev FS, it's also a good idea to disable /dev/pts filesystem support, as Dev FS automatically manages your ptys for you.

Before you recompile your kernel, copy all of the source code under the *drivers/* directory from Hermes AP over top of the existing drivers in the kernel (right over the files in *linux/drivers/net/wireless/*). Now build your kernel and modules as you normally would, and reboot.

Your Orinoco card should come up as normal with the new driver, but it won't support BSS master mode yet. First, cd to the Hermes AP source directory. To download a copy of the tertiary firmware from Proxim's site, run the *hfwget.sh* script in the *firmware/* directory. Next, build the *hfwload* utility by running make in the *hfw/* directory. This utility uploads the tertiary firmware to your card. Copy the utility and the card firmware somewhere handy (we keep ours in */usr/local/hermesap*), and run a command like this at boot time, before the interface comes up, replacing *eth1* with the actual interface name and FIRMWARE with the firmware filename (such as *T1085800.hfw*):

```
# cd /usr/local/hermesap; ./hfwload eth1 FIRMWARE
```

Note that the card must not be configured up when you load the firmware; if it is already up, an ifconfig *eth1* down brings it down for you. If all goes well, an iwconfig should show that eth1 is in master mode! You can now configure the radio with an ESSID, WEP keys, and any other features as you normally would.

Hermes AP is still beta software, but it seems to run quite well. For situations where you don't have the option of using HostAP and a Prism-based card, Hermes AP is a good alternative solution.

Agere Wlags49

Linux drivers for the Hermes cards have unfortunately hit a stopping point with the recent acquisition of the Orinoco line by Proxim. If you look for any information about Linux support on the Proxim web site, you will find that the latest Proxim-provided driver for Hermes-based cards is 6.20 from May 2002.

An interesting twist to this storyline is that Agere, who was originally spun off from Lucent and also produced Hermes-based radio cards, has updated drivers available on its web site dating from September 2003. If you browse to *http://www.agere.com/support/drivers*, you will find the Linux LKM Wireless Driver Source Code, Version 7.14 listed, which you can download from *http://www.agere.com/support/drivers/wl_lkm_714_release.tar.gz*.

If you dig into the README, you will find that this is a major update of the previously provided wavelan2_cs driver. It has been renamed wlags49, for reasons that are not clear. What is clear, however, is that the driver provides support for not only the classic Hermes I chipset that powers Orinoco Gold/ Silver cards, but the Hermes II chipset that is found in newer 802.11b PC Cards, MiniPCI, and CF adapters from Agere and Proxim.

Even more interesting is the list of new features in the release:

- Began updating the Wireless Extensions
- Added support for access point (AP) mode
- Added support for tertiary firmware downloads
- Added support for WDS in AP mode

The requirement for the driver is a 2.4.x kernel. The README does say that this driver should compile under architectures other than x86, but that has not been verified. You'll also need a working gcc compiler environment. If you have been able to compile kernels, pcmcia-cs, and the HostAP driver to this point, compiling this driver will not be a problem.

 If you already have the standard orinoco_cs or a compiled HostAP driver on your system, be warned: wlags49 does not play nice with these drivers. Once compiled and loaded as a module, wlags49 will be the default driver for any Hermes or Prism-based card in your system.

We recommend you use only wlags49 on a system where you are not going to use the orinoco_cs or HostAP drivers.

Getting the driver to compile is rather tricky. In order to configure the source code for compilation, you must first obtain the pcmcia-cs source code. In Chapter 2, we covered in detail how to compile and install pcmcia-cs. In brief, you can obtain the source code from *http://pcmcia-cs.sourceforge.net*.

You'll want to unpack the pcmcia-cs source somewhere. (On our Mandrake 9.2 system, we put the source in */usr/src/pcmcia-cs-3.2.7*.) Once you have done that, copy the gzipped Agere source into the *pcmcia-cs* directory and extract it:

```
# cp /root/download/wl_lkm_714_release.tar.gz pcmcia-cs-3.2.7
# cd pcmcia-cs-3.2.7
# tar xzvf wl_lkm_714_release.tar.gz
```

To configure the source for the driver, run ./Configure. This will look familiar to you if you have already compiled pcmcia-cs, because the *Configure*
script is part of the pcmcia-cs release. You must configure the wlags49
source this way, even if you have kernel tree PCMCIA enabled.

You don't have to completely reinstall pcmcia-cs once the configuration is
completed. To install the wlags49 default driver, which supports Hermes I
and II cards in both *STA* (station adapter or managed) mode and AP mode,
run the scripts that came with the wlags49 source:

```
./Build
./Install
```

Once installed, you must stop and restart the pcmcia-cs subsystem, unless
you have a MiniPCI Hermes II card, in which case you may want to simply
reboot.

The wlags49 source also gives you the option of building a driver that supports either Hermes I or II in *STA* or *AP* mode only. Instead of the ./Build
command, you can issue one of the following commands before ./Install:

```
# make -f wlags49.mk h1_cs_sta    # Hermes I, STA mode
# make -f wlags49.mk h1_cs_ap     # Hermes I, AP mode
# make -f wlags49.mk h2_cs_sta    # Hermes II, STA mode
# make -f wlags49.mk h2_cs_ap     # Hermes II, AP mode
```

If you only wish to build the driver to support a PCI/MiniPCI card in either
STA or *AP* modes, you can issue these commands:

```
# make -f wlags49.mk pci
# make -f wlags49.mk pci_install
```

Once the driver is loaded, you have the option of configuring wireless parameters in three different ways. The documentation seems to suggest that you
should perform all wireless configuration in the */etc/pcmcia/config.opts* file.
This is rather nonstandard, and we did not even attempt to go down this road.

The documentation goes on to say that you can also configure the driver
using a file in */etc/agere/iwconfig-eth1*. This directory was not created as part
of the installation, so we also did not attempt to use this method. We did
not have a Hermes II MiniPCI card to test with, but we suspect that this second method is the one that you would need to use.

Fortunately, the third method is to simply use the pcmcia-cs standard configuration by configuring the card in */etc/pcmcia/wireless.opts* and */etc/pcm-
cia/network.opts*. The *wlags49* driver takes advantage of the Wireless Tools,
so that setting up our Orinoco Silver card as an access point is just like using
HostAP:

```
# iwconfig eth1 essid myAP mode Master
```

As with Madwifi, the *wlags49* driver does not support MAC address filtering. We were able to set up a bridge using the Orinoco Silver card in *master* mode, using the example provided previously in the HostAP section of this chapter.

Linux-Powered Off-the-Shelf

Electronics manufacturers are increasingly turning to Linux to power all sorts of devices: e.g., TV set-top boxes, handheld computers, and mobile phones. Now wireless vendors have begun shipping products running a Linux kernel.

For example, Linksys is now selling the WRT54G Wireless Router. As the name implies, it uses an 802.11g radio. However, the name doesn't tell you that the box is really running a custom Linux kernel based on the 2.4.5 kernel code, running on a Broadcom processor, based on a 125 MHz MIPS processor core. As of this writing, a WRT54G can be purchased for as little as $70, making it probably the cheapest project in this book.

The Seattle Wireless folks have an excellent page on their web site detailing the work they have done peeking into the innards of this device. You can find it at *http://www.seattlewireless.net/index.cgi/LinksysWrt54g*. Even before Linksys began releasing the source code, people were hacking away at the WRT54G, trying to get a login shell and figure out what made it tick.

Hacking the WRT54G Hardware

In the fall of 2003, several of the NoCat folks were hacking away at a newly acquired WRT54G, attempting to learn how to get a login shell on the box. Early on, the Seattle Wireless group had determined that you could execute arbitrary code by using the *Ping.asp* web page, which is part of the administrative web pages shipped with the unit.

 If you're just looking for a quick way to upload new firmware, such as a custom Linux distribution, to the unit, skip ahead to "Hacking the WRT54G Firmware," later in this chapter.

It was then possible to upload arbitrary files to the unit, which we don't recommend for this reason: we managed to render our WRT54G completely useless by attempting to modify the administrative HTML pages. In other words, the configuration on the box was stuck that way, and we couldn't change it. Due to our error, none of the web pages were accessible, including *Ping.asp*, which was the only method at that time.

The box sat unhappily in a paper bag for a few months. Recently, while reading through the Seattle Wireless pages again, we became aware that someone had managed to solder the correct components on the mother-board of a WRT54G and had a working serial port. With a working serial console, you can interrupt the boot of the unit with Ctrl-C:

```
^C
PMON>
```

This puts you at the PMON bootloader prompt. From here, you can recover a crippled WRT54G by executing the following commands:

```
PMON> set boot_wait on
PMON> set nvram boot_wait
```

These commands tell the unit to wait at boot and to attempt to load firm-ware via TFTP. In order to take advantage of this, you need a tftp client that supports passwords. Standard tftp client software does not use authentica-tion, and the tftpd running on the WRT54G expects authentication. You can download a tftp client for Linux that supports authentication from *http://redsand.net/code/linksys-tftp.tar.bz2*. The code can be compiled with a sim-ple make. The WRTG54 assigns itself the IP address 192.168.1.1, so to con-nect to it, you must assign an IP address from the same subnet on the machine from which you want to run the tftp client.

When you are attempting a tftp upgrade of firmware or using the web-based firmware upgrade shown in the next section, you must make sure you have a reliable power connection. Interrupting the firmware upgrade process can corrupt the flash memory during a write and make your unit a very nice blue and black brick. It's also important to use an Ethernet connection to one of the LAN ports of the WRT54G when upgrading the firmware. While it is pos-sible to use the wireless connection, if *anything* interrupts the wireless trans-mission, you again run the risk of killing your flash memory and the unit.

Once you have set the boot_wait parameter, you can power-cycle the WRT54G. At this point, you have approximately three seconds to start the tftp client. In these three seconds, you must execute the following commands:

```
$ ./linksys-tftp 192.168.1.1
linksys-tftp> put firmware_image password
```

In the next section, we discuss alternate firmware images for the WRT54G.

Without a console on the Linksys unit, you cannot enter the bootloader. If you examine the motherboard of a WRT54G, you will find several empty surface mount sockets, a mount for a crystal, and two sets of standard pinouts marked UART1 and UART2 next to the WAN Ethernet port and the reset switch. Figure 6-9 shows a close-up of this area.

Figure 6-9. Close-up of WRT54G showing space for a UART

The Seattle Wireless web pages have a list of hardware that must be soldered on in the empty sockets:

- UART: National Semi PC16552DV
- Transceiver: Maxim MAS213CIA
- XTAL: 12.75MHZ

 The details in this section are relevant only for a Linksys WRT54GVersion 1.0. Version 1.1 hardware is different, and you can find a discussion on 1.1 serial port hardware at *http://www.sveasoft.com/postt44.html*. Look on the bottom of the WRT54G case to determine the hardware version: if your hardware is Version 1.1, it is printed there. 1.0 hardware has no identifier.

We ordered the first two sample parts from each manufacturer. For links to the order pages, see the Seattle Wireless WRT54G web page: *http://www.seattlewireless.net/index.cgi/LinksysWrt54g*. Search for "14 Booting your own kernel" to find the correct section.

As for the crystal, our hardware and soldering guru Brad Silva suggested that we should use an oscillator instead. This required a slightly different approach when we began construction, as you'll see below, but it worked well. We ordered a 12.8 MHz oscillator from Digikey (*http://www.digikey.com*).

Once all the parts had arrived, we set aside an evening to work on the unit in Brad's lab. He had the necessary soldering equipment plus an oscilloscope and a number of other tools that came in handy.

 Unless you really know what you're doing, soldering extra parts on your WRT54G is an excellent way to void your warranty and potentially destroy the unit. You need exceptional soldering skills for this project.

The first task was to solder the National Semi UART to the socket at U5. This was the most difficult part of the operation, as the socket is surface-mount technology that is designed to be soldered by a machine. The UART uses J-connectors, which curve inward under the chip. We held the chip in place with a piece of double-sided tape underneath, but it was still difficult for Brad. However, his soldering skills won out in the end.

Once we had the UART in place, we pulled out the oscilloscope so we could determine which of the two smaller sockets would need the Maxim transceiver installed. The correct socket turned out to be U1, which is strangely connected to the pinout for UART2, not to the pinout marked UART1/CON1 (which would seem to be indicative of the console).

We then soldered the transceiver in place at U1, and despite the small size, the soldering went much faster because the soldering iron simply wicked the existing solder into place on the chip.

Next up was the oscillator. As stated earlier, we chose an oscillator in place of a crystal. Either one should work, however. As Brad states, "Crystals are finicky devices. Oscillators are much more reliable and easier to work with." We mounted the oscillator on a small piece of breadboard.

In order to get signal flowing to the oscillator, we had to remove a resistor and a capacitor from the motherboard. These are located at R7 and C14 between the UART and the spot where a crystal would be mounted.

Lastly, we needed power and ground for the oscillator. We obtained these from ZN1 and DS1 next to the DC power input. Figure 6-10 shows an image of the motherboard with all the work completed up to this point.

During this process, we stopped at each step to use the oscilloscope to look at output from each new chip. Checking the output from the transceiver and doing a little math, we were able to determine that the eventual console serial speed would be at least 115 kbps.

The last requirement was to add a DB9 connector so we could connect to the serial port with a laptop. For this, we needed pins 2, 3, and 5 from the

Figure 6-10. WRT54G with added UART, transceiver, and oscillator

pinout marked UART2. It is important to note that unlike a standard RS-232 DB9 pinout, pins 2 and 3 are not crossed. The pinout to the DB9 is as follows:

- Pin 2: Pin 2 Transmit
- Pin 3: Pin 3 Receive
- Pin 5: Pin 5 Ground

Figure 6-11 shows the attached serial port close-up. We were not striving for attractiveness, just function. The intent was not to have the serial port permanently attached, because if the whole exercise were a success, we wouldn't have needed it afterwards.

This was the magic moment. Our monitoring with the oscilloscope was promising, in that we were definitely seeing a flood of output immediately after the unit was powered on. We hooked up a laptop to the DB9 port, fired up a minicom session, set the port speed to 115200, no RTS/CTS, no Xon/Xoff, applied power to the WRT54G, and voila!

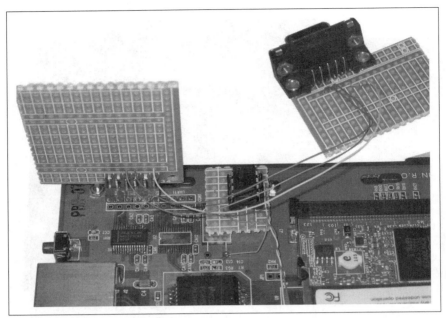

Figure 6-11. WRT54G with attached DB9 serial port

We were then able to use Ctrl-C to immediately interrupt the boot process, set the boot_wait parameter, and reboot. This time, the console showed a message indicating that it was waiting for network boot. Following the previous instructions, we ran the linksys_tftp client software and were able to flash the WRT54G with the latest Linksys firmware. We then went on to try out some alternate firmware, which we describe in the next section.

Hacking the WRT54G Firmware

At the time of this writing, you can find Linksys source code modifications at *http://www.linksys.com/support/gpl.asp*. Broadcom has not yet released any source code for the radio drivers, nor has it released the modifications that it has made to the gcc compiler.

Several Linux distributions for the WRT54G are available. Some of these depend on execution of arbitrary commands via *Ping.asp*. However, Linksys has fixed this "bug" with software release 1.42.2, which has made any release that depends on this feature unusable.

With the release of the modified source code for the WRT54G, it is possible for interested parties to compile the source themselves and learn how to build custom firmware that includes features that Linksys does not support in its product.

These new distributions are easy to install, because they are complete firmware releases based on the Linksys code. Linksys includes a firmware upgrade option in the administrative web pages for the WRT54G. Figure 6-12 shows the screen, which you can find by selecting the Administration tab in the web page and clicking on Firmware Upgrade.

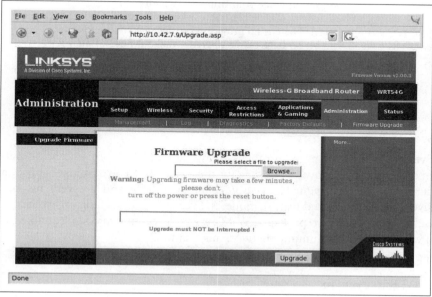

Figure 6-12. WRT54G firmware upgrade

You can also upgrade the firmware via TFTP, as we described in the "Hardware" section. Of course, on an unmodified WRT54G running Linksys firmware, the TFTP option is not possible. You must have a soldered-on serial port to enable the interrupt of the boot process, or you must flash the unit first with one of the alternative firmware images we discuss below. They both provide support for enabling the boot_wait option from the administrative web pages.

As of this writing, there are two well-developed distributions available that are based on the latest Linksys 2.0 source code. Each distribution appears to have a number of similar features, and as they continue to mature, it seems that they will continue to become more similar. Right now, however, both have different feature sets and appeal to somewhat different audiences. There is also a third distribution at sourgeforge.net (see "OpenWrt firmware" later in this chapter), which is built from the ground up and is not based on Linksys source code.

Linksys doesn't support firmware that you receive from other sources. While you many not be voiding your warranty by flashing the firmware with alternate versions from other sources, you should be aware that the process is not perfect. There is a possibility of corrupting the flash in your WRT54G and making it an expensive paperweight.

When you upgrade your firmware, whether it is a Linksys or alternative firmware file, the configuration in the WRT54G is erased. There is no provision for saving a configuration to NVRAM, so before you upgrade, make a note of all your settings.

Finally, it should be stressed that as of this writing, *all* of the alternative firmwares are in beta or testing modes, and are not as stable as the Linksys firmware.

Sveasoft firmware

Sveasoft is a company with offices in Sweden and California. It has developed a very nice firmware package for the WRT54G. The developers host an active forum at *http://www.sveasoft.com/forums.html* and are very responsive to bug reports and feature requests. Sveasoft is also selling in Sweden an outdoor-mountable repackaged WRT54G with its custom code, suitable for a wireless ISP or community network installation.

The Sveasoft firmware includes the following features:

- Telnet daemon
- SSH daemon
- OSPF routing from the Bird routing daemon
- 20 new iptables filters to support filtering P2P and other protocols
- QoS bandwidth management
- Local DNS caching daemon
- PPTP client and server capability
- Radio transmit power adjustment
- Antenna selection
- Client radio mode
- Signal strength and MAC addresses of radio clients
- WDS
- Added options in the Administrative web pages to enable/disable services
- Command shell from the Administrative web pages
- Replaced openssl with maxssl to free up 1 MB of flash
- Roaring Pengiun PPPoE module

Additional features planned for inclusion in the firmware are:

- SNMP support
- Kismet drone—a remote sniffer
- Remote monitoring package
- Dynamic DNS configuration
- Shorewall firewall
- NoCat-like captive portal
- Snort intrusion detection engine
- Complete IPSec client and server support
- 802.1X for client radio mode
- Simplified web interface
- Support for a dynamic download so that developers can update in packages rather than in a complete firmware reflash.

You can obtain the latest Sveasoft firmware from its FTP site: *ftp.sveasoft.com/pub*. As of this writing, the most current firmware is *Satori_v2_2.00.8.7sv-pre1.bin.zip*. When you uncompress this file:

```
$ unzip Satori_v2_2.00.8.7sv-pre1.bin.zip
```

you will receive a single *.bin* file that you can flash to the WRT54G using the Firmware Upgrade web page previously shown. Once you've clicked on the Upgrade button, do *not* interrupt the upgrade. Make sure you have reliable power and wired Ethernet connections to the unit from the PC that you are using.

Once the firmware upgrade is complete, you should hold down the reset button on the back of the unit for 8–10 seconds, until you see the LEDs on the front of the unit turn red and flash in a pattern. This ensures that you have cleared anything out of NVRAM that might have been put there by the previous firmware version.

When the unit resets, connect to it from a web browser; *http://192.168.1.1* is the default address for Linksys devices. As you can see from Figure 6-13, the firmware version in the upper-right corner is now a non-Linksys version.

The Sveasoft firmware offers another nice feature: the ability to select the receive and transmit antennas, as well as the ability to increase and decrease the transmit power of the radio card. In the web-based configuration, click on Wireless, and then on Advanced Settings. As shown in Figure 6-14, the last three options allow TX and RX antenna selection, and you can now increase the milliwatt output of the WRT54G radio card up to a maximum of 83 mW from the default of 28.

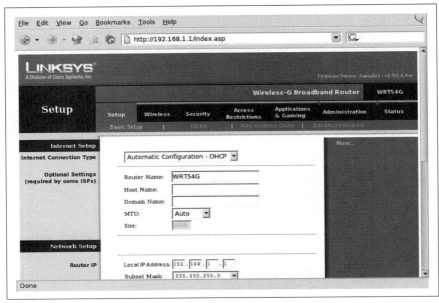

Figure 6-13. Sveasoft firmware main configuration screen

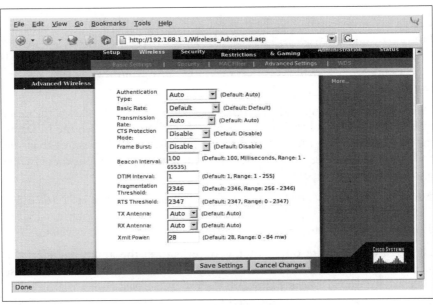

Figure 6-14. Sveasoft Advanced wireless configuration settings

If you have two WRT54G units, a Linux box with a Prism card and the HostAP driver, or an access point running the OpenAP/LinuxAP distributions (see "Running Linux on Non-Linux Devices" later in this chapter), you have the option of setting up WDS between your access points. If you choose to use a Prism card, it must have station firmware Version 1.50 or higher. See Chapter 4 for details on how to determine your station firmware version.

WDS is an 802.11 specification for using an 802.11 wireless connection as a distribution system. A special data frame with four addresses is defined for WDS. This allows layer 2 bridging of packets between two addresses. In other words, your access points continue to serve clients, but can also communicate with each other over a bridge. You can use this to set up a second access point that has no wired connection, only the bridged connection to another access point. This is most useful for extending the range of your network.

There are some caveats for using WDS. Your access points must use the same SSID, the same channel, and the same WEP keys (if you're using WEP). Currently, using WPA to encrypt WDS communications is not possible. Unless you use WEP, all of your bridged packets sent between the access points will be sent in the clear, and you could easily fall victim to a classic "man in the middle" attack where one of your MAC addresses is spoofed.

Another side effect of WDS will be decreased throughput. If both of your access points are serving clients while they are communicating via the WDS bridge, you will lose throughput due to increased radio utilization for WDS.

We did not have two WRT54G units with which to test this WDS, but we were able to set up a WDS link between our WRT54G running the Sveasoft code, and a notebook with a Prism card and the HostAP driver.

In order to set up the WDS link, we needed to install the *bridge-utils* package. On our Mandrake 9.2 system, this was installed using `urpmi bridge-utils`; Red Hat and Fedora users should be able to similarly use the rpm installation, and Debian users can do `apt-get install bridge-utils`.

It took some fits and starts to get WDS working between the WRT54G and our Mandrake box running HostAP. Figure 6-15 shows the WDS configuration screen in the Sveasoft firmware. Here, we entered the MAC address of the Prism card on the Mandrake system and assigned the WDS bridge an IP address and subnet mask.

However, when we first attempted to set this up and clicked on Save Settings on the WRT54G, our Prism card lost wireless communication with the Linksys. We were not able to bring up a bridge at that point. Later, as we continued to troubleshoot, we were able to figure out why: the MAC address we obtained from the WRT54G was *not* the MAC address that the WRT54G assigned to the WDS bridge.

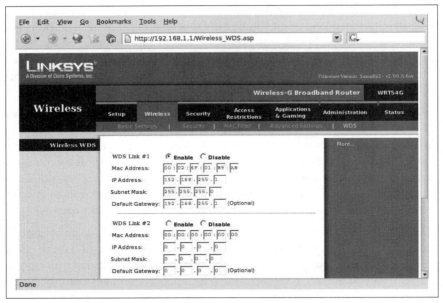

Figure 6-15. Sveasoft WDS configuration

On our WRT54G, the wireless MAC address is 00:06:25:B2:6B:D5. We entered this initially in the WDS configuration for the Prism card. However, once we obtained a console login on the Linksys, we found that the WDS interface was actually given a MAC address of 00:06:25:B2:6B:D7. Once we set up WDS for the Prism card with this interface, we were able to communicate over the WDS link.

> Once the WDS commands were entered for the Prism card, it took approximately 30 seconds for the WDS link to begin working. Don't give up if you can't ping across the link immediately.

In order to set up the WDS link on the Prism card running HostAP, we entered the following commands:

```
# iwpriv wlan0 wds_add 00:25:B2:6B:D7      # Creates a WDS interface
# brctl addbr br0                # Creates a bridge interface
# brctl addif wlan0              # Adds wlan0 to the bridge
# brctl addif wlan0wds0           # Adds the WDS interface to the bridge
# ifconfig wlan0 0.0.0.0         # Zeros out TCP/IP for wlan0
# ifconfig wlan0wds0 0.0.0.0      # Zeros out TCP/IP for the WDS interface
# ifconfig br0 192.168.255.2      # Assigns TCP/IP to the bridge interface
```

Note that you must have your Prism card in either managed or master mode for this to work. If you are in managed mode, you are essentially acting as a client to the bridge, and you must add another Ethernet or radio interface to make the bridge useful. If you are in master mode, your HostAP access point can continue to serve other clients while still participating in the WDS bridge.

The Sveasoft firmware enables many other interesting features, including Quality of Service (QoS) for bandwidth management, among other things. Those features are really outside the scope of this book, but one feature that is very handy is the SSH daemon.

To set up the SSH daemon, navigate to the Administration tab, and click on Management. Scroll down to the section titled SSHD. First, click on the radio button to Enable SSHD. Scroll down and click on Save Settings. Navigate back to the SSHD section and similarly enable Password Login. Click on Save Settings again. Reboot the WRT54G.

You can now use ssh to log in to the router using *root* as a username and the administrative password that you set in the web interface. (You *have* changed your administrative password from the default, haven't you?)

Wifi-Box firmware

The Wifi-Box firmware distribution was developed by Augustin Vu. It is also now based on the Linksys 2.0 firmware release, and the project web page is found at *http://sourceforge.net/projects/wifi-box*.

As we previously discussed, this project has much in common with the Sveasoft firmware, because many of the stated end goals of the project are similar. The current implementations, however, differ somewhat in their feature sets.

The Wifi-Box software includes the following features:

- Radio transmit power adjustment
- Antenna selection
- DHCP server can assign static DHCP addresses
- Supports Class A and Class B subnets
- Local caching DNS server
- SNMP daemon
- Support for VPN Passthrough—IPSec, PPTP, L2TP
- Server Profiles for multiple IP forwarding
- Telnet daemon
- Remote wake on LAN support
- Web-driven reboot and restart services commands
- Enhanced status pages

Additional features planned for inclusion in the firmware include:

- WDS bridging
- SSH daemon
- QoS bandwidth management
- IPSec client and server
- PPTP client

You can download the firmware from the SourceForge web site. As of this writing, the most current version is *code_2.02.pre1-wfb.zip*. Use the unzip command to extract the single *.bin* file contained in the compressed download.

The procedure for installing the Wifi-Box firmware is identical to flashing any other firmware to the WRT54G (see "Hacking the WRT54G Firmware" and "Sveasoft firmware" earlier in this section). You can use the web interface, or, if you have already tried the Sveasoft firmware, you can set the boot_wait option in the Administration tab and flash the router via tftp on the next reboot.

As you can see from Figure 6-16, the only noticeable difference to the Wifi-Box firmware is again in the upper-right corner of the main screen.

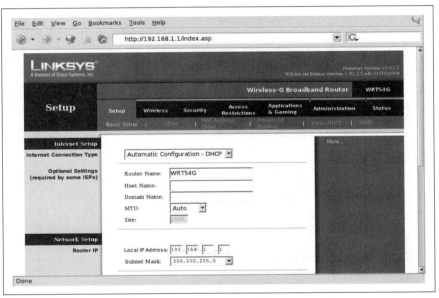

Figure 6-16. Wifi-Box firmware main configuration screen

The current Wifi-Box firmware has fewer enhancements to the wireless side of the router and more added features in the TCP/IP department. Wifi-Box does include the antenna selection and radio transmit power adjustments in the same location as Sveasoft: Click on the Wireless tab and select Advanced Wireless Settings.

One feature that will appeal to anyone already running MRTG, Cacti, or any other SNMP-based network data gathering tool is the inclusion of an SNMP daemon. To configure SNMP, click on the Setup tab and then select SNMP. The documentation is incomplete, and there is no help file for this page, so it is unclear if the SNMP daemon supports SNMP v1, v2, v3, or a combination of these.

The Security tab adds new VPN settings to allow passthrough of the three most widely used VPN protocols. In the Applications & Gaming tab you can define Server Profiles that allow you to forward many commonly used ports to different servers on the LAN side of the WRT54G.

In the Administration section, you can enable the Telnet daemon. Here you can also click to reboot the router or restart all services on the router without a reboot.

All in all, the Wifi-Box firmware is a nice upgrade from the standard Linksys firmware. As of this writing, it appears that the Sveasoft firmware has more wireless features enabled, and it also does have the advantage of a working SSH daemon. Both firmware packages are worth investigating for your use.

OpenWrt firmware

The OpenWrt firmware project is taking a completely different approach. Its firmware is not based on the Linksys code at all, and its statement of goals at *http://openwrt.sourceforge.net* states some very specific goals:

- Create a usable and functional development environment for the WRT54G that exposes the full capability of the 2.4.20 kernel.
- Firmware must have failsafe modes so that configuration errors do not prevent the unit from booting.
- As much flash as possible should be dedicated to read/write filesystems for installation of functional modules.
- The Linksys/Broadcom/Cisco copyrighted configuration utilities are *not* included.

The OpenWrt developers are hard at work on the beta version of their firmware. As of this writing, they have not released any packages on their SourceForge project site. Follow the directions at *http://openwrt.sourceforge.net* to obtain their latest beta.

As the login file to the #wrt54g IRC channel states: "Newbies need not apply." The OpenWrt firmware is not complete. OpenWrt is still working on a development platform base. If you want a fully functional access point with all the features shipped in the Linksys firmware, this is not for you. If, however, you want to hack on a fully open source Linux distribution for the WRT54G, read on.

As with the previous firmwares, you can load the OpenWrt firmware by using the Upgrade Firmware option in the Administration web pages, or, if you have loaded Sveasoft or Wifi-Box firmware, you can set boot_wait and use the tftp client to flash the WRT54G firmware.

OpenWrt changes the flash filesystem layout of the Linksys firmware. It contains a small read-only *squashfs* filesystem and a larger writable *jffs2* (Journaling Flash Filesystem). The *squashfs* partition has a failsafe boot routine, which you can trigger by holding the reset button during boot. This failsafe mode boots entirely from the *squashfs* partition, and configures the LAN and wireless networks to 192.168.1.1. So if you manage to munge up the *jffs2* partition, you can always recover and start over.

OpenWrt attempts to set up the networking of the WRT54G using configuration stored in NVRAM. So your LAN, WAN, and wireless network information should remain the same after flashing.

OpenWrt implements a Telnet daemon for administrative access. The developers plan to have ssh available as a package once the basic development environment is done. The *busybox* environment implements telnetd by default, so this is a simple way to proceed with development.

On the first boot after flashing, the *jffs2* filesystem does not exist. You must telnet to 192.168.1.1, run the firstboot command at this point, and then restart the system. This initializes the *jffs2* filesystem and allows you to boot completely into OpenWrt.

When fully booted, the *squashfs* partition is remounted as */rom* with the *jffs2* partition mounted as /. Symlinks are made from the root filesystem to files contained in */rom*. If you want to modify any of the files on *jffs2*, you must remove the symlink and copy the file or create the file on the root partition.

OpenWrt uses VLAN interfaces to represent the LAN and WAN ports. On a v1.x WRT54G, the following interfaces are created:

- vlan1: WAN interface
- vlan2: LAN interface
- eth2: Wireless interface

For more detailed information on the innards of this beta version, you should consult the README. Check out the IRC channel and the Source-Forge project pages for updates. The developers hang out on #wrt54g, so it's the best place at the moment for help with the firmware.

You now have a small Linux-powered router. Although the OpenWrt firmware is still in early development, we think it has the most potential of the alternative firmwares currently available for the WRT54G. The Linksys-based firmware version have some impressive features, to be sure, but Open-Wrt will definitely be the most flexible firmware distribution of the three, due to its stated goals.

Other Linux-Powered Devices

Aside from the WRT54G, there are other Linux-powered devices now on the market. Some of them appear to be even more capable internally than the WRT54G. Some of them have serious limitations that would make it difficult or impossible to modify the kernel source. We touch on a few of these devices here. If you're a dedicated hardware or kernel hacker, these boxes could use your time and expertise.

The Linux-powered device world is constantly changing, so by the time you read this, other wireless devices with Linux under the hood will probably be available.

Linksys WRV54G

This is a Linksys wireless VPN router. It has nothing in common with the WRT54G, in that the internal processor is a 266 MHz Intel ISP425 ARM-based CPU and the MiniPCI wireless card is a PrismGT 802.11G chipset. The MiniPCI card is soldered to the MiniPCI connector for grounding purposes. There are open source issues with the Intel Ethernet driver for the ISP425. The Intel Access Software Library license expressly forbids any code in the Library from being released under the GPL or BSD licenses.

The Seattle Wireless folks have been hard at work on a WRV54G. As of this writing, however, there is no alternative firmware available, and the firmware has not yet been hacked. You can find all of their current information at *http://seattlewireless.net/index.cgi/LinksysWrv54g*. Linksys has released the source code, and the various versions are available at *http://www.linksys.com/support/opensourcecode/wrv54g*.

Dell TrueMobile 1184

The Dell TrueMobile 1184 was released in early 2003. It has a Prism 3 802.11b chipset inside and runs a 2.2 Linux kernel. It appears that Dell contracted with another vendor to develop this product, and when it was released, there was no acknowledgment that the device was Linux based, nor was there any source code released.

Dell was persuaded by a user to release the source code. However, since that time it has been discovered that the released source is not actually the correct source for the internal ARM processor or Ethernet chipset.

As of this writing, there does not yet appear to be a viable solution to run any custom Linux kernels on the Dell hardware. Dell has since discontinued this unit, and information and source code are no longer available on the Dell web site. You can follow the Dell 1184 threads at the LinuxAP mailing list for more information: *http://ksmith.com/pipermail/linuxap-dev/2003-July*. Lastly, if you follow this threaded discussion, it appears that the Dell is so difficult to work with, any development has been abandoned to look for easier hardware to hack: *http://ksmith.com/pipermail/linuxap-dev/2003-October/ 000522.html*.

Running Linux on Non-Linux Devices

Ever since 802.11b access points began shipping, people have been taking them apart to find out what makes them tick. In many cases, especially with early models, the internals were i386-compatible chips, which made the challenge of attempting to run Linux on these machines impossible to ignore. There are some serious caveats to running Linux on any of these devices:

- These systems need a small kernel. 2.4 series kernels, even stripped to the bare bones, just take up too much space on a device that has 2 or 4 MB of RAM. 2.2 series kernels are then the choice for all of the following distributions.

- With some of these devices, there isn't enough room to store a usable Linux system on the flash, so the root filesystem must be kept on an NFS server. While this isn't out of the question, it does mean you must have an NFS server running.

- The minimal amount of RAM in these systems means that application space is very limited. It's possible to run things like telnetd, but sshd or any other larger applications are out of the question.

- The cards in these access points are based on chipsets that do not support *master* mode. Even though you have Linux running on them, you are restricted to *managed* or *ad-hoc* modes, and can't use the AP as an actual access point.

Apple AirPort

When the Apple AirPort 802.11b access point was first released, people naturally opened it up to find out what was inside. The guts of the unit are an AMD ELAN processor running at 33 MHz. The ELAN is an i386-compatible processor that is very popular with embedded device manufacturers.

Of course someone took the challenge of getting the AirPort to run Linux, because it runs i386 binary code. Til Straumann has an excellent web page detailing the steps necessary to run a Linux 2.2 kernel on the AirPort: *http://www-hft.ee.tu-berlin.de/~strauman/airport/airport.html*.

The AirPort has only 4 MB of flash RAM, so you must boot and load software from a network share to make Linux run. To do this, you need a tftp server, NFS server, and DHCP server. In addition, you must reflash your AP with boot code that makes it look for the Linux software on the network. This is not easy to set up, so we recommend that you read completely through the web page listed in the previous paragraph before attempting to run Linux on your AirPort or RG-1000.

Orinoco RG-1000

The Lucent Orinoco RG-1000 is internally identical to the Apple AirPort. Seattle Wireless uses Linux-powered AirPorts and RG-1000s extensively in its citywide wireless network. More information on its projects can be found at *http://www.seattlewireless.net/?AirportLinux*.

Seattle Wireless AirportLinux is based on the code by Til Straumann for the AirPort, with some modifications. While both of these distributions are fun hacks, they are not nearly as practical as using vanilla PC hardware or flashing a Linksys router. They both require a dedicated server to boot from. If you have such an environment, great! You can pick up used RG-1000 units on Ebay for very little money.

Eumitcom WL11000

While you will never find a consumer product with this name on it, this motherboard was the basis for these early models of 802.11b access points:

- US Robotics (USR 2450)
- SMC EZconnect (2652W)
- Addtron (AWS-100)

There have been two Linux distributions developed for these access points. They are both still available, although the first, OpenAP, does not appear to be under active development. OpenAP is available from *http://opensource.instant802.com*. As stated, it runs only on this single hardware platform. It is increasingly difficult to find these access points, but if you have one, this is a fun little project.

In order to flash these access points, you need a linearly mapped memory card. The OpenAP site recommends a MagicRAM Industrial SRAM Memory card that is 2 MB in size and readable at 3.3 V. You must also connect a null modem cable to the RS-232 serial port on the access point, and a terminal program to communicate with the Linux distribution.

For information and complete instructions, see the *Getting Started* page on the OpenAP web site: *http://opensource.instant802.com/getting_started.php*.

We mentioned LinuxAP in the "Software" section earlier in this chapter. While LinuxAP is designed to run on the Soekris hardware platform, and indeed can be made to run on any Intel-compatible small-board PC, it also supports the WL11000-based access points. You can find LinuxAP at *http://linuxap.ksmith.com*. This site also hosts an active mailing list at *http://linuxap.ksmith.com/mailman/listinfo/linuxap-dev*, and a recent posting of the LinuxAP FAQ can be found in the mailing list archives: *http://ksmith.com/pipermail/linuxap-dev/2004-February/000675.html*.

## CHAPTER 7

Bluetooth

Bluetooth is a wireless cable-replacement technology that uses low-power signals in the 2.4 GHz band. Using Bluetooth, devices can transfer up to 720 kbps. This bandwidth is restricted in comparison to those obtainable from 802.11 wireless technology, and while networking is one application of Bluetooth, it is not the primary application area.

Bluetooth's goal is to be a low-cost, low-power, and, above all, pervasive technology. As well as to increase convenience for the user, its aim is also to reduce the cost to the manufacturer by eliminating the need to supply cables with devices. As opposed to single-use cables, a Bluetooth transceiver sustains multiple connections, and, for most applications, the bandwidth constraints are not an issue.

As befits a cable-replacement technology, many of Bluetooth's applications are in areas where infrared, USB, or serial connections were previously used: in connecting peripherals, PDAs, cell phones, and other portable devices. One much-trumpeted application that bucks this general trend is mobile phone headsets, which use Bluetooth to carry the audio to and from the user, who is liberated from the tiresome cable.

Support for Bluetooth in the Linux kernel is mature, being present in both the 2.4 and 2.6 series of stable kernels. Popular core functions of Bluetooth, such as emulated serial connections and networking, are well-supported. More recent Bluetooth technologies, such as keyboard and mice support, have less well-developed support and require more involvement from the user. User-level applications that support Bluetooth on Linux are of varying maturity: applications simply requiring an emulated serial port work out of the box, whereas specialized Bluetooth tools are under heavy development.

This chapter first introduces the core Bluetooth concepts that will aid a Linux system administrator in his deployment, discusses kernel configuration and system-level tools, and finally covers user-level applications.

Quick Start

We tested a Belkin Bluetooth USB adapter with several Linux distributions on an IBM ThinkPad A20m. In all cases, we got it up and running to the point where we created a serial port connection between a Bluetooth cell phone (Nokia 3650) and the Linux machine.

After we set up Bluetooth on each distribution, we completed the following steps (all of this is explained in detail throughout the chapter):

1. Set the pinin */etc/bluetooth/pin* to a numeric-only pin (1234)
2. Restarted the hcid daemon with `killall -HUP hcid`
3. Plugged in the adapter
4. Discovered the cell phone's Bluetooth address with `hcitool scan`
5. Configured the serial port (*/dev/rfcomm0*) with:

    `# rfcomm bind 0 bluetooth_address`

Upon completion, we conversed with the phone over the serial port using Kermit (see "Phones and Cards" in Chapter 9).

The following sections describe our distribution-specific notes. Even if your distribution isn't listed here, check these notes out.

Debian 3.0r1

We abandoned the older 2.4.18 kernel that was the latest 2.4 kernel available for Debian 3.0, and we compiled kernel 2.4.24 according to the instructions in "Configuring the kernel," later in this chapter. To get Bluetooth to the point where we could make an rfcomm connection, we follow these steps:

1. Edited */etc/apt/sources.list* according to the instructions at *http://bluez.sourceforge.net/download/debian/APT-README*.
2. Next, we completed an `apt-get update` and then installed the following packages:
    - bluez-hcidump
    - bluez-pan
    - bluez-sdp
    - bluez-utils
    - hotplug

3. The bluez-utils and bluez-sdp packages configured themselves to start in runlevel 3 and 5. After installing these packages, we started them with the following commands (but we could also have rebooted):

```
/etc/init.d/bluez-utils  start
/etc/init.d/bluez-sdp start
```

4. The */dev/rfcomm** devices already exist, so we didn't need to create them.

SuSE 9.0

We used SuSE 9.0 (FTP install) with the latest available kernel package (2.4.21-166-default). To enable Bluetooth, we followed these steps:

1. Installed the following packages using YaST:
   - bluez-bluefw
   - bluez-libs
   - bluez-pan
   - bluez-sdp
   - bluez-utils

2. The packages configured themselves to start in runlevels 3 and 5. After installing these packages, we started them with /etc/init.d/bluetooth start (but we could also have rebooted).

3. The */dev/rfcomm** devicesdid not exist, so we created them as shown in Example 7-4.

Mandrake 9.2 and RedHat 9

On Mandrake, we used the latest available kernel package (2.4.22-10mdk), but on Red Hat, we rebuilt the kernel the same way we built it for Debian. For rfcomm to work on RedHat and Mandrake, we followed these steps:

1. Downloaded the following RedHat RPMs from *http://bluez.sourceforge.net*:
   - bluez-bluefw
   - bluez-hcidump
   - bluez-libs
   - bluez-pan
   - bluez-sdp
   - bluez-utils

2. Next, we ran rpm --test -ivh bluez-*, and all looked well, so we installed them with rpm -ivh bluez-*.

3. To make sure that the Bluetooth scripts were started on boot, we ran `chkconfig --add bluetooth`.

4. We ran `/etc/init.d/bluetooth start` (we could also have rebooted).

5. The *\/dev\/rfcomm** devices did not exist, so we created them as shown in Example 7-4.

Troubleshooting

Generally, following the previous steps went smoothly, but we did run into some problems. Here are some tips that should help you out:

Start hcid in the foreground
> By default, the startup scripts launch hcid in the background. If you want to see verbose messages from it, kill it and then start it with `-n`:
>
> ```
> # killall hcid
> # hcid -n
> ```
>
> This helps you figure out what's going on with failed PIN requests.

Restart hcid after PIN changes
> If you edit the PIN in *\/etc\/bluetooth\/pin*, restart hcid (`killall -HUP hcid` should do the trick).

Replace bluepin
> In theory, the bluepin utility should either use the PIN in *\/etc\/bluetooth\/pin* or prompt you when it needs a PIN. However, on Mandrake, the PIN exchange was silently failing. So, we replaced bluepin with a script that spat out the PIN in *\/etc\/bluetooth\/pin*:
>
> ```
> #!/bin/sh
> # file: /usr/local/bin/bluepincat
>
> echo -n "PIN:"
> cat /etc/bluetooth/pin
> ```
>
> Then we set the `pin_helper` line in *\/etc\/bluetooth\/hcid.conf*:
>
> ```
> pin_helper /usr/local/bin/bluepincat
> ```

Make sure the rfcomm module is loaded
> When we installed Bluetooth support on Mandrake and Red Hat, the rfcomm module wasn't loaded automatically, so we received a complaint when we ran `/etc/init.d/bluetooth start`:
>
> ```
> "Can't open RFCOMM control socket: Address family not supported by
> protocol"
> ```
>
> So, we added `modprobe rfcomm` to the `start( )` section of the *\/etc\/init.d\/ bluetooth* script and rebooted to make sure everything worked OK.

Double-check your kernel configuration

If you're compiling the kernel from source, be sure everything is configured the way it should be. For example, one of us was testing the examples in this chapter and received an Operation not supported error when we tried to make a connection over *∕dev∕rfcomm0*. We hadn't configured RFCOMM TTY support (CONFIG_BLUEZ_RFCOMM_TTY) in the kernel. Well, we had, but it was configured as a module rather than statically compiled into the kernel. Although make menuconfig showed [*], a peek inside our *.config* file showed:

```
CONFIG_BLUEZ_RFCOMM_TTY=m
```

So we changed m to y, recompiled the kernel, installed it, and rebooted, and all was well.

Bluetooth Basics

Bluetooth Special Interest Group (SIG), a consortium of telecommunications, electronics, and computer manufacturers, develops Bluetooth. The founding members were Ericsson, Nokia, IBM, Intel, and Toshiba. The first version of the Bluetooth specification was formally adopted by the SIG in 1999.

The first revisions of the Bluetooth specification had a mixed reception, because implementations were dogged by interoperability problems. The 1.1 release, published in 2001, eliminated the gray areas from the 1.0b specification and, as a result, improved device interoperability. Over two years since the 1.1 release, Bluetooth is well on its way to becoming a ubiquitous technology in portable devices. At the time of writing, the current approved revision of the Bluetooth specification is Version 1.2, released in November 2003.

The Bluetooth specification itself covers the many levels involved in getting a signal between two applications, from the radio through link control to application-level protocols. Figure 7-1 shows just some of the various strata specified by Bluetooth, which we encounter in this chapter. Further details, including the specifications themselves, can be obtained from *http://www.bluetooth.org*.

Bluetooth hardware typically takes the form of one or two microchips, which are embedded in devices. Computers are increasingly shipping with integrated Bluetooth adapters, but the prevailing way of adding Bluetooth support is by adding an external adapter, typically via the USB or PC card ports. Before a device can sport the Bluetooth logo and use the Bluetooth trademarks, it must be put through a series of tests known as *qualification*. Qualification involves tests for all parts of the Bluetooth specification, from radio testing to protocol conformance.

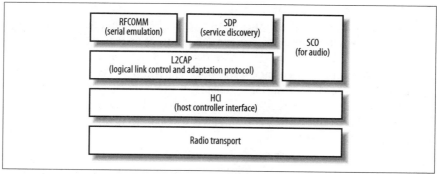

Figure 7-1. Some layers of the Bluetooth specification

What You Can Do with Bluetooth

As Bluetooth is intended to replace cable, it can be used for more or less the same purposes as a cable, within the bandwidth constraints of the technology. All the following usage scenarios are supported within Linux and are discussed in this chapter:

Serial port

Bluetooth's serial port emulation enables the connection of modems (such as in cell phones) and printers. Serial emulation is also an easy way of writing simple data exchange applications using Bluetooth.

Object exchange (OBEX)

Facilitated by implementing the OBEX protocol, object exchange is used for "beaming" data objects between devices, such as contacts from address books. It is the main way that cell phones exchange data and is often implemented by Bluetooth-enabled printers.

Synchronization

Devices that implement the IrMC specification permit synchronization of data sources, such as calendars and address books. Many Bluetooth-enabled cell phones have this feature. More modern devices implement the SyncML specification, which requires a networking connection.

Networking

Bluetooth supports two different forms of networking. The most basic and commonly implemented form is dial-up networking using PPP over a serial connection. In addition, there is BNEP, an encapsulation of Ethernet networking, which allows Bluetooth devices to join a network in a manner much more analogous to Wi-Fi networking.

Input devices

Bluetooth supports an array of input devices similar to USB. Major manufacturers such as Apple and Microsoft are shipping Bluetooth-enabled mice and keyboards.

Audio

Audio is one of the most-promoted aspects of Bluetooth by cell phone manufacturers; it is possible to support bi-directional audio connections to headsets over Bluetooth.

Concepts

The following sections describe essential Bluetooth concepts that you need to be aware of. These include the Bluetooth address, which uniquely identifies a Bluetooth adapter; the protocols and profiles that define the communication techniques and device capabilities; bonding, discoverability, and device classes, which Bluetooth devices use to find each other and communicate their abilities; and piconets, scatternets, masters, and slaves, which describe the topology of Bluetooth networks and the relationships of one device to another.

Bluetooth address

Each Bluetooth interface has a *Bluetooth address*, also known as its *BDADDR*. These addresses look very much like Ethernet interface MAC addresses, and follow the same address allotments that the ANSI/IEEE 802 standard, administered by the IEEE, has laid down. The first three octets of the Bluetooth address denote the organizationally unique identifier (OUI). For instance, the address 00:80:98:23:15:6E has an OUI of 008098, which is registered to the TDK Corporation.

 OUIs can be looked up online using the IEEE's search interface at *http://standards.ieee.org/regauth/oui/*. As some device manufacturers subcontract to others, it may not always be possible to determine the manufacturer of a device from its OUI.

In addition, Bluetooth adapters have a programmable name used to present to the user in interactions. Example 7-2 shows both the Bluetooth addresses and the names that are discovered in a device scan.

Protocols

The Bluetooth specification defines some protocols of its own and also reuses some existing standards. A protocol is an agreement about the way data is exchanged. It is on top of these protocols that all applications of Bluetooth are built. An in-depth knowledge of the protocols is not necessary to deploy Bluetooth, but passing familiarity with them helps in troubleshooting situations.

Confusingly, some of the protocols have very similar names to the *profiles* in which they are used and are listed next. (Additionally, some protocols are layered on top of lower-level protocols. This happens elsewhere in computing—for example, when a computer connects to the Internet via a modem, it uses the RS232 protocol to communicate serial port data, the PPP protocol on top of that to facilitate a network connection, and TCP/IP on top of that to carry the data.)

Link Manager Protocol (LMP)
    Provides basic control of interdevice communication links

Logical Link Control and Adaptation Protocol (L2CAP)
    Provides logical channels of communication to higher protocol layers

Radio Frequency Communication (RFCOMM)
    Provides emulated serial connections

Object Exchange (OBEX)
    A simple file transfer protocol

Bluetooth Network Encapsulation Protocol (BNEP)
    Provides Ethernet encapsulation for wireless networking

Service Discovery Protocol (SDP)
    Enables the querying and reporting of services that a device supports

Telephony Control Protocol Specification (TCS)
    Provides call control for voice and data telephone calls

Profiles

A *profile* is the name given to the implementation of one more protocols to provide a particular application service. Bluetooth devices advertise profiles. Many of the profiles build on each other—for instance, the OBEX profile builds on the serial port profile.

Commonly implemented profiles include:

Service Discovery Access Profile (SDAP)
    Enables a device to discover the profiles supported by other devices

Serial Port Profile (SPP)
    Emulates a serial port connection

Hardcopy Cable Replacement (HCRP)
Emulates a parallel port connection for the purposes of printing

Dial-up Networking Profile (DUN)
A connection to a modem or cell phone, which connects to an Internet access point

LAN Access Profile (LAP)
A point-to-point (PPP) access to a network

Headset Profile (HS)
A combination voice and control channel, which provides a link between a cell phone and audio headset

Generic Object Exchange Profile (GOEP)
A file exchange, which exchanges business cards on cell phones

File Transfer Profile (FTP)
Analogous to Internet FTP, which allows navigation and access to a filesystem

Synchronization Profile (SP)
An address book and calendar synchronization, which uses the IrMC protocol

Human Interface Device Profile (HID)
A connection to a keyboard, mouse, joystick, barcode scanner, or other input devices

Personal Area Networking (PAN)
An Ethernet-like access to a network

Basic Printing Profile (BPP)
Enables devices to print text, as well as formatted documents; useful for low-powered devices such as phones or pagers

Bonding

Bonding, also called pairing, is the process by which trust is established between two Bluetooth devices. The user is required to input matching codes, called *personal identification numbers* (PINs), into the two devices. In some situations, one of the devices may have the PIN pre-set—for example, some headsets come with a PIN of 0000. PINs are typically a sequence of digits; they provide little security, and they are intended only for the initial pairing.

Given a successful match of PIN, the devices negotiate a *link key*, a much more cryptographically secure code, which is used thereafter as an access control mechanism between the two devices.

Discoverability

A Bluetooth device is *discoverable* if it can be found by another device's inquiry. During discovery, the inquiring device broadcasts a specially coded message. As remote devices receive the message, they send a return message indicating their presence. In most circumstances, you must make a device discoverable in order to initiate bonding.

Bluejacking

Cell phone owners who inadvertently leave their phones discoverable may suffer from "bluejacking," the phenomenon in which unknown people send data transfers such as address cards. The address card carries a message in place of contact details. Although a remote device can never force a data transfer on another device, leaving devices discoverable makes the user vulnerable to these half technical, half social-engineering attacks. And it's possible for bluejacking to go beyond pranks: one early smartphone operating system had a bug that caused the phone to lock up if it was sent a GIF image file constructed in a particular way.

Device classes

Bluetooth devices fulfill many functions, so there should be a way that a device can quickly indicate its primary function. As we have already mentioned, the SDP exists to provide a complete description of running services. However, Bluetooth provides an additional way for a device to describe itself: the *device class*. Although the SDP provides the description of the running services, the device class provides the *purpose* of them.

The device class code is a 24-bit number that incorporates three subcodes: the major device type, the minor device type, and additional service codes, which broadly indicate the services available. Table 7-1 shows the meaning of the useful major device types (other types are reserved or undefined), and Table 7-2 shows the useful service class bits. The meaning of the minor device type bits (bits 7–0) depends on the major device type. You can find a full explanation of these values on the Bluetooth Special Interest Group web site at *http://www.bluetoothsig.org/assigned-numbers/baseband.htm*.

Table 7-1. Major device types as expressed in the device class

Bit pattern (bits 12–8)	Meaning
0 0 0 0 0	Miscellaneous
0 0 0 0 1	Computer (from desktop to PDA)

Table 7-1. Major device types as expressed in the device class (continued)

Bit pattern (bits 12–8)	Meaning
0 0 0 1 0	Telephone (cell phone, payphone, cordless phone)
0 0 0 1 1	Network access point
0 0 1 0 0	Audio/video device (headset, speakers)
0 0 1 0 1	Peripheral (keyboard, mouse, joystick)
0 0 1 1 0	Imaging (printer, camera, scanner)
1 1 1 1 1	Uncategorized

Table 7-2. Service classes as expressed in the device class

Bit	Meaning if set
16	Positioning (location information, e.g., GPS)
17	Networking
18	Rendering (printer, speakers)
19	Capturing (scanner, microphone)
20	Object transfer
21	Audio (speaker, microphone, headset)
22	Telephone (modem, cordless telephone, headset)
23	Information (web server)

Piconets and scatternets, and masters and slaves

A *piconet* is a network of Bluetooth devices created by a master connecting to one or more slaves. The master is the device that initiates the connection. Figure 7-2 shows the topology of a piconet. A master may be connected to as many as seven slaves simultaneously.

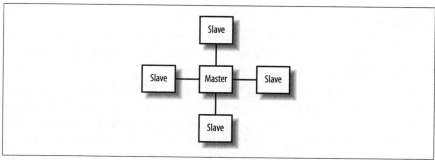

Figure 7-2. Topology of a piconet

Various applications such as LAN access points require the master/slave relationship to be the same as the server/client relationship. For this reason, a client device, which serves as a master, initiates a connection to the access point; once connected, a *role-switch* occurs, and the client device now becomes a slave. For most applications of Bluetooth on Linux, you do not need to be aware of these distinctions, but the knowledge of their existence may be useful in debugging scenarios. Some Bluetooth hardware has restricted role-switching ability.

Sometimes, a slave in one piconet is connected to a master of another piconet. The linking together of multiple piconets in this way is called a *scatternet*.

Bluetooth Hardware

There is a wide variety of hardware available for adding Bluetooth support to your computer. Devices fall into several categories:

USB dongle
Plugs into the USB port. This device is the most common and economical.

Built-in
Increasingly, laptops are shipping with a Bluetooth transmitter built in. Typically this device appears to the operating system as if it were a USB device.

PC card
Plugs into a laptop's PCMCIA slot and provides a serial interface to the Bluetooth transmitter.

CF card
Behaves in the same way as a PCMCIA card, and it is used with PDA devices.

Serial dongle
A Bluetooth transmitter that plugs into the serial port. In the early days of Bluetooth deployment, it was a popular choice; today, however, it is not a recommended option.

Compatibility between Linux and Bluetooth hardware is good. A comprehensive table of verified device compatibility can be found on Marcel Holtmann's web site, at *http://www.holtmann.org/linux/bluetooth/devices.html*. This table includes information for laptops with built-in Bluetooth, too. If you have no specific overriding criteria, it is best to choose a USB dongle. Due to the standardization of the Bluetooth USB interface, compatibility is very good.

If you dual-boot your computer between Linux and the manufacturer's operating system, such as Windows XP or Mac OS X, you may want to use the Bluetooth device your vendor recommends. Both the Apple-sold D-Link USB dongle and Microsoft-manufactured USB dongle are known to work with Linux. If in doubt, consult the Linux device compatibility list.

When choosing a Bluetooth device, be aware of the difference between *Class 1* and *Class 2* Bluetooth devices. Class 1 devices have a more sensitive radio and work up to distances of 100 meters, whereas Class 2 devices work up to 10 meters and are cheaper.

Linux Bluetooth Support

As with many emerging technologies, there are competing implementations of Linux Bluetooth support. The main two implementations are Affix and BlueZ. Affix was originally developed by Nokia and is now hosted as an open source project at SourceForge (*http://affix.sourceforge.net*). BlueZ is also hosted at SourceForge is (*http://bluez.sourceforge.net*) and the official Bluetooth stack of the Linux kernel.

Although Affix is a mature and functional project, BlueZ receives more testing and has more widespread adoption. For this reason, this chapter focuses on the uses of the BlueZ Linux Bluetooth stack and libraries.

This section includes all the information that you need to install and configure Bluetooth support from scratch. It is possible that your Linux distribution already contains preconfigured Bluetooth support, which will save you effort. However, the installation instructions provide useful background information for troubleshooting.

Distributions

As Bluetooth is a relative newcomer to Linux, BlueZ support across commercial distributions varies. Generally speaking, if the kernel shipping with your distribution is older than 2.4.22, it is a good idea to upgrade it. Users of "bleeding-edge" distributions such as Debian Unstable and Gentoo should find that Bluetooth is adequately supported.

Configuring the Kernel

Bluetooth support under Linux requires a recent kernel. If your kernel is Version 2.4.22 or better, or a 2.6 series kernel, then you're all set. Otherwise, you must upgrade your kernel. Alternatively, if you do not wish to upgrade, and have kernel 2.4.18 or better compiled from source, you can apply the patches from the "kernel patches" area of the BlueZ web site (*http://bluez. sourceforge.net*). Regardless, it's worth checking out the patches, because there are often improvements available that have not yet been merged into the main Linux kernel source.

Patching the Kernel

To patch the kernel, first download the most recent patch for your kernel version from the BlueZ web site (for example, *patch-2.4.22-mh1.gz*), and place it somewhere convenient, such as */usr/src/*. Change into the directory where your kernel source is unpacked, typically */usr/src/linux*, and apply the patch:

```
cd /usr/src/linux
gzip -dc ../patch-2.4.22-mh1.gz | patch -p1
```

Next, run this command:

```
find . -name '*rej'
```

If any of the patches were rejected, you'll find some files ending in *.rej*. If they were, delete the kernel source, extract it again (be sure that you have the correct patch for your kernel version), and try the patch again.

You can then proceed with configuring your kernel for Bluetooth by running make menuconfig, make xconfig, or make config.

Chapter 2 explains how to configure and compile a kernel. Table 7-3 and Table 7-4 show the options that must be set in your kernel configuration to enable Bluetooth support. You can either configure Bluetooth support to be compiled into the kernel or to be loadable on-demand in the form of modules. Many Linux distributions choose to ship with modules, so we proceed on the assumption that you will use modules. This removes the need to recompile your kernel if you acquire a different type of Bluetooth device.

Figure 7-3 and Figure 7-4 show the Bluetooth configuration options from the 2.4.24 kernel.

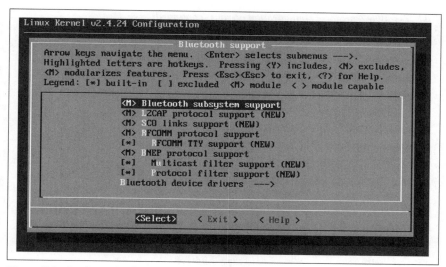

Figure 7-3. Configuring Bluetooth support in the Linux kernel

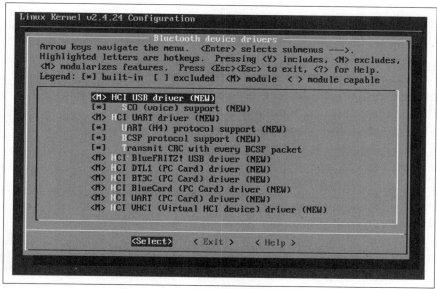

Figure 7-4. Configuring Bluetooth hardware support in the Linux kernel

Table 7-3. BlueZ protocol configuration options

Option	Purpose	Recommended value
Bluetooth subsystem support	Enables the entire BlueZ stack	m
L2CAP protocol support	A basic Bluetooth protocol	m

Table 7-3. BlueZ protocol configuration options (continued)

Option	Purpose	Recommended value
SCO links support	Bluetooth Audio	m
RFCOMM protocol support	Serial data transfer	m
RFCOMM TTY support	Maps Linux terminal devices (e.g., */dev/rfcomm0*) to Bluetooth serial ports	y
BNEP protocol support	Personal area networking	m
BNEP Multicast filter support, protocol filter support	Advanced filtering for networking	y

Table 7-4. BlueZ hardware support configuration options

Option	Purpose	Recommended value
HCI USB driver	Support for USB dongles	m
SCO (voice) support	Audio transmission support	y
USB zero packet support	Workaround for buggy USB devices	n
HCI UART driver	Support for serial dongles: either PCMCIA, CF, or RS232 serial port	y
UART (H4) protocol support	Serial protocol used for most PCMCIA and CF cards	y
BCSP protocol support	Serial protocol used for PCMCIA and CF cards based on the CSR BlueCore chipset	y
Transmit CRC with every BCSP packet	Improves reliability of BCSP support, at a slight cost to efficiency	y
HCI BlueFRITZ! USB driver	Support for BlueFRITZ! Bluetooth ISDN	m
HCI VHCI (Virtual HCI device) driver	Support for a virtual Bluetooth device for testing purposes	m

 You should not enable the Bluetooth device support in the USB drivers section of your kernel configuration (CONFIG_USB_BLUETOOTH). This is a vestigial driver from very early Bluetooth work and will prevent the BlueZ Bluetooth stack from operating. If you are using a distribution's pre-compiled kernel, this corresponds to the *bluetooth* kernel module, and you should prevent it from being loaded. This can be done either by ensuring the BlueZ *hci_usb* module is loaded instead of the USB Bluetooth module or by disabling the module by adding its name to hotplug's configuration list (*/etc/hotplug/blacklist*).

Once your kernel is compiled and you have rebooted, you must configure Linux so it knows how to load the appropriate Bluetooth protocol modules. Most modern distributions come with */etc/modules.conf* already set up for Bluetooth use, but you may be missing the required configuration.

To verify this, ensure that the contents of Example 7-1 are present in */etc/modules.conf*. If you need to change this file, run `depmod -a` to ensure automatic loading of modules by the kernel. You must be the root user to perform this operation.

Example 7-1. Module configuration for BlueZ

```
# BlueZ modules
alias net-pf-31 bluez
alias bt-proto-0 l2cap
alias bt-proto-2 sco
alias bt-proto-3 rfcomm
alias bt-proto-4 bnep
alias tty-ldisc-15 hci_uart
alias char-major-10-250 hci_vhci
```

 Linux distributions may vary in the way they manage the */etc/modules.conf* file. Debian GNU/Linux, for example, requires you put the contents of Example 7-1 in a separate file in */etc/modutils* and run `/sbin/update-modules`; however, if you use the pre-packaged Debian BlueZ utilities, this file is already provided for you.

Supporting Subsystems

Depending on your hardware configuration, you must ensure you are running some extra supporting software to initialize your Bluetooth device.

PCMCIA

If your Bluetooth adapter is a PC card or a CF card, you must have kernel support for PCMCIA and the PCMCIA card services software installed. This software is responsible for initializing your adapter when it is plugged in and loading the required drivers into the kernel.

BlueZ requires PCMCIA card services to be Version 3.2.2 or higher. If your Linux distribution has an older version, you can update it from *http://pcmcia-cs.sourceforge.net*. See Chapter 2 for complete instructions on compiling pcmcia-cs from source.

Hotplug

The Linux hotplug subsystem enables you to plug in a device and have it immediately ready to use. It is similar in function to the card manager from PCMCIA card services, except it is generalized to include USB, Firewire (IEEE 1394), and network devices. The 2.6 series of Linux kernels adds hotplug capability to even more subsystems, such as SCSI and input devices.

When hotplug detects a new device, it loads the necessary driver modules into the kernel, and it runs any scripts the user has configured. In the case of BlueZ, hotplug is required for certain Bluetooth devices that require firmware downloaded to them, such as the USB dongles based on the Broadcom chipset.

Hotplug ships with most Linux distributions. Version 2002_08_26 or later is required. If you need to install it separately, download it from *http://linux-hotplug.sourceforge.net/*.

Installing the BlueZ Utilities

In addition to the kernel support, you must install a set of utility programs to help you manage your Bluetooth devices. Table 7-5 shows the names of the packages and their purpose. You can either install the versions of these tools that come with your Linux distribution, or compile and install them from source.

Table 7-5. BlueZ software packages

Package	Purpose
bluez-libs	The application library that all other Bluetooth tools require in order to function
bluez-utils	Main utilities that enable you to initialize and control Bluetooth devices
bluez-sdp	Service discovery protocol tools that enable the advertisement and discovery of Bluetooth services
bluez-pan	Tools that enable personal area networking using Bluetooth
bluez-hcidump	A debugging tool that permits the monitoring of Bluetooth packets
bluez-bluefw	The firmware for Broadcom chipset-based Bluetooth devices

If you are compiling the tools from source code, compile and install in the order shown in Table 7-5 to avoid dependency problems.

Precompiled version of the utilities can be obtained for Red Hat Linux as RPMs, for Debian stable as *.deb* packages (the latest BlueZ utilities are an integral part of Debian unstable), and as packages suitable for the Sharp Zaurus Linux PDA. These can be downloaded, along with the source code packages, from the BlueZ download page at *http://bluez.sourceforge.net/*.

In order to determine whether your Bluetooth system is working, you only need to install the bluez-libs and bluez-utils packages, and also bluez-bluefw if your dongle contains a Broadcom chip (you can determine this from Marcel Holtmann's Bluetooth hardware page at *http://www.holtmann.org/linux/bluetooth/devices.html*). Install the rest when you have verified that everything is working properly.

Basic Configuration and Operation

The bluez-utils package contains the tools you need to configure and test your Bluetooth setup. Once you've installed the package, run the init script (/etc/init.d/bluez-utils start on Debian, /etc/init.d/bluetooth start on Red Hat) to start the Bluetooth subsystem. These scripts normally run on boot, so they may have been started already if you installed from RPMs or Debian packages.

The *hcid* daemon should now be running. This program controls the initialization of Bluetooth devices on the system and handles the bonding process with other devices. We discuss configuration of *hcid* later in this chapter.

The prefix "hci" derives from the name of the interface between the computer and the Bluetooth device, the Host Controller Interface.

Examining Local Devices

The *hciconfig* tool allows the configuration of the characteristics of your Bluetooth adapter. If you are familiar with the configuration of network interfaces, you will find it parallel in operation to *ifconfig*. Use -a to display extended information about each Bluetooth device attached to the computer:

```
# hciconfig -a
hci0:   Type: USB
        BD Address: 00:80:98:24:15:6D ACL MTU: 128:8  SCO MTU: 64:8
        UP RUNNING PSCAN ISCAN
        RX bytes:4923 acl:129 sco:0 events:168 errors:0
        TX bytes:2326 acl:87 sco:0 commands:40 errors:0
        Features: 0xff 0xff 0x05 0x00
        Packet type: DM1 DM3 DM5 DH1 DH3 DH5 HV1 HV2 HV3
        Link policy: HOLD SNIFF PARK
        Link mode: SLAVE ACCEPT
        Name: 'saag-0'
        Class: 0x100100
        Service Classes: Object Transfer
        Device Class: Computer, Uncategorized
        HCI Ver: 1.1 (0x1) HCI Rev: 0x73 LMP Ver: 1.1 (0x1) LMP Subver: 0x73
        Manufacturer: Cambridge Silicon Radio (10)
```

From this output, you can observe several things, which have been rendered in bold text in the example.

- Bluetooth interfaces are referred to as *hci0*, *hci1*, etc. in the same way as Ethernet interfaces are generally named *eth0*, *eth1*, etc.
- The unique Bluetooth address of our device is *00:80:98:24:15:6D*.
- The *hci0* device in question is activated, that is, UP.

- Other Bluetooth devices will see this computer as saag-0. This name is configurable, as explained in Table 7-6.
- The chipset is manufactured by Cambridge Silicon Radio (CSR). The CSR chipset is the most commonly used chipset for USB dongles.

When diagnosing and reporting problems to kernel driver authors, you may be asked for the output of hciconfig -a. Note that you must be the root user to use some of the features of *hciconfig*.

Table 7-6 shows the most useful options of the *hciconfig* tool.

Table 7-6. Common usages of the hciconfig tool

Command	Description
hciconfig hci0 up hciconfig hci0 down	Activates or deactivates the Bluetooth device. Normally, in *hcid* does this for you when you plug the device.
hciconfig hci0 reset	Sends a reset command to the Bluetooth device.
hciconfig hci0 name *myname*	Sets the device's public name to *myname*.
hciconfig hci0 features	Shows a human-readable list of the Bluetooth features the device supports. The most useful feature is *SCO link*, required in order to use audio.

Scanning for Remote Devices

The acid test is, of course, to see if your computer can detect other Bluetooth devices. The *hcitool* toolcan be used to do this. Switch on your other Bluetooth device, and ensure it is in "discoverable" mode. Issue the command hcitool scan and wait (see Example 7-2). You don't need to be root in order to run this command.

Example 7-2. An example scan of remote Bluetooth devices

```
$ hcitool scan
Scanning ...
        00:0A:D9:15:CB:B4       ED P800
        00:40:05:D0:DD:69       saag-1
```

Example 7-2 shows a typical output of a scan. In this case, the author's cell phone, "ED P800," and second Bluetooth adapter, "saag-1," are shown as discoverable.

The *hcitool* and *hciconfig* programs produce similar output for the remote devices. You must be root to use this option of *hcitool*. Here's an example session with *hcitool* where we specify the Bluetooth address of the P800 cell phone discovered in Example 7-2:

```
# hcitool info 00:0A:D9:15:CB:B4
Requesting information ...
```

Why Isn't Scanning Instantaneous?

The reason scanning can take a long time is because a Bluetooth *inquiry* is being performed. As Bluetooth devices frequency-hop, inquiry cannot be instantaneous. The device performing the inquiry transmits a special code on two consecutive frequencies. When the other devices' hop patterns take them onto those frequencies, they listen for a repetition of that code and then indicate their presence to the inquirer.

```
BD Address:   00:0A:D9:15:CB:B4
Device Name: ED P800
LMP Version: 1.1 (0x1) LMP Subversion: 0x9040
Manufacturer: Ericsson Mobile Comunications (0)
Features: 0xff 0xfb 0x01 0x00
          <3-slot packets> <5-slot packets> <encryption> <slot offset>
          <timing accuracy> <role switch> <hold mode> <sniff mode>
          <park mode> <RSSI> <SCO link> <HV2 packets>
          <HV3 packets> <u-law log> <A-law log> <CVSD>
```

Pinging a Remote Device

The *ping* command is an incredibly useful tool for discovering whether remote computers are reachable over a TCP/IP network. BlueZ has an analog to *ping*, called *l2ping*. Its name refers to the fact that it attempts to create a connection to the device using the *logical link control and adaptation protocol* (L2CAP), the lowest-level link-based protocol in Bluetooth.

In other words, before despairing because you cannot connect to a device, check it with *l2ping*. There may be a fault with software higher up the chain; *l2ping* enables you to determine whether a basic connection can be established with a remote device. Here's an example of *l2ping* in action (you need to run *l2ping* as root):

```
# l2ping 00:0A:D9:15:CB:B4
Ping: 00:0A:D9:15:CB:B4 from 00:80:98:24:15:6D (data size 20) ...
0 bytes from 00:0A:D9:15:CB:B4 id 200 time 54.85ms
0 bytes from 00:0A:D9:15:CB:B4 id 201 time 49.35ms
0 bytes from 00:0A:D9:15:CB:B4 id 202 time 34.35ms
0 bytes from 00:0A:D9:15:CB:B4 id 203 time 28.33ms
4 sent, 4 received, 0% loss
```

If you have not yet paired your computer with the device with which you are testing, using *l2ping* may result in a "permission denied" error. To remedy this, you must either pair your device with the computer (see "Bonding/Pairing" later in this chapter) or ensure that the remote device is discoverable.

Configuring hcid

The *hcid* daemon handles various low-level aspects of a system's Bluetooth devices, including activating and configuring the Bluetooth interfaces, and handling device bonding. *hcid* should be running at all times on your system, and it is usually started by initialization scripts installed along with the rest of the tools from the bluez-utils package.

The configuration file for *hcid*, */etc/bluetooth/hcid.conf*, has two parts: global configuration and Bluetooth device configuration. In normal operation, most of the default options are acceptable. In this chapter, we cover only the options that are most useful to change.

Global options

This section is introduced by the options keyword in the configuration file and controls the behavior of the *hcid* program. The most useful option in this section is pin_helper, which tells the computer the program to run in order to obtain a PIN code when pairing. The default PIN helper that ships with bluez-utils is a Python script, which uses the Python bindings to the GTK graphical toolkit. Unless you have Python and the Python-GTK package installed on your computer, this helper will not work, and you will not be able to pair your computer with other Bluetooth devices. (See the "Troubleshooting" section earlier in this chapter for instructions on replacing the PIN helper with one that returns the same PIN code every time.)

A better-looking PIN helper is available separately from bluez-utils, in a package called bluez-pin. Installing this package is recommended, and several Linux distributions ship it as a default. If you install bluez-pin, you must amend the pin_helper option accordingly. Figure 7-5 shows bluez-pin in action.

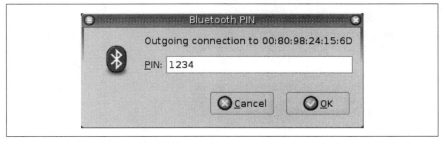

Figure 7-5. A request for a PIN from bluez-pin

Device options

This section is introduced by the devices keyword, which controls the configuration that *hcid* gives to each Bluetooth device as it is activated. This has the same effect as if you were to manually configure the device with *hciconfig*. Table 7-7 explains the most useful options available in this section.

Table 7-7. Useful device-level options from /etc/bluetooth/hcid.conf

Option	Explanation
name	The name of the adapter as it appears to other devices. The special sequence %h is replaced by the machine's hostname, and %d is replaced by the interface number.
class	The Bluetooth device and service class advertised to other devices. The default is hex 0x000100, indicating a *computer* device class, with no special service class. Depending on how the Bluetooth adapter is to be used, it may be helpful to amend this value. For more information, see the section at the beginning of this chapter entitled "Device classes."
iscan pscan	These two options control whether the adapter responds to inquiry and page scans. If inquiry scanning (iscan) is enabled, the adapter is discoverable by other devices. If page scanning (pscan) is enabled, the computer permits adapter connections from remote devices.

Bonding/Pairing

Many devices require that bonding, or pairing, is performed before a Bluetooth connection is established. Bonding may be initiated by the computer or by the remote device.

If the computer initiates bonding—usually by making an outgoing connection—then the pin_helper program (usually *bluepin*) will present a graphical dialog box to the user requesting that he input a PIN, which should match the code set on the remote device. If the remote device initiates bonding, then the remote device is required to provide a PIN to match that set in the file */etc/bluetooth/pin*.

> In some distributions of bluez-utils, the PIN code is set to the alphabetical string BlueZ. This is troublesome, because many Bluetooth devices, including most cell phones, are only capable of delivering numeric PINs. It is therefore recommended that you alter the contents of */etc/bluetooth/pin* to a numeric code.

If bonding is successful, the *hcid* daemon will store the resulting link key, used to authenticate all future connections between the two devices concerned, in the database file */etc/bluetooth/link_key*.

Service Discovery

Bluetooth devices implement the service discovery profile (SDP) in order to describe to other devices how their services may be accessed. SDP is generally used in two ways: browsing and searching. An SDP *browse request* causes a device to respond with a list of services that it supports. A *search request* is a query for details of a particular service.

Two tools found in the bluez-sdp package handle SDP on Linux. The first is *sdpd*, which provides an SDP server and allows remote devices to query the computer. The second, *sdptool*, allows administration of the SDP server and querying of the remote device.

 Not all Bluetooth-enabled devices support SDP browsing—for example, the Palm Tungsten-T PDA. Applications that wish to connect to these devices must instead search for the services they wish to use, as shown in the following section.

Using sdptool

The simplest invocation of *sdptool* is sdptool browse. This performs an inquiry and then browses each available device. Example 7-3 shows the result of this command.

Example 7-3. Results of an SDP browse

```
$ sdptool browse
Inquiring ...
Browsing 00:80:98:24:15:6D ...
Service Name: SDP Server
Service Description: Bluetooth service discovery server
Service Provider: BlueZ
Service RecHandle: 0x0
Service Class ID List:
  "SDP Server" (0x1000)
Protocol Descriptor List:
  "L2CAP" (0x0100)
    PSM: 1
    Version: 0x0001
Language Base Attr List:
  code_ISO639: 0x656e
  encoding:    0x6a
  base_offset: 0x100

Service Name: Public Browse Group Root
Service Description: Root of public browse hierarchy
Service Provider: BlueZ
Service RecHandle: 0x804d008
Service Class ID List:
```

Example 7-3. Results of an SDP browse (continued)

```
  "Browse Group Descriptor" (0x1001)
Language Base Attr List:
  code_ISO639: 0x656e
  encoding:    0x6a
  base_offset: 0x100

Service Name: LAN Access Point
Service RecHandle: 0x804d6f0
Service Class ID List:
  "LAN Access Using PPP" (0x1102)
Protocol Descriptor List:
  "L2CAP" (0x0100)
  "RFCOMM" (0x0003)
    Channel: 3
Profile Descriptor List:
  "LAN Access Using PPP" (0x1102)
    Version: 0x0100

Service Name: OBEX Object Push
Service RecHandle: 0x804d7f0
Service Class ID List:
  "OBEX Object Push" (0x1105)
Protocol Descriptor List:
  "L2CAP" (0x0100)
  "RFCOMM" (0x0003)
    Channel: 4
  "OBEX" (0x0008)
Profile Descriptor List:
  "OBEX Object Push" (0x1105)
    Version: 0x0100
```

The output from the browse command shows a list of service descriptions obtained from the SDP server. In this case, you can see that the device is running an SDP server, has support for public browsing of the SDP server contents, is offering network access via PPP, and supports OBEX via OBEX PUSH. The two profiles that use RFCOMM as a base protocol also indicate the RFCOMM channel on which the service is available. The term "channel" is somewhat overloaded in radio technologies such as Bluetooth, so you may find it helpful to consider each RFCOMM channel a virtual serial port number.

If the BDADDR of the device to query is known, it can be specified on the command line: sdptool browse 00:80:98:24:15:6D.

The *sdptool* program is also used to search for devices supporting a particular service. For instance, sdptool search OPUSH returns the service descriptor for OBEX PUSH support from any available device supporting it. Unfortunately, unlike the browse command, there is no way of searching only one device with the current version of *sdptool*; it must perform an inquiry and search for the service on every device. Table 7-8 shows the service abbreviations that *sdptool* understands.

Table 7-8. Service abbreviations for sdptool

Abbreviation	Service
SP	Serial port
DUN	Dial-up networking
LAN	LAN access
HSET	Headset profile
FAX	Fax profile
OPUSH	Object push
FTRN	Object file transfer protocol
NAP	Network access point
GN	Ad-hoc peer networking
HID	Human interface device
CIP	Common ISDN access
CTP	Cordless telephony

Although the use of *sdptool* appears clumsy, in practice it is normally required only for diagnostic purposes. Bluetooth application software generally performs its own SDP requests to determine how to connect to a service on a remote device.

Configuring sdpd with sdptool

Unlike *hcid*, *sdpd* does not remember its settings by use of a static configuration file. The service directory is dynamic, allowing services to register and deregister themselves as they come and go. Most applications do this by using the BlueZ SDP libraries, but on occasion, it is useful to configure this manually using *sdptool*.

To see which services the system's SDP daemon is advertising, use the special Bluetooth address FF:FF:FF:00:00:00, which refers to the local Bluetooth device: sdptool browse FF:FF:FF:00:00:00.

The add subcommand of *sdptool* registers a service via SDP. It takes the service name as a parameter, with an optional parameter for the RFCOMM channel. For instance, to advertise a serial port connection on RFCOMM channel 3, use the following command: sdptool add --channel=3 SP. Obviously, the channel option makes sense only for those services based on serial emulation, such as dial-up networking, OBEX, and fax.

Removing a service is slightly more complex, requiring the identifying "handle" of the record. In the output from an SDP browse in Example 7-3, there is a Service RecHandle entry for each record; the del command requires this number. So, assuming Example 7-3 refers to a local SDP server, you could remove the object push record with the command sdptool del 0x804d7f0.

The *sdptool* command provides even more granular control over the SDP records through the use of setattr and setseq, which adjust particular parameters. Use of setattr and setseq require knowledge that is likely to be useful only if you are writing sophisticated Bluetooth programs.

Serial Connections

Using BlueZ's RFCOMM implementation, it is possible to create and use emulated serial port connections over Bluetooth. RFCOMM actually underlies many Bluetooth profiles such as dial-up networking and OBEX.

As with SDP, BlueZ provides both application libraries, so programs can create and utilize RFCOMM connections and an administrative tool for the user to set up connections herself.

Ensuring RFCOMM is set up

To use RFCOMM connections, you must ensure that:

- The *rfcomm* kernel module is either compiled into the kernel or available to load
- The */dev/rfcomm** devices exist on your machine

Kernel configuration was covered in "Configuring the Kernel" earlier in this chapter. Most Linux distributions should automatically create the RFCOMM device entries for you, but if they don't exist, create them using the script in Example 7-4, which must be run as the root user.

Example 7-4. Creating the /dev/rfcomm devices

```
#!/bin/sh
# script: mkrfcomm

C=0;
while [ $C -lt 256 ]; do
  if [ ! -c /dev/rfcomm$C ]; then
    mknod -m 666 /dev/rfcomm$C c 216 $C
  fi
C=`expr $C + 1`
done
```

Connecting to a cell phone

To see an example of RFCOMM usage, you could set up a serial connection to a cell phone's modem and try some commands on it. First, you must discover the RFCOMM channel that dial-up networking uses on the phone. For this, use sdptool browse *ADDR* (where *ADDR* is a Bluetooth address you retrieved with sdptool browse):

```
$ sdptool browse 00:0A:D9:15:CB:B4
...
Service Name: Dial-up Networking
Service Description: Dial-up Networking
Service Provider: Sony Ericsson
Service RecHandle: 0x10002
Service Class ID List:
  "Dialup Networking" (0x1103)
Protocol Descriptor List:
  "L2CAP" (0x0100)
  "RFCOMM" (0x0003)
    Channel: 3
```

The phone uses channel 3 for dial-up networking. A virtual serial port on the Linux machine must be bound to this channel on the phone. As the root user, use the *rfcomm* command to bind the port and then again to confirm that the port is bound, as shown in Example 7-5.

Example 7-5. Binding to and checking an RFCOMM serial port

```
# rfcomm bind 0 00:0A:D9:15:CB:B4 3
# rfcomm
rfcomm0: 00:0A:D9:15:CB:B4 channel 3 clean
```

The 0 in bind 0 corresponds to the 0 in the device */dev/rfcomm0*, which can now be used with applications in the same way that traditional serial ports (known as */dev/ttyS0*, etc.) are used. A terminal emulation package, such as the popular minicom, can be used to confirm that the phone's modem is working, as shown in the following listing. The command ATI3 usually returns useful model information for a remote modem.

```
OK
ATI3
P800 Bluetooth (TM) Modem
OK
```

 For more information on minicom, see *http://alioth.debian. org/projects/minicom/*. You must create a configuration file for minicom referencing */dev/rfcomm0* or change the serial device to */dev/rfcomm0* from within minicom's option screens, which you can find by running minicom -s. You can also use Kermit, as shown in Chapter 9.

Internet access via a cell phone

By creating PPP connections with RFCOMM serial ports, you can use your cell phone for Internet access. (To learn how to do this with GPRS cell phones, see Chapter 9.) For example, to connect to AT&T Wireless's GPRS network with a Nokia 3650 (see "GSM/GPRS Phone with Data Cable" in Chapter 9), use the *peers* script shown in Example 7-6. Be sure to use rfcomm bind as shown in Example 7-6. You can use the *attws-connect* and *attws-disconnect* scripts from Chapter 9.

Example 7-6. PPP peer settings for AT&T Wireless and the Nokia 3650 over Bluetooth

```
# File: /etc/ppp/peers/attws-rfcomm
#
/dev/rfcomm0  # Nokia 3650
115200        # speed
defaultroute  # use the cellular network for the default route
usepeerdns    # use the DNS servers from the remote network
nodetach      # keep pppd in the foreground
nocrtscts     # no hardware flow control
lock          # lock the serial port
noauth        # don't expect the modem to authenticate itself
local         # don't use Carrier Detect or Data Terminal Ready

connect    "/usr/sbin/chat -v -f /etc/chatscripts/attws-connect"
disconnect "/usr/sbin/chat -v -f /etc/chatscripts/attws-disconnect"
```

Object Exchange

OBEX is a simple file transfer protocol. It is used when you "beam" files from one device to another. This is known as OBEX PUSH. Some devices also support OBEX FTP. As its name suggests, OBEX FTP behaves similarly to the Internet FTP protocol, allowing file uploads and downloads to a device.

The OBEX protocol was introduced as part of the group of technologies created for infrared device connections. Its implementation in devices such as cell phones is widespread but not without its quirks. OBEX itself is a binary protocol layered on top of a serial connection. With Bluetooth, it is layered on top of an RFCOMM connection. Example 7-3 shows an entry for the OBEX PUSH profile, using RFCOMM channel 4.

Some older cell phones don't actually provide OBEX implementation in this way. Instead, they have extended AT commands accessible from a serial connection to their internal modem, as described in the previous section. These commands place the connection into OBEX mode. We do not cover this use, often called "cable OBEX," but rather focus on the Bluetooth OBEX profiles.

OBEX FTP over Bluetooth is not very well supported on Linux. The most popular package, obexftp, still has Bluetooth support in development at the time of writing. We advise you to check the project's home page at *http://triq.net/obex*.

OBEX PUSH is better supported and is more practical since it is consistently implemented in consumer devices such as cell phones. There are several graphical programs available to support OBEX PUSH on Linux, as we shall see later. First, we look at the command-line tools available to perform file transfers.

Basic support

OBEX support on Linux is implemented through a project called OpenOBEX. Any OBEX-related program requires you to have these libraries installed. They can be obtained and compiled from the project's home page at *http://openobex. sourceforge.net/* or installed through your Linux system's package management system.

 If your Linux distribution is relatively old, be aware that OpenOBEX might not have been compiled with Bluetooth enabled. If you are encountering inexplicable errors in starting up OBEX applications, this may well be the case, and you should contact your Linux distribution vendor.

The OpenOBEX libraries have a companion package called openobex-apps. The openobex-apps package contains a set of basic test programs that you can use to get started. They are by no means production quality, but they enable you to test your setup. We'll use the obex_test program to test receiving and sending files.

To send a file to a remote device, you must first discover the RFCOMM port the OBEX PUSH support uses, as shown in Example 7-3. Use sdptool to discover this, and then run obex_test. Let's suppose our remote device has the address *11:22:33:44:55:66* and uses RFCOMM port 3 for OBEX PUSH. Here is an imaginary session:

```
$ obex_test -b 11:22:33:44:55:66 3
> c
> p localfilename remotefilename
```

This session presents two arguments to the p command: the location of the file you want to send and the name of the file to use when it reaches the remote device.

To receive a file from a remote device, use the test program in server mode. (This is shown in the following listing.) You can then push a file to your computer from a remote device.

```
$ sdptool add --channel=4 OPUSH
$ obex_test -b ff:ff:ff:00:00:00 4
> s
```

Note that some devices require the OBEX capability to be reflected in your Bluetooth device's device class setting before they allow transfers to be made to your computer. (See the section "Device classes" for a detailed discussion on the exact values that this can take.) In most cases, it is sufficient to set the class to service_class_obex | device_class_computer (0x100100). This can be set in */etc/bluetooth/hcid.conf* or by dynamically using the *hciconfig* command.

The test applications that come with the OpenOBEX libraries are necessarily very rough and require you to do the legwork. Happily, more polished applications are available. These applications form part of the KDE and GNOME desktop projects, and are mentioned later in this chapter.

Other software meriting investigation can be found on the Web. These programs include ussp-push, obextool, and the OBEX PUSH daemon. They can be found either by searching the Web or visiting a page on Linux and Bluetooth, created by BlueZ maintainer Marcel Holtmann, at *http://www.holtmann.org/linux/bluetooth*.

PPP Networking

Point-to-point networking is useful for networking two computers together. If one of the peers permits routing or bridging to a wider network, then the other gains access to that network. This is what happens when you dial up your Internet service provider on a traditional modem.

PPP networking is used in the implementation of the Bluetooth LAN access profile. Here is what an SDP record for the LAN access profile looks like:

```
Service Name: LAN Access over PPP
Service RecHandle: 0x804dae0
Service Class ID List:
  "LAN Access Using PPP" (0x1102)
Protocol Descriptor List:
  "L2CAP" (0x0100)
  "RFCOMM" (0x0003)
    Channel: 2
Profile Descriptor List:
  "LAN Access Using PPP" (0x1102)
    Version: 0x0100
```

You can use LAN access to provide Bluetooth devices with access to your local network. Many PDA devices support this connection method, both for purposes of synchronization over TCP/IP and general Internet access.

In order to use LAN access, you need the bluez-pan package installed on your computer. This contains two tools: *dund* and *pand*. LAN access is provided by *dund*, which we discuss here. You also need PPP support in your Linux kernel, and the PPP daemon *pppd* installed on your computer. With most Linux distributions, this is already installed.

While no *pppd* expertise is assumed in this section, you are strongly recommended to familiarize yourself with its documentation. The Linux PPP HOWTO at *http://www.linux.org/docs/ldp/howto/PPP-HOWTO* is a good starting point.

The *dund* daemon can be used to manage both sides of the LAN connection. It provides PPP access to a remote device or connects to a provider. Acting as the server, it listens on a specific RFCOMM channel, and when a connection is made, it invokes *pppd* to establish the network connection. Acting as the client, it establishes a connection over Bluetooth to a remote device and then invokes *pppd* to handle the network connection.

Creating a LAN access server

The simplest invocation of *dund* is dund --listen --persist. You should run this command from the account of a user with permission to run *pppd* (as a fallback, you can always run it as the root user.) This command line causes *dund* to register the LAN access profile with the local SDP server and listen for incoming connections as a daemon. (For debugging purposes, *dund* can be given the --nodetach argument, which causes it to run in the foreground like a normal program.) The *persist* option causes the daemon to continue running after a connection has terminated and await new connections. You can check the system log */var/log/syslog* for status messages from *dund*.

When a connection is established, *dund* invokes *pppd* with its default options. You can normally find these in */etc/ppp/options*. Some systems use */etc/pppd* instead of */etc/ppp*. However, it's better to create a separate configuration file especially for your connections. Anything you pass to *dund* on the command line after its own configuration options is sent straight to *pppd*. Create a file called *dun* in */etc/ppp/peers* with the content shown in Example 7-7.

Example 7-7. PPP daemon configuration for LAN access

```
noauth
debug
```

Example 7-7. PPP daemon configuration for LAN access (continued)

```
crtscts
lock
local
proxyarp
ms-dns 192.168.0.5
# local : remote
192.168.7.1:192.168.7.2
```

You may want to adjust the last two entries in the configuration to suit your setup: the ms-dns line specifies the IP address of your DNS server. This will become useful when you enable routing. The two colon-separated addresses are the local IP address and the IP address to give the remote device. You should choose addresses in the 10.x.x.x or 192.168.x.x ranges that don't clash with any of your internal subnets.

The *dund* program can then be invoked with dund --listen --persist call dun. When a remote device connects, the PPP connection is brought up. Because of the "debug" option to *pppd*, you should see a verbose report of the connection in the system log. To confirm that a connection has been established, run the *ifconfig* command and look for the ppp0 network interface. Invoke the *ping* command to confirm that your remote device is reachable:

```
$ ping 192.168.7.2
PING 192.168.7.2 (192.168.7.2): 56 data bytes
64 bytes from 192.168.7.2: icmp_seq=0 ttl=255 time=77.8 ms
64 bytes from 192.168.7.2: icmp_seq=1 ttl=255 time=80.5 ms
64 bytes from 192.168.7.2: icmp_seq=2 ttl=255 time=78.3 ms
```

The final step is to ensure that your Linux box can route for the remote device, so it can take advantage of your network facilities. Various Linux distributions have their own way of doing this in their network configuration, but to test you can enable it by issuing the command echo 1 > /proc/sys/net/ipv4/ip_forward. Further instructions on routing can be found on the iptables home page (*http://www.netfilter.org*) and also in "Sharing a Network Connection over IrDA" in Chapter 8. There are a few ways to set up this kind of routing, depending on your distribution and kernel version, but make sure that other machines on your network know how to route to your connected Bluetooth device.

If you are connecting to a device running Microsoft software, you should pass the --ms-dun option to *dund*. This enables the extra negotiation required to talk to the Windows dial-up networking implementation.

Our setup so far has no security considerations. There are several steps one can take to improve the security situation:

- Require username/password authentication for the PPP setup; see the *pppd* documentation for how to do this.
- Configure your Bluetooth device to always use link-level encryption in *hcid.conf*.

You should rely on neither of these to provide more than basic security. Bluetooth is still a relatively new technology, and its security measures have not yet been subjected to many attacks in the wild. It's always best, if the remote device is capable of it, to assume link-level security is weak and to use secure connection tools such as *ssh* to encrypt your network traffic at the application layer.

Connecting to a LAN access server

The *dund* program can be configured to connect to a known LAN access point or to search for one and connect to it. Here are the command lines for these two functions:

```
dund --connect 11:22:33:44:55:66
dund --search
```

You can also specify a PPP configuration file by appending the call keyword and the name of the configuration in */etc/ppp/peers/* to the command line.

Personal Area Networking

While you can achieve much with file transfers via OBEX and point-to-point networking with PPP, devices can take the full advantage of being inter-linked in the same way that Ethernet networks are. They can then run protocols such as IPv4, IPv6, and IPX. For this reason, the Bluetooth specifications define a protocol called Bluetooth Network Encapsulation (BNEP). BNEP is used by the Personal Area Networking (PAN) profiles.

The PAN profiles cover two basic modes of networking. The first profile is a *network access point* (NAP). NAPs provide network access in the same way that an access point for a Wi-Fi network does. They are typically connected to a wider network and provide bridging. Figure 7-6 shows the structure of a NAP network. Clients connect using a profile called *PAN user* (PANU).

The second PAN profile is a *group ad-hoc network* (GN). GNs are not intended to provide access to any further network but can be used to create ad-hoc networks among a group of devices. Figure 7-7 shows the structure of a GN.

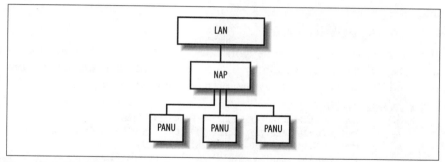

Figure 7-6. Structure of a network connected to a NAP

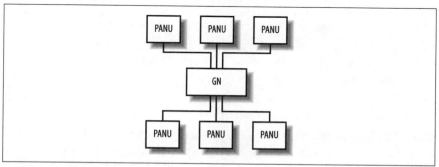

Figure 7-7. Structure of a GN

Both of these types of network are supported under Linux. To set them up, you must have some familiarity with Linux network administration.

Creating a GN

GNs are easier to create, so they are good starting points to test PAN functionality. To set up a GN or NAP, the bluez-pan package must be compiled and installed. You must also ensure that your kernel has the BNEP module compiled (Table 7-3). Load the BNEP module with `modprobe bnep`.

On the server machine, run this command as root:

```
# pand --master --listen --role GN
```

On the client machine, run this command, substituting the Bluetooth address of the master machine:

```
# pand --connect 11:22:33:44:55:66
```

As usual, you can check for status reports from *pand* in the system log file. To bring a network up, configure the interfaces' network addresses. On the master:

```
# ifconfig bnep0 192.168.7.1
```

and on the client:

```
# ifconfig bnep0 192.168.7.2
```

If you use the *192.168.7.x* network locally, substitute other suitable IP addresses. Test the connection by using *ping* to verify the connection from each end. Use *ifconfig* to display the interface configuration:

```
# ifconfig bnep0
bnep0     Link encap:Ethernet  HWaddr 00:80:98:24:15:6D
          inet addr:192.168.7.1  Bcast:192.168.7.255  Mask:255.255.255.0
          inet6 addr: fe80::280:98ff:fe24:156d/64 Scope:Link
          UP BROADCAST RUNNING MULTICAST  MTU:1500  Metric:1
          RX packets:0 errors:0 dropped:0 overruns:0 frame:0
          TX packets:5 errors:0 dropped:0 overruns:0 carrier:0
          collisions:0 txqueuelen:1000
          RX bytes:20 (20.0 b)  TX bytes:188 (188.0 b)
```

You may not want to specify the GN host's Bluetooth address on the client. By default, *pand* registers the GN or NAP service with the master host's SDP server. To make the client find its access point via SDP, give the client the following command line:

```
# pand --role PANU --search --service GN
```

Omitting the service argument causes *pand* to search for the NAP by default. Specifying the --persist option to the client's *pand* line causes it to search for the GN whenever it is not connected. Using this option, you can configure a machine to automatically connect to the network whenever it comes in range of the master machine.

To automate the IP address configuration, use the methods provided by your Linux distribution. On Red Hat, this means creating suitable scripts to go into */etc/sysconfig/network-scripts*. On Debian, you should edit */etc/network/interfaces*. The BNEP network interfaces are not present at boot time, but they will be initialized by the hotplug utility when a BNEP connection is made. For further details of this configuration, read the manpages on your system for *ifup*, *interfaces* (Debian only), and *hotplug*.

The ideal configuration is to give the GN master a static IP address and require the clients to use DHCP. If your DHCP server is running on the GN master, you may need to run a command to cause it to take note of the new network interface to listen on. This should be possible through your system's network configuration.

Bridging interfaces

As you will discover if you attempt to connect more than one client machine to your host, each connection is given its own network interface: *bnep0*, *bnep1*, *bnep2* and so on. Not only is it a nuisance to specify multiple configurations on the master side for each interface, but it leaves the client devices unable to communicate with each other. The solution to this is called bridging. Bridging enables multiple network devices to appear as one interface on a network by tying, on the master side, all the *bnep** devices into one interface.

The first step is to ensure that bridging is enabled in your Linux kernel; bridging is supported in both the 2.4 and 2.6 series of kernels. This option can be found under "Networking options" from the kernel's menu configuration and is called 802.1d Ethernet Bridging. You also need the bridge-utils software package installed. If this is not part of your Linux distribution, download it from *http://bridge.sourceforge.net/*.

Once you have the kernel modules and tools installed, you can bring up and configure a bridge interface:

```
# brctl addbr pan0
# ifconfig pan0 192.168.7.1
# brctl setfd pan0 0
# brctl stp pan0 disable
```

This bridged interface then handles all the BNEP interfaces. The latter two commands disable two features of Ethernet bridging known as Listening and Learning States and Spanning Tree Protocol. For noncomplex networks, they are not required and may cause delays to initializing the network. Further information on these features can be found on the O'Reilly Network web site at *http://www.oreillynet.com/pub/a/network/2001/03/30/net_2nd_lang.html*.

The second part of the trick is to get *pand* to add each interface to the bridge as it comes up. Create a script, as shown in Example 7-8, and save it to */etc/bluetooth/pan/dev-up*. Ensure it is executable.

Example 7-8. A script to add each BNEP network interface to the bridge

```
#!/bin/sh
brctl addif pan0 $1
ifconfig $1 0.0.0.0
```

The bridging method provides another advantage: you don't need to inform your DHCP server of the existence of a new interface whenever a BNEP connection is made.

Here is the configuration of the network interfaces after a bridged network connection has been established with one NAP and two PANU clients:

```
bnep0     Link encap:Ethernet  HWaddr 00:40:05:D0:DD:69
          inet6 addr: fe80::240:5ff:fed0:dd69/64 Scope:Link
          UP BROADCAST RUNNING MULTICAST  MTU:1500  Metric:1
          RX packets:11 errors:0 dropped:0 overruns:0 frame:0
          TX packets:13 errors:0 dropped:0 overruns:0 carrier:0
```

```
               collisions:0 txqueuelen:1000
               RX bytes:789 (789.0 b)  TX bytes:880 (880.0 b)

bnep1          Link encap:Ethernet  HWaddr 00:80:98:24:15:6D
               inet6 addr: fe80::280:98ff:fe24:156d/64 Scope:Link
               UP BROADCAST RUNNING MULTICAST  MTU:1500  Metric:1
               RX packets:49 errors:0 dropped:0 overruns:0 frame:0
               TX packets:72 errors:0 dropped:0 overruns:0 carrier:0
               collisions:0 txqueuelen:1000
               RX bytes:6453 (6.3 KiB)  TX bytes:9019 (8.8 KiB)

pan0           Link encap:Ethernet  HWaddr 00:40:05:D0:DD:69
               inet addr:192.168.7.1  Bcast:192.168.7.255  Mask:255.255.255.0
               inet6 addr: fe80::200:ff:fe00:0/64 Scope:Link
               UP BROADCAST RUNNING MULTICAST  MTU:1500  Metric:1
               RX packets:11 errors:0 dropped:0 overruns:0 frame:0
               TX packets:13 errors:0 dropped:0 overruns:0 carrier:0
               collisions:0 txqueuelen:0
               RX bytes:700 (700.0 b)  TX bytes:1254 (1.2 KiB)
```

Creating a network access point

If you intend to incorporate PAN networking as part of your network's infra-structure, you will want to set up a NAP. The initial part of NAP configuration is exactly the same as for the aforementioned GN configuration, except it specifies --role NAP to the *pand* command line rather than --role GN.

The remaining configuration required is to set up the routing in your network to ensure that the client machines and the rest of your LAN know how to reach each other. To illustrate, consider a network where the LAN uses the *10.x.x.x* subnet and your NAP machine has the IP *10.0.3.2*. The Bluetooth access point you just set up uses the *192.168.7.x* subnet with *192.168.7.1* as your NAP machine. On your client machines, you must run:

```
# route add -net 10.0.0.0 netmask 255.0.0.0 gw 192.168.7.1
```

On the LAN router, you must run the following command, or insert an equivalent configuration in the case of a non-Linux router:

```
# route add -net 192.168.7.0 netmask 255.255.255.0 gw 10.0.3.2
```

As with the configuration for *dund*, you must also ensure your NAP machine has IP forwarding enabled.

Finally, for further information, you should consult the "PAN HOWTO" document, available from the documentation area of the BlueZ web site (*http://www.bluez.org/documentation.html*). This document serves as the source for much of the information in this section.

Experimental Features

The uses of Bluetooth covered so far in this chapter are the widespread applications of the BlueZ stack. In this section, we cover the more experimental uses: printing over Bluetooth, connecting Bluetooth mice and keyboards, and using audio with Bluetooth headsets. If you're not afraid of some system configuration, happy with compiling programs from source, and understand how to use CVS, this section is for you.

Printing over Bluetooth

The Common Unix Printing System (CUPS) is a popular solution for managing printers on Linux systems. If you run CUPS, you can add a Bluetooth printer to your system. Assuming you don't already have a Bluetooth-enabled printer, you can buy Bluetooth-to-Centronics dongles that plug into the back of your printer. These devices are produced by several manufacturers, which include AnyCom, Axis, HP, and TDK.

To configure CUPS to use a Bluetooth printer, you must first download and install Marcel Holtmann's software from *http://www.holtmann.org/linux/bluetooth/cups.html*. Once you have compiled and installed the software as per Marcel's instructions, you can configure the CUPS backend.

Edit the file */etc/bluetooth/printers.conf* and add an entry similar to the following:

```
default {
    # Bluetooth address of the device
    device 00:40:8C:5E:5D:A4;

    # Bluetooth printing protocol
    protocol serial;

    # Description of the connection
    comment "My Bluetooth printer";
}
```

Restart your CUPS system, and you should then see the printer ready for administration. The Bluetooth backend performs an SDP inquiry on the target printer to discover the RFCOMM channel on which to send data.

Connecting input devices

Vendors such as Apple and Microsoft both produce Bluetooth-connected mice and keyboards. There is experimental support available from the BlueZ project for these devices, and they will be supported more fully in the 2.0 release of the BlueZ tools.

Input device support entails enabling the user-level driver support in the Input device drivers section of your Linux kernel. As its name suggests, this allows regular programs to inject events into the system's input device channels. Secondly, you must compile and configure the development version of BlueZ:

```
# cvs -d :pserver:anonymous@cvs.bluez.sourceforge.net login
# cvs -z3 -d :pserver:anonymous@cvs.bluez.sourceforge.net \
      co libs2 utils2
# cd libs2
# ./bootstrap
# ./configure --prefix=/opt/bluez2
# make && make install
# cd ../utils2
# ./bootstrap
# ./configure --prefix=/opt/bluez2 --with-bluetooth=/opt/bluez2
# make && make install
# echo /opt/bluez2/lib >> /etc/ld.so.conf
# ldconfig
```

Put BlueZ into */opt/bluez2* to avoid conflict with earlier, production-quality versions of the BlueZ tools. We suggest that you don't put */opt/bluez2/bin* in your path, but invoke the 2.0 tools with their full path. When BlueZ 2.0 is released, however, feel free to use them with wild abandon.

Next, you must verify that the user-level input module is working. Check that the device */dev/misc/uinput* exists. If not, create it with mknod /dev/misc/ uinput c 10 223. Load the module with modprobe uinput.

If you use your mouse with the XFree86 windowing system, ensure that it has a suitable entry. If you already use a USB mouse, you should have this already. Here is a configuration appropriate for the Microsoft Bluetooth mouse, supporting its scroll wheel:

```
Section "InputDevice"
    Identifier "MSMouse"
    Driver "mouse"
    Option "Protocol" "IMPS/2"
    Option "Device" "/dev/input/mice"
    Option "ZAxisMapping" "4 5"
    Option "Buttons" "5"
    Option "Emulate3Buttons" "false"
EndSection
```

Additionally, ensure that InputDevice "MSMouse" "SendCoreEvents" is added to the ServerLayout section of your XFree86 configuration.

Adding Bluetooth input devices to your system is now a matter of invoking the */opt/bluez2/bthid* program. This runs once as a daemon, and then you should invoke it again, each time to add a device:

```
# /opt/bluez2/bin/bthid -d
# /opt/bluez2/bin/bthid -c 11:22:33:44:55:66
```

Note that the input devices need to be paired before they will connect. With mice, the manufacturer presets the PIN, usually to 0000. With keyboards, you enter a PIN and press return on the Bluetooth keyboard. As ever, keep an eye on the system log to help diagnose failures.

Connecting to Bluetooth ISDN modems

Marcel Holtmann has written the necessary tools to interface with Bluetooth-enabled ISDN modems. The relevant software and instructions can be found on his web site at *http://www.holtmann.org/linux/bluetooth/cmtp.html*.

Graphical Applications

Linux has several popular graphical user interface systems, the most well-known being KDE and GNOME. These projects both have tools that provide an easy-to-use interface to your system's Bluetooth devices. At the time of writing, neither project is an official part of the KDE or GNOME desktop, but both will be integrated in future. This section presents a brief survey of the tools available and where to get them.

KDE

The KDE Bluetooth Framework's home page is at *http://kde-bluetooth. sourceforge.net/*. Its features include:

- A control center plug-in to configure Bluetooth devices
- An OBEX server application
- An OBEX sending client
- Graphical exploration of remote devices
- Cell phone handsfree implementation using your computer's microphone and speakers
- Proximity-based screen locking

The KDE Bluetooth Framework can be downloaded from the project's web page. Figure 7-8 and Figure 7-9 show KDE's Bluetooth applications in action.

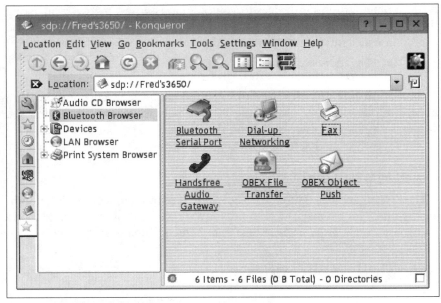

Figure 7-8. Browsing a device's services in KDE

Figure 7-9. Receiving a file via OBEX in KDE

GNOME

The GNOME Bluetooth subsystem's home page is available at *http://usefulinc.com/software/gnome-bluetooth*. Download it from the project's home page. RPM and Debian packages are also available. Features of the GNOME Bluetooth subsystem include:

- An OBEX server application
- An OBEX sending client
- A phone manager application allowing sending and receiving of SMS messages
- Graphical exploration of remote devices
- Programming libraries for creating Bluetooth-aware applications in C, Python, or C#

Figure 7-10 and Figure 7-11 show GNOME's Bluetooth features in action.

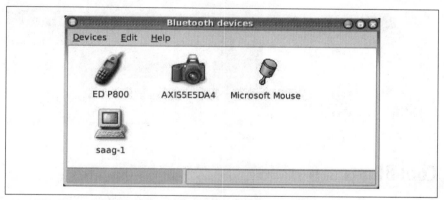

Figure 7-10. Exploring nearby Bluetooth devices in GNOME

Synchronization

If your PDA uses Bluetooth and you use Ximian Evolution as your calendar and contacts management tool, you can synchronize the two over Bluetooth using the Multisync application. Multisync is available in most Linux distributions, and you can download it from its home page at *http://multisync.sourceforge.net*.

Figure 7-11. Sending a file via OBEX in GNOME

Cool Bluetooth Tricks

Aside from the everyday file management and connectivity, Bluetooth on Linux provides scope for some fun applications. This section outlines a few of them, mostly involving interfacing a cell phone with your computer.

Use a Bluetooth Cell Phone to Control Presentations

Wireless devices that control presentations have been available for some time, but at a relatively hefty price tag, they're probably not worth the investment for the occasional presenter. Instead, why not program your cell phone to do the work?

This trick works with Ericsson phones, such as the T610, T68i, and R520m. These phones provide an advanced ability to map keypad presses to output over an RFCOMM serial connection. In turn, a program running on the Linux side can translate these codes into system input events.

You can find the code at *http://www.hackdiary.com/projects/bluetoothremote.*

Controlling Music Players

Using a similar trick as mentioned previously, the popular MP3-playing application XMMS can be controlled from a suitable Ericsson phone. The *bluexmms* program even supports display of the MP3 playlist on the phone's screen. You can find instructions and a download at *http://linuxbrit.co.uk/ bluexmms.*

Proximity-Sensitive Screen Blanking

The BlueZ Bluetooth stack reports the signal strength of an active Bluetooth connection. The KDE Bluetooth Framework has a program that takes advantage of this and activates your screensaver when you take your cell phone out of range.

If you don't run the KDE desktop, then try Jon Allen's Perl script to do a similar task, available from *http://perl.jonallen.info/bin/view/Main/ BluetoothProximityDetection.*

CHAPTER 8
Infrared

Infrared is a legacy technology that won't die any time soon. Sure, it has lousy range and can be a hassle to set up, but sometimes, it's the only common communications medium between your Linux box and something you want to talk to.

If you have ever used a remote control, you have used infrared technology. Infrared is a wireless communication technology that makes use of the invisible spectrum of light that is just beyond red in the visible spectrum. It's suitable for applications that require short-range, point-to-point data transfer. Because it uses light, line of sight is a prerequisite for using infrared. Despite this limitation, infrared is widely used in household equipment and is increasingly popular in devices such as digital cameras, PDAs, and notebook computers.

Founded in 1993 as a nonprofit organization, the Infrared Data Association (IrDA) is an international organization that creates and promotes interoperable, low-cost infrared data interconnection standards that allow users to transfer data from one device to another. The Infrared Data Association standards support a broad range of appliances, computing, and communications devices.

 The term IrDA is typically used to refer to the protocols for infrared communications, not exclusively to the nonprofit body.

There are currently four versions of IrDA; their differences are mainly in the transfer speed:

Serial Infrared (SIR)
   The original standard with a transfer speed of up to 115 kbps

Medium Infrared (MIR)

Improved transfer speed of 1.152 Mbps; it is not widely implemented

Fast Infrared (FIR)

Speed of up to 4 Mbps; most new computers implement this standard

Very Fast Infrared (VFIR)

Speed of up to 16 Mbps; it is not widely implemented yet

When two devices with two different IrDA implementations communicate, one steps down to the lower transfer speed.

In terms of operating range, infrared devices can communicate up to one or two meters. Depending on the implementation, if a device uses a lower power version, the range can be stepped down to a mere 20 to 30 cm. This is crucial for low-power devices.

A Cyclic Redundancy Check (CRC), which uses a number derived from the transmitted data to verify its integrity, protects all exchanged data packets. CRC-16 is used for speeds up to 1.152 Mbps, and CRC-32 is used for speeds up to 4 Mbps. The IrDA also defines a bi-directional communication for infrared communications.

An infrared connection operates at a range of 0 to 1 meter, with peak intensity within a 30-degree cone (see Figure 8-1). With more power, a longer operating range is possible with a reduction in transfer speed. In addition, an infrared connection requires a visual line of sight in order to work, so there cannot be any direct obstruction between the two communicating devices.

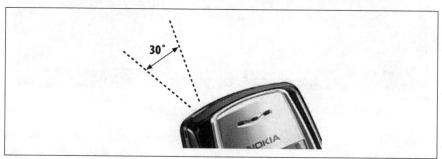

Figure 8-1. The 30-degree cone for peak power intensity of an infrared port

Setting up Infrared with Linux can be tricky. Jean Tourrilhes's Linux-IrDA Quick Tutorial (*http://www.hpl.hp.com/personal/Jean_Tourrilhes/IrDA/IrDA.html*) lists 24 common pitfalls that await the unsuspecting user.

If your hardware supports SIR mode, this is usually straightforward. FIR configuration is still somewhat arcane, unless you have a system that's supported right out of the box. Most modern notebooks support FIR by default, but you can often go into the BIOS setup and change it to SIR. Even if you want FIR to work, be sure to try SIR first, because it's usually the simplest.

IrDA in the Kernel

Most modern kernels have all the support that you need to get infrared to work. If you build your own kernel, make sure that you've enabled infrared support. Most of the infrared support is configured under the IrDA (Infrared) Support section that appears in the kernel configuration. Figure 8-2 shows the *make menuconfig* kernel configuration screen open to the IrDA Support section. (You may need to select Prompt for development and/or incomplete code/drivers under the top-level Code maturity level options section of the kernel configuration to see all the available options.)

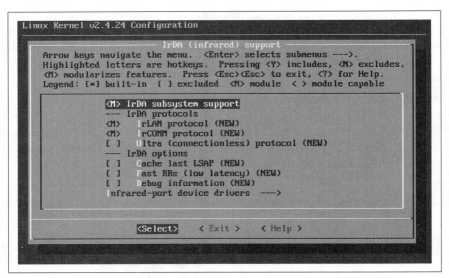

Figure 8-2. Configuring IrDA support with make menuconfig

You'll definitely want to configure IrDA Subsystem Support (CONFIG_IRDA) as well as the IrCOMM Protocol (CONFIG_IRCOMM), which lets you use the IrDA port as a serial port via one of the */dev/ircommN* ports. We suggest that you compile these as modules and go into Infrared-port Device Drivers and select every driver that it offers you, configuring each as a module.

PC Laptop with Built-In IrDA

There is a lot of hardware out there, and it's all put together slightly differently. We got infrared working under a couple of different distributions, both with a dongle and the internal infrared. Your configuration should be similar, but if you run into any trouble, check out Jean Tourrilhes's Linux-IrDA Quick Tutorial at *http://www.hpl.hp.com/personal/Jean_Tourrilhes/IrDA/IrDA.html*.

 To make sure you are up to date with the most recent bug and security fixes, make sure you've installed the most recent updates that are available for your Linux distribution, especially for the kernel and associated modules.

Out of the box, we were unable to get infrared working in SIR or FIR mode on our computer, a ThinkPad A20m. On a whim, we went into the BIOS and tried different IRQ and port settings. The combination of IRQ 4 and port 0x3E8 did the trick. The ThinkPad didn't let us switch from FIR to SIR mode in the BIOS, but it let us use SIR mode without any complaints under several Linux distributions.

On all of the Linux distributions described in the following list, we performed some initial steps to discover the infrared port. First, we booted the system, and then inspected the output of *dmesg* to get a list of serial ports:

```
debian:~# dmesg | grep tty
ttyS01 at 0x02f8 (irq = 3) is a 16550A
ttyS02 at 0x03e8 (irq = 4) is a 16550A
```

We used this information to figure out which serial devices corresponded to the infrared hardware. If there are a lot of serial devices on your system, this may involve some guesswork or at least a look around the BIOS settings. In this infrared port, we knew that the first serial devices listed (*/dev/ttyS1*) corresponds to the 9-pin serial port on the back of the computer, so that left */dev/ttyS2*.

In each of the following examples, we rebooted after making the changes to ensure that everything worked. If you'd like to preserve your uptime, try running /etc/init.d/irda restart after making the changes instead of rebooting.

Debian 3.0r1

Because the latest 2.4 kernel-image package (2.4.18-14.1) was showing its age, we compiled and installed the latest kernel from source (2.4.24). Other than that, we worked with a stock 3.0r1 install with the latest updates. To get infrared working, we installed the irda-common and irda-tools packages, and edited */etc/irda.conf*, setting IRDADEV=/dev/ttyS2.

irda-common sets up */etc/init.d/irda* to start in all runlevels, so we didn't need to modify any startup scripts. However, Debian did not put our mortal user into the correct group (dialout) to access serial ports, so we fixed that with usermod -G dialout *username.*

SuSE 9.0

The *irda* package, which was installed by default, provided all the utilities we needed for IrDA support. We set IRDA_PORT="/dev/ttyS2" in */etc/sysconfig/irda.* Next, we ran insserv /etc/init.d/irda to enable IrDA support to start at boot time.

Mandrake 9.2

To get infrared working, we installed the *irda-utils* package and edited */etc/sysconfig/irda,* setting DEVICE=/dev/ttyS2. *irda-utils* sets up */etc/init.d/irda* to start in all runlevels, so we didn't need to modify any startup scripts. Mandrake did not put our mortal user into the correct group (uucp) to access serial ports, so we fixed that with usermod -G uucp *username.*

RedHat 9

The *irda-utils* package, which was installed by default, provided all the utilities we needed for IrDA support. We set DEVICE=/dev/ttyS2 in */etc/sysconfig/irda.* Next, we ran chkconfig --level 5 irda on to enable IrDA support to start in runlevel 5, the default runlevel for Red Hat Linux running in graphical mode (check your */etc/inittab* to see the default runlevel for your system or use the runlevel command to see your current runlevel). Red Hat did not put our mortal user into the correct group (uucp) to access serial ports, so we fixed that with usermod -G uucp *username.*

Gentoo 1.4

We installed the infrared utilities with emerge irda-utils and set IRDADEV=/dev/ttyS2 in */etc/conf.d/irda.* Next, we enabled the *irda* startup script with rc-update add irda default. The *ircomm* devices were owned by root, so we gave the uucp group access to them with chgrp uucp /dev/ircomm* and chmod g+rw /dev/ircomm*, and then gave our mortal user access with usermod -G uucp *username.*

Infrared Dongle

If you don't have built-in infrared support, or if you can't get the built-in infrared to work, use an infrared dongle. If your dongle is compatible with the USB and IrDA specifications, it should just work. We tested the WINIC W-USB-180 IrDA dongle (*http://www.winic.com.tw/180.htm*), which is available in the U.S. from MadsonLine (*http://www.madsonline.com/*).

The most compelling reason to use an external dongle is the awkward placement of infrared ports on devices. Figure 8-3 shows how we had to position an HP iPaq upside down to use it with the ThinkPad's built-in IrDA port. Figure 8-4 shows a much more relaxed positioning using the W-USB-180..

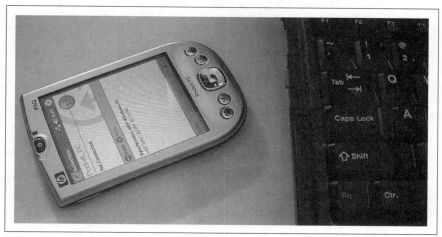

Figure 8-3. Awkward infrared port placement

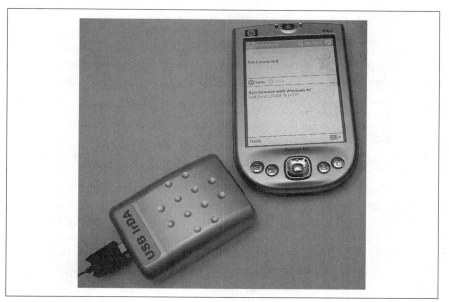

Figure 8-4. Taking things into your own hands with an external IrDA adapter

At the time of this writing, support for USB infrared dongles was experimental. We suggest you compile the latest kernel available in the series you are using and configure *irda-usb* as a module (CONFIG_USB_IRDA). You should also disable *ir-usb*, which conflicts with *irda-usb*. See "IrDA in the Kernel" earlier in this chapter

We got the W-USB-180 adapter to work by following these steps:

1. We stopped *irda*, just in case it had been started earlier:

   ```
   # /etc/init.d/irda stop
   ```

2. We disabled the *ir-usb* module, which appears in some recent kernels and conflicts with the driver that we should be using, *irda-usb*:

   ```
   # cd /lib/modules/
   # find . -name ir-usb.o
   # cd ./2.4.21-166-default/kernel/drivers/usb/serial/
   # mv ir-usb.o ir-usb.o.unused
   ```

3. (Optional.) If you've already plugged in the dongle in the *ir-usb* module may have already claimed it. You can convince that module to release the dongle with this command (you may have to run it more than once if there are some other dependencies that prevent the modules from unloading):

   ```
   # rmmod ircomm-tty ircomm irtty ir-usb irda-usb irda
   ```

4. Next, we *modprobe*ed the *irda-usb* module, and *dmesg* showed that the device *irda0* had come up (the actual device name may vary on your system):

   ```
   # modprobe irda-usb
   # dmesg | grep irda
   usb.c: registered new driver irda-usb
   IrDA: Registered device irda0
   ```

5. A device name of *irdaX* (where X is some number) indicates that you've loaded the IrDA device as a network device. So, instead of putting the pathname to a device (such as */dev/ttyS2*) in your IrDA configuration file, you should put just the device name alone. For example, under Debian 3.0r1, we set IRDADEV=irda0 in */etc/irda.conf* (for a list of some Linux distributions and the IrDA configuration files used by each, see the Debian entry in "PC Laptop with Built-In IrDA" earlier in this chapter).

6. After this, we rebooted, but we could have also started IrDA support with /etc/init.d/irda start.

For more information on using infrared dongles with Linux, including serial port dongles, see the sections on dongles in the Linux Infrared HOWTO (*http://www.tuxmobil.com/Infrared-HOWTO/Infrared-HOWTO.html*).

For specific details on using USB dongles, see the IrDA and USB section of the Linux Infrared HOWTO at *http://www.tuxmobil.com/Infrared-HOWTO/ infrared-howto-s-irda-usb.html.*

Sharing a Network Connection over IrDA

If you want to accept PPP connections from other IrDA-enabled devices, start *pppd* listening on the *ircomm* device that corresponds to your IrDA adapter (these devices are numbered *ircommN*, where *N* is a number from 0 to one less than the number of IrDA adapters on your system). See Chapter 7.

In most cases, you'll want more than just a PPP connection. If you want to connect to the Internet from the other device, you'll need your Linux box to act as a NAT router, and you'll also need to tell the PPP client device where it can find its name server. We've found that the following script works well (you may need to customize $LOCAL, $REMOTE, $DNS, $INTERFACE, and $IRDEV):

```
#!/bin/sh

LOCAL=192.168.2.1      # IP address for the server running pppd
REMOTE=192.168.2.2     # IP address for the device
DNS=192.168.254.1      # A DNS server
INTERFACE=wlan0        # Interface that connects to the network
IRDEV=/dev/ircomm0     # Infrared device

# Set up forwarding.
#
echo 1 > /proc/sys/net/ipv4/ip_forward
/usr/sbin/iptables -t nat --flush
/usr/sbin/iptables -t nat -A POSTROUTING -o "$INTERFACE" -j MASQUERADE

# Start the PPP link.
#
/usr/sbin/pppd $IRDEV 115200 local \
    $LOCAL:$REMOTE ms-dns $DNS \
    silent noauth persist nodetach \
```

Connecting from Linux

To connect from another IrDA-enabled Linux device, align the infrared ports and then issue the following command:

```
# pppd /dev/ircomm0 115200 usepeerdns local nodetach defaultroute
```

You may need to bring down any existing network interfaces, because the defaultroute option generally does not override existing default routes. Some versions of Linux ship with a modified *pppd* that lets you use the replacedefaultroute option to replace any existing default route.

Connecting from Palm OS

To set up the connection to the Linux system:

1. Select Prefs → Communication → Network (Figure 8-5)
2. The Network preferences appear, which list the existing services; click New.
3. Give the new service a name and select IR to a PC/Handheld under Connection as shown in Figure 8-6.

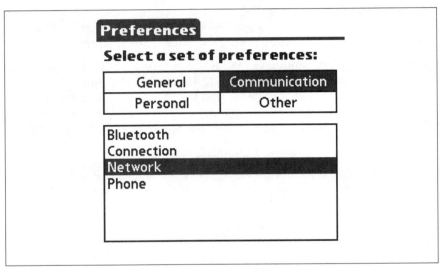

Figure 8-5. Opening Network Preferences on the Palm

To connect, align the infrared ports of your Linux system and the Palm. Return to Network preferences, select the service you created in Step 3, and click Connect. When you are done with the network connection, return to the Network preferences and click Disconnect.

To test out your connection, ping a remote host. To do this, stay in the Network preferences after the connection is made and select Menu → Options → View Log. Scroll to the bottom of the log, use Graffiti to write ping *hostname* and then use the Graffiti stroke for a carriage return (a diagonal stroke in the ABC region from upper right to lower left). If you've made the network connection successfully, you'll be able to ping a remote host, as shown in Figure 8-7. (Be sure that the remote host accepts pings and that your network does not block them).

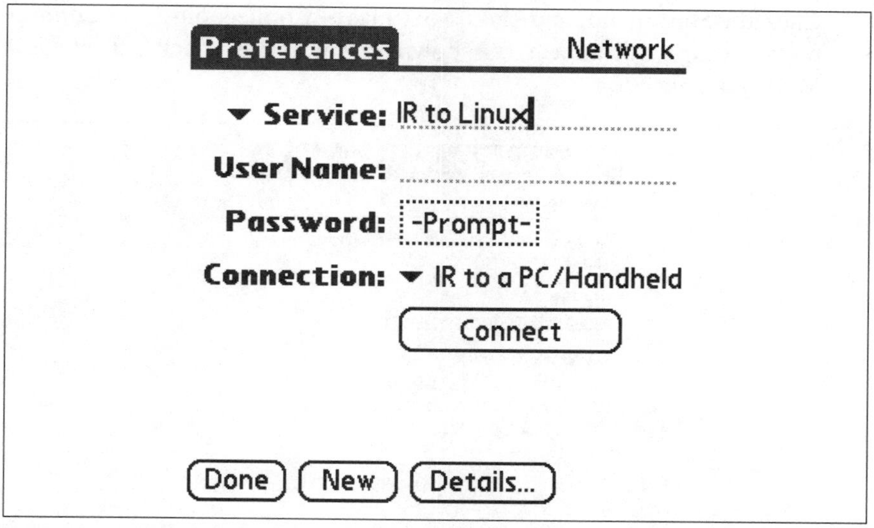

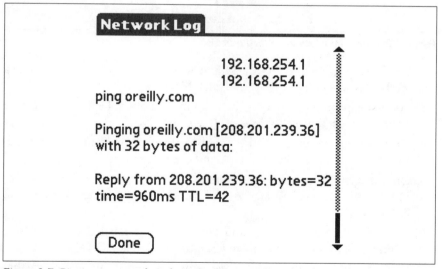

Figure 8-6. Setting up a new network connection on the Palm

Figure 8-7. Pinging a remote host from the Palm

Connecting from Pocket PC

Making a simple PPP connection is more complicated under the Pocket PC than under Palm OS. To set up the connection to the Linux system with Windows Mobile 2003.

1. Click the Start menu, and choose Settings → Connections. The Connections settings will appear, as shown in Figure 8-8. Click Add a New Modem Connection.

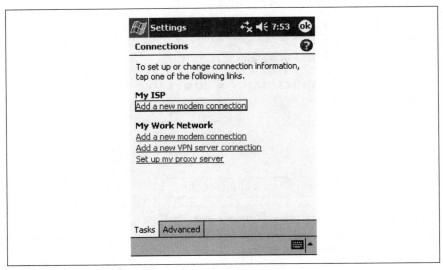

Figure 8-8. Connection settings on the Pocket PC

2. You'll be prompted to choose a name for the connection and to select a modem. Select Generic IrDA and click Next.

3. You'll be prompted to type in a phone number. Pick anything you want—it's just a placeholder—and then click Next.

4. On the next screen, you'll be asked to supply a username, password, and domain. Leave these all blank and click Advanced.

5. On the General tab of the advanced settings, set the Baud rate to 115200 and uncheck Wait for Dial Tone before Dialing, as shown in Figure 8-9.

6. Click the Port Settings tab and check the box labeled Enter Dialing Commands Manually, as shown in Figure 8-10. Click OK.

7. You'll be back at the dialog (username, password, and domain) that you originally saw in Step 4. Click Finish to return to the Connections settings.

To connect to the Linux system, align your infrared ports, and then:

1. Click the Start menu and choose Settings → Connections. Click Manage Existing Connections under the same section where you created the connection originally.

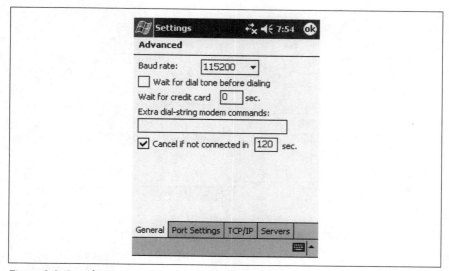

Figure 8-9. Specifying general settings on the Pocket PC

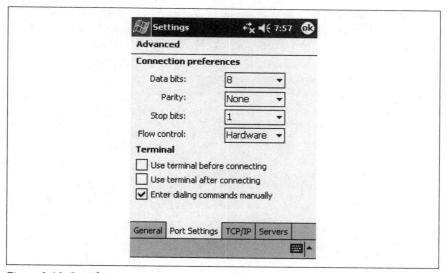

Figure 8-10. Specifying port settings on the Pocket PC

2. A list of connections appears, showing the connection that you created. Tap and hold on it to bring up a context menu and select Connect, as shown in Figure 8-11.

3. You'll be prompted for a username, password, and domain. Leave these blank and click Save Password to have this (hopefully) never bother you again, and then click OK.

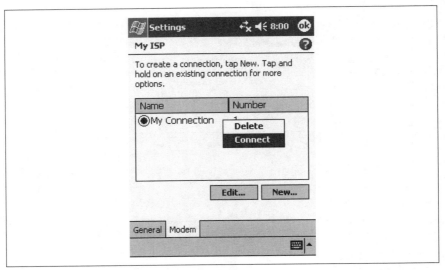

Figure 8-11. Making the connection on the Pocket PC

4. After a few seconds, the Manual Dial Terminal should appear full of PPP gibberish, as shown in Figure 8-12. Click OK, and you should get confirmation of your connection, as shown in Figure 8-13.

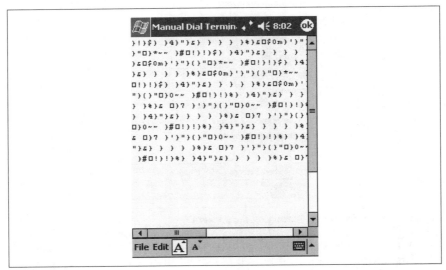

Figure 8-12. The Manual Dial Terminal on the Pocket PC

You can hide this notification and make it reappear by clicking its icon at the top of the screen. Use the Disconnect button to disconnect when you are finished. Test your connection by visiting a web site with Pocket Internet Explorer.

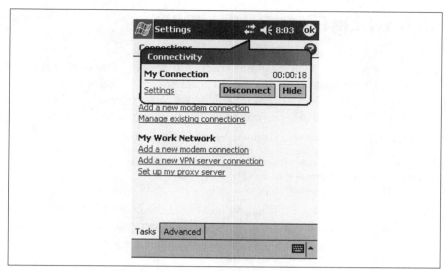

Figure 8-13. Confirming the connection on the Pocket PC

Connecting to the Internet with a Cell Phone

Making an Internet connection over infrared is really no different from making it over any other serial port, which is described in detail in Chapter 9. For example, to connect to AT&T Wireless's EDGE network with a Nokia 6200 (see "GSM/GPRS Phone with Data Cable" in Chapter 9), use the *peers* script as shown in Example 8-1. You can use the same *attws-connect* and *attws-disconnect* scripts as shown in Chapter 9.

Example 8-1. PPP peer settings for AT&T Wireless and the Nokia 6200 over IrDA

```
# File: /etc/ppp/peers/attws-irda
#
/dev/ircomm0   # Nokia 6200
115200         # speed
defaultroute   # use the cellular network for the default route
usepeerdns     # use the DNS servers from the remote network
nodetach       # keep pppd in the foreground
nocrtscts      # no hardware flow control
lock           # lock the serial port
noauth         # don't expect the modem to authenticate itself
local          # don't use Carrier Detect or Data Terminal Ready

connect    "/usr/sbin/chat -v -f /etc/chatscripts/attws-connect"
disconnect "/usr/sbin/chat -v -f /etc/chatscripts/attws-disconnect"
```

Transferring Files with OpenOBEX

OBEX (Object Exchange) is an IrDA standard (*http://www.irda.org/standards/standards.asp*) for transferring files between devices. OpenOBEX (*http://sourceforge.net/projects/openobex/*) is an open source implementation of this standard. To install OpenOBEX, download the latest release (*openobex-x.y.z.tar.gz*), extract the tarball, then configure, compile, and install it:

```
bjepson@linux:~/Documents> tar xfz openobex-1.0.1.tar.gz
bjepson@linux:~/Documents> cd openobex-1.0.1/
bjepson@linux:~/Documents/openobex-1.0.1> ./configure
bjepson@linux:~/Documents/openobex-1.0.1> make
bjepson@linux:~/Documents/openobex-1.0.1> sudo make install
```

You'll also want the applications, so download the latest release of the apps (*openobex-apps-x.y.z.tar.gz*), and go through the same steps:

```
bjepson@linux:~/Documents> tar xfz openobex-apps-1.0.0.tar.gz
bjepson@linux:~/Documents> cd openobex-apps-1.0.0/
bjepson@linux:~/Documents/ openobex-apps-1.0.0> ./configure
bjepson@linux:~/Documents/ openobex-apps-1.0.0> make
bjepson@linux:~/Documents/ openobex-apps-1.0.0> sudo make install
```

(You may need to add */usr/local/lib* to */etc/ld.so.conf* and run *ldconfig* as root for everything to work.)

After you've installed the applications, you can transfer files with the *irobex_palm3* utility. Don't let the "palm" in the name put you off; we've used it with cellular phones as with well as a Palm (you should be able to use any infrared device that supports OBEX). To receive files, start *irobex_palm3*, initiate sending a file from your device, and align the ports. After *irobex_palm3* receives the file, it exits. Here's a session where *irobex_palm3* receives a business card from a Nokia phone:

```
bjepson@linux:~ > irobex_palm3
 Send and receive files to Palm3
Waiting for files

..HEADER_LENGTH = 220
Filename = Nokia.vcf
Wrote /tmp/Nokia.vcf (108 bytes)
```

To send a file, be sure that your device is configured to receive files via infrared, align the ports, and use irobex_palm3 *filename*:

```
bjepson@linux:~> irobex_palm3 sample.png
Send and receive files to Palm3

name=sample.png, size=11439
...........

PUT successful
```

Synchronizing with a Palm

There are several tools that you can use to synchronize your Palm and Linux system. pilot-xfer, which is part of the pilot-link (*http://www.pilot-link.org/*) package, lets you synchronize your Palm to a directory. You can synchronize to KDE address books, calendars, etc. with KPilot (*http://www.slac.com/pilone/kpilot_home/*). GNOME-Pilot (*http://www.gnome.org/projects/gnome-pilot/*) lets you do the same with GNOME applications.

In each of these applications, you'll be asked to press the HotSync button somewhere along the way. When this happens, launch HotSync on your Palm, select IR to a PC/Handheld, and click the on-screen HotSync button (not the HotSync button on your cable or cradle), as shown in Figure 8-17.

KPilot

You can use KPilot as a free alternative to the Palm Desktop software for Windows and Mac OS X. To set up KPilot with your Palm over infrared:

1. Launch KPilot (select it from a menu or run the command kpilot). The main window appears as shown in Figure 8-14.

2. Click Settings → Configure KPilot. The settings window appears, as shown in Figure 8-15. Specify */dev/ircommN* (where *N* is the number of your infrared device, usually 0) as the Pilot device and click OK.

3. The main window should update to display the following (if it doesn't, check your IrDA configuration):

       13:05:54 Trying to open device...
       13:05:54 Device link ready.

4. Next, click Settings → Configure Conduits to choose the kind of information you want to synchronize. The conduit configuration window appears, as shown in Figure 8-16. Select each conduit you want, and click Enable. Click OK when you are done.

To synchronize with your Palm:

1. Place your Palm's infrared port in range of that of your Linux system.

2. On your Palm, click the on-screen HotSync button as shown in Figure 8-17.

3. The first time you sync, you may get a dialog indicating that the Palm already has a username associated with it. If you haven't synced the Palm before, the dialog may be slightly different.

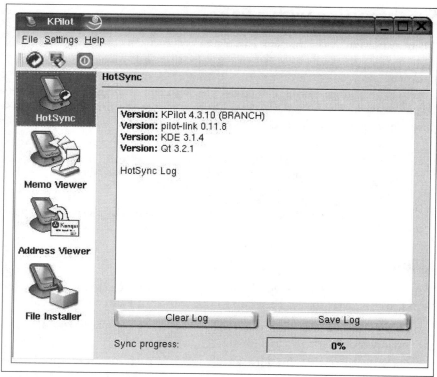

Figure 8-14. The KPilot main window

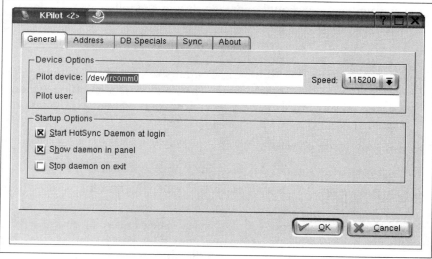

Figure 8-15. Setting the Pilot device in KPilot

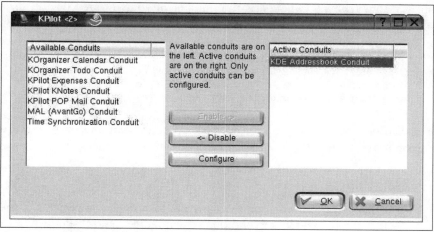

Figure 8-16. Selecting which conduits to use in KPilot

The KPilot window shows the progress of the HotSync as it continues.

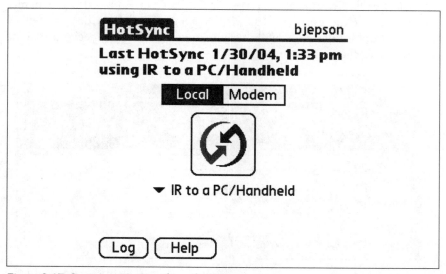

Figure 8-17. Starting a HotSync from the Palm

pilot-link

Use the pilot-xfer utility to back up, sync, or restore your Palm (see the pilot-xfer manpage for a complete list of options and features). For example, to sync your Palm into the ~/Palm directory, use the --sync option and specify */dev/ircommN* (where *N* is the number of your infrared device, usually 0) as the port with the -p option:

```
bjepson@linux:~> pilot-xfer -p /dev/ircomm0 --sync ~/Palm
    Listening to port: /dev/ircomm0
Please press the HotSync button now... Connected
Synchronizing /home/bjepson/Palm/Novarra-19.txt.pdb
Synchronizing /home/bjepson/Palm/Novarra-19.nod.pdb
...
```

You can use the --backup option to back up your Palm and the --restore option to restore it.

GNOME-Pilot

GNOME-Pilot lets you synchronize your Palm to various components of the GNOME desktop, including Evolution. To configure GNOME-Pilot:

1. Launch GNOME-Pilot (*gpilotd-control-applet*). You'll see a Welcome screen. Click Next.

2. The Cradle Settings appear (Figure 8-18). Give your settings a name, then select the port, such as */dev/ircommN* (where *N* is the number of your infrared device, usually 0), and speed (115200). Specify a type of IrDA and click Next.

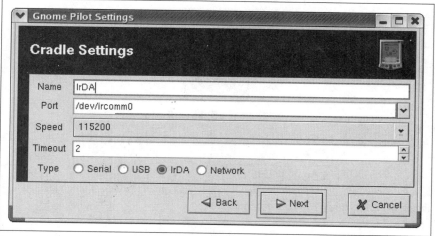

Figure 8-18. GNOME-Pilot cradle settings

3. The Pilot Identification appears. Here you must specify whether you've synced this Palm before. If not, provide a username and ID. Click Next.

4. If you have synced the Palm before, the Initial Sync screen appears, and GNOME-Pilot will try to retrieve the username and ID. Click Next after it has retrieved the name and ID (see Figure 8-19).

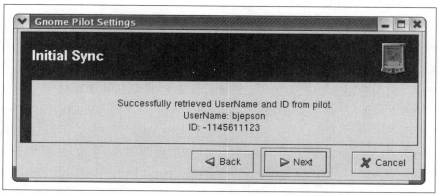

Figure 8-19. GNOME-Pilot retrieving the username and ID

5. The Pilot Attributes screen appears, as shown in Figure 8-20. You can specify a name, working directory, and action to perform on syncing. You should set the Sync Action to Use conduit settings and click Next.

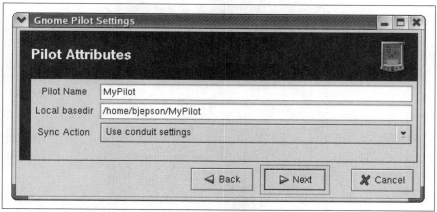

Figure 8-20. GNOME-Pilot displaying the Pilot Attributes

6. The final screen appears, which should indicate success. Click Finish, and the Pilot Link dialog appears, as shown in Figure 8-21.

7. (Optional.) If GNOME-Pilot retrieved a negative ID in Step 3, you should change it now. Select your Palm in the Pilot Link dialog and click Edit.

8. The Pilot Settings appear, as shown in Figure 8-22. Set the ID to a reasonable number (just to be safe, choose an integer between 1 and 254) and click Send to Pilot. You'll need to press the on-screen HotSync as shown earlier in Figure 8-17.

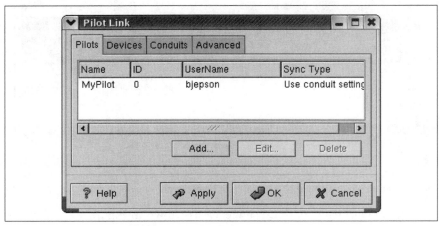

Figure 8-21. The Pilot Link dialog

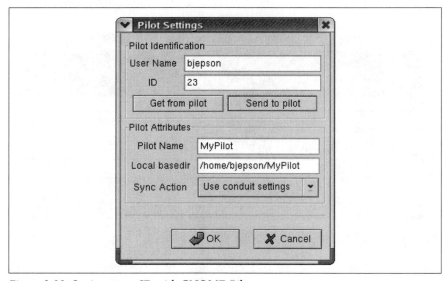

Figure 8-22. Setting a new ID with GNOME-Pilot

9. Select the Conduits tab (see Figure 8-23), and for each conduit you want to enable, select the conduit name and click Enable.

10. Click OK when you are done.

Now, when you press the onscreen HotSync button, you may not see anything on the screen unless you've added a panel item for GNOME-Pilot. However, the Palm will show you what's happening as the HotSync progresses.

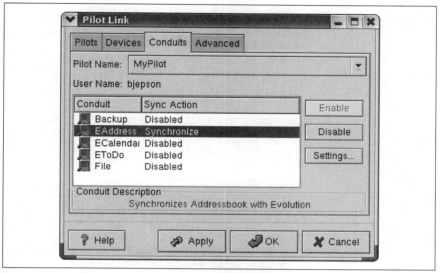

Figure 8-23. Specifying conduit settings in GNOME-Pilot

Pocket PC

You can sync with a Pocket PC using SynCE (*http://synce.sourceforge.net/synce/*). If SynCE is not available with your distribution, follow the excellent instructions at the SynCE site for installing and configuring the software.

After it's installed, you can generally start SynCE with synce-serial-config ircomm*N* (where *N* is the number of your infrared device, usually 0) and then use synce-serial-start (run these as root):

```
# synce-serial-config ircomm0
```

You can now run synce-serial-start to start a serial connection.

```
# synce-serial-start
```

Once synce-serial-start is running, you should run the *dccm* utility as the mortal user who wants to play with the Pocket PC (this utility communicates with the *synce* process that you started as root):

```
bjepson@linux:~> dccm
```

Now, align your Pocket PC's infrared port with that of your Linux system, and launch ActiveSync. Click Tools → Connect via IR, and your Pocket PC should make an ActiveSync connection, as shown in Figure 8-24. Note that the progress bar never goes anywhere. It's just a live link between the two; it's not actually syncing.

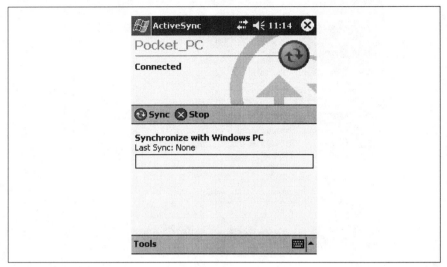

Figure 8-24. Never-ending ActiveSync

To move data between your Linux system and your Pocket PC, you can use commands like pls to list files on the Pocket PC and pcp (may be Pcp on some systems) to copy files to and from the Pocket PC. Note that you must prefix the root of the filesystem with ":" when you use pcp.

```
bjepson@linux:~> pls /My\ Documents/
AC--------      57727  Thu Jul 31 20:00:02 2003   000013a8  Sample4.jpg
AC--------      67617  Thu Jul 31 20:00:02 2003   00001393  Sample3.jpg
AC--------      45053  Thu Jul 31 20:00:02 2003   00001386  Sample2.jpg
AC--------      64168  Thu Jul 31 20:00:02 2003   00001374  Sample1.jpg
Directory              Thu Jul 31 20:00:02 2003   0000134a  Business/
Directory              Thu Jul 31 20:00:02 2003   00001349  Personal/
Directory              Thu Jul 31 20:00:02 2003   00001287  Templates/
bjepson@linux:~> Pcp ":/My Documents/Sample1.jpg"
File copy of 64168 bytes took 0 minutes and 7 seconds, that's 9166 bytes/s.
```

The SynCE site includes a number of other tools, such as Orange (extract *.cab* files from Pocket PC installation packages) and a plug-in for MultiSync (*http://multisync.sourceforge.net/*).

Cellular Networking

The widest of the wide area wireless networks are the cellular networks. They're also among the slowest, unless you're in one of the markets where third-generation (3G) cellular networks are available. At the time of this writing, San Diego and Washington, D.C. users could receive between 300 and 500 kbps from Verizon for $80 a month. The rest of the United States, and much of the world, is still plodding along at between 30 and 130 kbps, depending on several variables: the type of network, capabilities of their terminal (a phone or PC Card), and quality of coverage. This chapter explains these variables to help you make the best choice in cellular data service, and also talks about configuring a cellular phone or PC Card with Linux (although this is usually just a small matter of PPP chat scripting).

Cellular Data

There are several types of cellular data networks. The most popular are General Packet Radio Services (GPRS) and 1x Radio Transmission Technology (1xRTT). At the time of this writing, slightly faster Enhanced Data rates for GSM Evolution (EDGE) and 1x Evolution Data Only (1xEV-DO) networks are emerging.

CSD

You use Circuit Switched Data (CSD) when you use your cellular phone as a dial-up modem. When you do this, you use your voice plan. Generally, this is not the best option: CSD calls typically don't receive the full throughput that's available to a data connection. However, there is a high-speed variant called High Speed CSD (HSCSD) that can provide you with better speeds.

Unless you need to dial into a private network using a modem, we suggest that you use a packet-switched protocol, such as GPRS, EDGE, 1xRTT, or 1xEV-DO, to make your data connection. With these technologies, you're not dialing a bank of modems; rather, you're effectively using your cellular carrier as your ISP and your phone as a network adapter. Additionally, CSD calls are billed by the minute; with the exception of one plan offering from Verizon Wireless (Express Network NationalAccess) that we're aware of, packet-switched data connections are billed by the amount of data used, rather than the amount of time you spend online (unless you have an unlimited plan, in which case you are paying a flat rate).

If your cellular carrier and GSM device supports it, you can make an HSCSD at speeds up to 40 kbps. To enable this capability, you must issue the command AT+CBST=*speed*,0,1, where *speed* is a value supported by your phone (you can enumerate the supported values by issuing the AT+CBST=? command). For example, request 14.4 kbps with AT+CBST=14,0,1.

The isdn4linux FAQ has some information on using HSCSD with ISDN: *http://www.mhessler.de/i4lfaq/i4lfaq-6.html#config_gsmv110*. The following sites have information on HSCD commands, although support varies from device to device, and some providers do not support HSCD at all (contact your cellular provider if you are unsure):

> *http://www.gcrsoft.com/data.html*
> *http://www.nc9210.de/9210/tipps/at_hscsd.htm*
> *http://www.zelaskowski.de/pda/hscsd.html*

GPRS and EDGE

GPRS sits on top of Global System for Mobile communications (GSM), a cellular networking protocol that breaks a channel into timeslots so that up to eight users can share the same channel; at any given time, a channel is dedicated to one user only. A channel is 200 kHz of bandwidth within the 850, 900, 1,800, or 1,900 MHz bands. GSM is the most widespread digital cellular technology with 970 million users at the end of 2003. It's available in the U.S., much of Asia, Europe, and many other places.

Although a given timeslot supports a slow data rate (typically between 9.6 and 13.4 kbps), one timeslot is sufficient for each side of a voice conversation. GPRS phones and PC Cards combine multiple GSM timeslots (up to eight in theory, but the equipment we've seen maxes out at four) and typically support a downstream data rate of 40 kbps (we have found that this translates to a peak of 30 kbps for HTTP transfers). Upstream data rates are typically less, as low as 9.6 kbps, but this is governed by the number of timeslots your device supports for upstream data, as well as by the number of timeslots your cellular carrier makes available for this purpose.

EDGE is an improvement over GSM in that it increases the data rate per timeslot significantly. Instead of 9.6 kbps to 13.4 kbps, EDGE supports between 48 and 70 kbps per timeslot. However, to take advantage of EDGE speeds, you need a handset or PC Card that supports EDGE, such as the Nokia 6200 cell phone or the Sony Ericsson GC82 PC Card Modem. EDGE devices are backward-compatible with GSM and GPRS, so if you're in a location without EDGE coverage, you can still connect at the slower GPRS speeds.

GSM devices require the installation of a Subscriber Identity Module (SIM). You (or the salesperson) insert this card when you first get the phone. If you have more than one phone, you can swap SIMs and use the phone that is currently holding the SIM. However, most cellular providers lock the device to their network, so you can use the phone onlwith them. So, if you buy a phone from AT&T Wireless and insert the SIM you bought from T-Mobile, you'll receive an error message. However, there are many ways to remove this lock. Some carriers will do it for you if you contact their customer support and ask; this is usually done for customers who have been with the carrier for a while, have an account in good standing, and are planning to use the phone overseas (you can save money by buying a pay-as-you-go SIM from a local cellular provider and swapping SIMs while you are abroad). Figure 9-1 shows a Nokia 6200 that is being inserted with an AT&T Wireless SIM card (that's the battery next to it, which we had to remove to get at the SIM).

1xRTT and 1xEV-DO

1xRTT is an improvement to CDMAone, the first version of Code Division Multiple Access (CDMA), a digital cellular protocol that supported data rates up to 14.4 kbps. 1xRTT cranks it up to 144 kbps upstream and downstream. Instead of slicing up cellular channels by timeslots, CDMA uses spread-spectrum technology to support multiple users in each 1.25 MH–wide CDMA channel within the 800 and 1900 MHz bands. Each user within a given CDMA channel is associated with a code, and their signals (tagged with the associated code) are spread across the channel. although CDMA is not as widespread as GSM, there are still many users (188 million at the end of 2003). It's available in the U.S., parts of Asia, Latin America, and Europe.

1xEV-DO improves on 1xRTT by supporting burst speeds up to 2.4 Mbps while still keeping channels only 1.25 MHz wide. At the time of this writing, Verizon Wireless has begun 1xEV-DO trials in San Diego and Washington, D.C. (priced the same as its 1xRTT offering). Initial reports indicate that 300–500 kbps are the likely real-world speeds.

Figure 9-1. Inserting a SIM card into a Nokia 6200

CDMA phones do not use SIM cards. As a result, you can't move your account to a new phone as easily as you can with GSM phones. You must contact your cellular provider, deactivate the old phone, and activate the new one. (Your carrier may also allow you to do this through its customer support web site).

Some Cellular Carriers

There are major cellular carriers around the world; This section looks at some of the major U.S. providers. Of the ones described here, we have hands-on experience with Sprint, Verizon Wireless, AT&T Wireless, and T-Mobile.

To connect to the Internet using a GPRS carrier, you must specify an Access Point Name (APN), which is the name of a gateway on the carrier's network that gets you on the Internet. After that, dial *99#***1# to connect. APNs for networks not listed here can be found in a variety of places online, but your best bet is to contact your cellular provider. Opera Software maintains a list of user-submitted carriers and APNs at *http://www.opera.com/products/ smartphone/docs/connect/*.

All plans and prices listed in the following sections are accurate as of this writing, but are subject to change.

AT&T Wireless

AT&T Wireless (*http://www.attwireless.com*) offers GSM service with GPRS under a variety of plans. Its consumer-oriented mMode plan tops out at 8 megabytes of data per month for $19.99, with additional megabytes costing about six dollars each.

mMode plans must be accompanied by a voice plan. However, AT&T Wireless offers standalone Mobile Internet data plans starting at $29.99 for 10 megabytes (about three dollars per additional megabyte), going up to $79.99 a month for unlimited data (you can also add these plans to service with an existing voice plan). In late 2003, AT&T rolled out support for EDGE on its North American network.

AT&T Wireless uses a GPRS APN named proxy, which also works with its EDGE data service. You can set your APN with the following AT command sequence:

```
AT+CGDCONT=1,"IP","proxy"
```

AT&T Wireless maintains online support forums at *http://forums. attwireless.com/attws* that are valuable more for the community discussion than for the actual tech support that goes on there. Check out the mMode and GSM(TM)/GPRS/EDGE General Discussion forums for insights into AT&T Wireless' data services.

At the time of this writing, Cingular has just purchased AT&T Wireless, and it is expected to merge its network with AT&T's by the end of 2004. Whether that changes any of the AT&T Wireless–related instructions in this chapter remains to be seen. For more information, consult this book's errata at *http://www.oreilly.com/catalog/lnxunwired*.

T-Mobile

T-Mobile (*http://www.t-mobile.com*), formerly VoiceStream, offers GSM and GPRS in a number of markets across the globe. Its unlimited (T-Mobile Internet Unlimited) data plans are available as an add-on to voice service or as separate plans. You can add unlimited GPRS data for $19.99 a month with a qualifying voice plan ($29.99 and higher). Otherwise, unlimited GPRS data is $29.99 a month.

Don't confuse T-Mobile's t-zones plan with its T-Mobile Internet Unlimited plan. The $4.99 and $9.99 a month t-zones plans are designed for users who use the Internet exclusively from their handset, and some users have reported that services such as SSH (and practically anything that isn't HTTP, SMTP, or POP3) don't work with these plans.

As of late 2003, T-Mobile had not rolled out EDGE in any of the markets we tested.

T-Mobile uses two different APNs: `internet2.voicestream.com` and `internet3.voicestream.com`. `internet2.voicestream.com` gives you a private network IP address, which may cause headaches with VPN connections, and `internet3.voicestream.com` gives you a public IP address, which may cause headaches when people to try break into your machine. If you want to use `internet3.voicestream.com`, you must be on the T-Mobile Internet Unlimited VPN plan, which costs the same as T-Mobile Internet Unlimited. If you aren't sure which plan you are on, contact T-Mobile customer service to find out. You can set your APN with one of the following AT command sequences:

```
AT+CGDCONT=1,"IP","internet2.voicestream.com"
AT+CGDCONT=1,"IP","internet3.voicestream.com"
```

Cingular Wireless

Cingular Wireless (*http://www.cingular.com*) is also a GSM/GPRS provider. Its Wireless Internet Express pricing plans are similar to AT&T's mMode and Mobile Internet plans: for $24.99 a month, you can get 10 megabytes of data, and each additional megabyte is about four dollars. Its unlimited plan is $74.99 per month.

As of late 2003, Cingular Wireless had rolled out trial EDGE support in one market (Indianapolis).

Cingular Wireless uses a GPRS APN named `isp.cingular`. You can set your APN with the following AT command sequence:

```
AT+CGDCONT=1,"IP","isp.cingular"
```

Verizon Wireless

Verizon Wireless (*http://www.verizonwireless.com*) offers CDMA service with 1xRTT and 1xEV-DO for data. Its advertised data plans are available as add-ons to a voice plan or as standalone data plans. Although it is not advertised on its site, many users have reported that the America's Choice voice plan minutes can be used for data; but many users have reported that Verizon does not permit this, so unless you get something in writing that indicates your plan allows this, we suggest that you use an add-on data plan.

Verizon Wireless has a number of data plans. Its NationalAccess plan lets you pay by the minute. This means that you're paying even when your network connection is idle. However, it also has plans that let you pay by the megabyte, starting at 20 megabytes for $40 a month with each additional megabyte for about four dollars. You can go up from there to unlimited data for $79.99 a month.

Verizon Wireless' 1xRTT service is available across its national network. As of late 2003, 1xEV-DO trials were underway in San Diego and Washington, DC.

 An APN is not required for 1xRTT or 1xEV-DO; you can generally just dial #777 to make the connection. For more details, see "CDMA Phone with Data Cable" and "CDMA PC Card" later in this chapter.

Sprint

Sprint PCS (*http://www.pcsvision.com*) offers CDMA cellular service. It offers unlimited 1xRTT data service, which it calls PCS Vision, as an add-on to a voice plan for $15 a month. However, there are reports that say that these plans are not intended for users who want to connect a laptop to their cell phone, and that Sprint may charge users who use the service in this way as much as $10 a megabyte.

However, Sprint does offer by-the-megabyte plans starting from $40 a month for 20 megabytes, going up to $100 for 300 megabytes. Additional megabytes are two dollars each under all their megabyte plans. Although Sprint had offered an unlimited data plan for $80 a month in the past, it is not advertising such a plan at the time of this writing.

As of late 2003, Sprint was reported to be testing 1xEV-DO, but it was not marketing it or selling 1xEV-DO cards or phones.

Phones and Cards

The following sections describe the cards and phones that we tested with Linux. They include an assortment of devices that can talk CDMA 1xRTT, GPRS, and EDGE. Each section includes the information you need to make a data call.

Table 9-1 contains the results of the testing with these devices. In each download test, we moved a 384 KB compressed datafile down from an HTTP server using wget 1.8.1 (*wget_1.8.1-6.1_i386.deb*) and recorded the transfer rate. In each upload test, we uploaded the same file using Debian's ftp client (*ftp_0.17-9_i386.deb*) and recorded the transfer rate.

Table 9-1. Download and upload speeds with various devices

Device	Carrier	Signal[a]	Download test 1	Upload test 1	Download test 2	Upload test 2
Merlin C201	Sprint	65%	12.64 KB/sec	8.7 KB/sec	12.86 KB/sec	9.0KB/sec
Motorola v120e	Verizon Wireless	97%	13.94 KB/sec	5.7 KB/sec	13.3 KB/sec	7.5 KB/sec
Nokia 6200	AT&T Wireless[b]	55%	11.05 KB/sec	6.0 KB/sec	11.31 KB/sec	6.0 KB/sec
Nokia 6200	T-Mobile[c]	65%	2.61 KB/sec	2.8 KB/sec	1.74 KB/sec	2.6 KB/sec
Merlin G100	T-Mobile	32–54%	4.26 KB/sec	1.4 KB/sec	5.09 KB/sec	1.4 KB/sec

[a] Reported by AT+CSQ and divided by 31.
[b] Connected in an EDGE-enabled AT&T Wireless market.
[c] At the time of this writing, T-Mobile does not support EDGE.

These devices use a basic Hayes command set but also support an extended command set (IS-707 AT command set). You can use this command set to ask the modem about signal strength and the type of network to which it's connected. For example, if you issue the command AT+CSQ?, the phone will respond with the signal strength (on a scale of 0–31) and the frame error rate, which will be zero if you haven't had any network activity.

Table 9-2 shows some of the commands and sample responses from the Novatel Wireless Merlin C201 (you should be able to use these commands with any CDMA or GPRS device described later in this chapter). To issue one of these commands, use minicom or Kermit; type the command and then press Enter. Example 9-1 shows a session where we set the serial speed and then run Kermit to have a conversation with the modem. If your user account does not have the correct permissions, you must set the permisions appropriately (on Debian, we add the bjepson user to the dialout group).

Example 9-1. Kermit session with the Novatel Wireless Merlin C201

```
bjepson@debian:~$ setserial /dev/ttyS2 baud_base 230400
bjepson@debian:~$ kermit
C-Kermit 7.0.196, 1 Jan 2000, for Linux
 Copyright (C) 1985, 2000,
   Trustees of Columbia University in the City of New York.
Type ? or HELP for help.
(/home/bjepson/) C-Kermit>set line /dev/ttyS2
(/home/bjepson/) C-Kermit>set speed 115200
/dev/ttyS2, 115200 bps
(/home/bjepson/) C-Kermit>connect
Connecting to /dev/ttyS2, speed 115200.
```

Example 9-1. Kermit session with the Novatel Wireless Merlin C201 (continued)

```
The escape character is Ctrl-\ (ASCII 28, FS)
Type the escape character followed by C to get back,
or followed by ? to see other options.
------------------------------------------------------
at
OK
at+csq?
+CSQ: 22, 00000000,00000000

OK
```

 If you can't see the commands you are typing but are still getting a response, the modem is probably set to not echo the commands that you type. You can reset this with the command ATE1 or reset the modem to its defaults with ATZ.

Table 9-2. Some of the AT commands recognized by cellular modems

Command	Syntax	Sample response from C201
Get battery charge information	AT+CBC?[a]	+CBC: 0,65 (First integer: 0=running on battery, 1=charging, 2=status no available, 3=power fault; second integer: percentage charge remaining) Not applicable to the C201, because it's powered by the PCMCIA bus
Get manufacturer information	AT+GMI	+GMI: Novatel Wireless Inc.
Get mobile model	AT+GMM	+GMM: CDMA Merlin 1900MHz
Get model revision	AT+GMR	+GMR: F/W VER: 1065 S/W VER: BM3.0.10 Jun 11 03 14:45:56 BOOT VER: 1-1
Get serial number	AT+GSN	+GSN: 00000000
Get service information (analog or digital)	AT+CAD?[b]	+CAD: 1 (0=no service, 1=CDMA digital, 2=TDMA digital, 3=analog)
Get serving system information	AT+CSS?[b]	+CSS: 1,1 4106 (First integer: 0=unknown band, 1=800MHz, 2=1900MHz; second integer: mobile station block; third integer: system identifier)
Get signal quality	AT+CSQ?[a]	+CSQ: 5, 00000291,00000241 (First integer: signal strength from 0–31; last integers: frame error rate)

[a] Do not include the ? for GSM phones or modems.
[b] Not supported by the GSM phones or modems that we tested.

The Tao of Mac maintains a list of GSM AT commands at *http://the. taoofmac.com/space/AT%20Commands*.

Although the example PPP peers file and chat scripts show examples for a particular provider, you should be able to adapt these to providers and phones other than the ones covered in this chapter. If you decide to change the name of the files, be sure that the connect and disconnect entries in your peers file match the new filenames. For CDMA providers, you shouldn't need to make any change unless your cellular carrier requires a username and password. For GSM providers other than the ones described in this chapter, you need to change the APN (and perhaps set a username and password). If you are using a different type of phone that uses a different file in the */dev* directory, you need to change the device name.

When you make a connection as directed in the following sections (running the command pppd call *provider* as root), you should see something similar to the following:

```
Serial port initialized.
Starting CDMA connect script
Dialing...
Serial connection established.
Using interface ppp0
Connect: ppp0 <--> /dev/ttyS2
kernel does not support PPP filtering
Cannot determine ethernet address for proxy ARP
local  IP address 68.29.37.40
remote IP address 68.28.97.6
primary   DNS address 68.28.122.11
secondary DNS address 68.28.114.11
```

When you're done with your connection, press Ctrl-C to disconnect.

PPP Troubleshooting

If you see a message that the pppd command is "not replacing existing default route," it means you have another network connection active. You should temporarily bring this network connection down before making the PPP connection or manually adjust the routing to your liking.

If your link is dropping due to LCP Echo errors, try setting the interval to something really high in the */etc/ppp/peers* file:

```
lcp-echo-failure 4
lcp-echo-interval 65535
```

Also, some phones may have trouble with the default compression scheme that PPP uses. If you are having problems negotiating a connection, try adding novj and novjccomp, as shown in Example 9-5 later in this chapter.

For more information on PPP configuration, see the Linux PPP HOWTO: *https://secure.linuxports.com/howto/ppp/*.

CDMA PC Card

The Novatel Wireless Merlin C201 (Figure 9-2) is a CDMA 1xRTT PC Card offered by Sprint that is automatically recognized by all the versions of Linux we tested (Mandrake 9.2, Gentoo 1.4, and Debian 3.0). It appears as two serial ports starting at the highest unused serial port. So, on a ThinkPad A20m running Debian 3.0, there were already two serial ports (*ttyS0* and *ttyS1*). When we plugged in the C201 card, two more were detected: *ttyS2*, which is the CDMA modem, and *ttyS3*, a status port for the modem (whose purpose is unknown to us but is not necessary to connect to the Internet).

Figure 9-2. The Novatel Wireless Merlin C201 card

As of this writing, there is no way to provision (perform the initial activation with the Sprint network) this card without a PC running Microsoft Windows. Novatel Wireless technical support confirmed this but mentioned that upcoming firmware may come out that supports provisioning on any operating system. Unless that happens, you must get access to a Windows notebook long enough to install the software that comes with the card, activate it, and verify that you can connect to the network before trying it with Linux.

To get online with the Merlin C201, use a PPP connection and the phone number #777. If you use a regular phone number, you'll end up making a CSD call, which may incur per-minute charges. When you dial #777, you'll incur whatever charges are applicable under your data plan. To set up a data connection with the C201, first create the */etc/ppp/peers/sprint-pcs* file shown in Example 9-2. You must change the first two lines to specify your device (for example, */dev/ttyS2*).

Example 9-2. PPP peer settings for Sprint PCS and the Merlin C201

```
# File: /etc/ppp/peers/sprint-pcs
#
/dev/YOUR_DEVICE    # device
init "setserial /dev/YOUR_DEVICE baud_base 230400"

115200       # speed
defaultroute # use the cellular network for the default route
usepeerdns   # use the DNS servers from the remote network
nodetach     # keep pppd in the foreground
crtscts      # hardware flow control
lock         # lock the serial port
noauth       # don't expect the modem to authenticate itself

# scripts for connection/disconnection
connect    "/usr/sbin/chat -v -f /etc/chatscripts/sprint-connect"
disconnect "/usr/sbin/chat -v -f /etc/chatscripts/sprint-disconnect"
```

 The Merlin C201 is a bit of an oddball. You must use *setserial* to specify twice the actual speed you want to use. (Thanks to the folks at tummy.com for this information, found on *http://www.tummy.com/articles/laptops/merlin-c201/*)

Next, create the */etc/chatscripts/sprint-connect* and */etc/chatscripts/sprint-disconnect* scripts, shown in Example 9-3 and Example 9-4.

Example 9-3. PPP connect script for Sprint PCS and the Merlin C201

```
# File: /etc/chatscripts/sprint-connect
#
TIMEOUT 10
ABORT   'BUSY'
ABORT   'NO ANSWER'
ABORT   'NO CARRIER'
SAY     'Starting CDMA connect script\n'
```

Example 9-3. PPP connect script for Sprint PCS and the Merlin C201 (continued)

```
# Get the modem's attention and reset it.
''      'ATZ'

# E0=No echo, V1=English result codes
OK      'ATE0V1'

# Dial the number
SAY     'Dialing...\n'
OK      'ATD#777'
CONNECT ''
```

Example 9-4. PPP disconnect script for Sprint PCS and the Merlin C201

```
# File: /etc/chatscripts/sprint-disconnect
#
""      "\K"
""      "+++ATH0"
SAY     "CDMA disconnected."
```

After you've set up these scripts, issue the command pppd call sprint-pcs as root. Press Ctrl-C to invoke the disconnect script and hang up the PPP connection.

> If your carrier requires a username and password, set the user and remote_name options as shown in Example 9-5, and create a *chap_secrets* file, as shown in Example 9-6.

CDMA Phone with Data Cable

The Motorola v120e (see Figure 9-3) is a CDMA 1xRTT phone offered by Verizon Wireless. You must modprobe or insmod the *acm.o* (the USB Abstract Control Model drive) module for this phone to be recognized. The v120e appears as a serial port *named /dev/ttyACM0*.

> The Motorola v120e does not require the provisioning step typically required of PCMCIA cards (see "CDMA PC Card" earlier in this chapter). Simply using the data connection for the first time provisions the phone.

To get online with this phone, create a PPP connection using the phone number #777. You can also use this phone to connect to dial-up service (see "CSD" earlier in this chapter), but per-minute charges will apply, and you'll get a maximum speed of 14.4 kbps. To set up a data connection for this phone, first create the */etc/ppp/peers/verizon* file shown in Example 9-5. Be sure the device name corresponds to that of your phone (use dmesg to see

Figure 9-3. The Motorola v120e CDMA phone

which device the phone was associated with), although it will probably be /*dev/ttyACM0*. You must supply your phone number followed by @vzw3g.com as your username in the *verizon* file, and specify vzw as your password in the */etc/ppp/chap-secrets* file shown in Example 9-6 (the verizon in the server column in *chap-secrets* corresponds to the remote_name specified in the */etc/ppp/peers/verizon* file).

Example 9-5. PPP peer settings for Verizon Wireless and the Motorola v120e

```
# File: /etc/ppp/peers/verizon
#
```

Example 9-5. PPP peer settings for Verizon Wireless and the Motorola v120e (continued)

```
/dev/ttyACM0    # device

# The following two settings need a corresponding entry in
# /etc/ppp/chap-secrets.
user YOUR_CELLULAR_PHONE_NUMBER@vzw3g.com
remotename verizon

115200         # speed
defaultroute   # use the cellular network for the default route
usepeerdns     # use the DNS servers from the remote network
nodetach       # keep pppd in the foreground
crtscts        # hardware flow control
lock           # lock the serial port
noauth         # don't expect the modem to authenticate itself

novj
novjccomp

# scripts for connection/disconnection
connect    "/usr/sbin/chat -v -f /etc/chatscripts/verizon-connect"
disconnect "/usr/sbin/chat -v -f /etc/chatscripts/verizon-disconnect"
```

Example 9-6. CHAP password for Verizon wireless connection

```
# File: /etc/ppp/chap-secrets
#
# Secrets for authentication using CHAP
# client                              server   secret   IP addresses
YOUR_CELLULAR_PHONE_NUMBER@vzw3g.com  verizon  vzw      *
```

Next, create the */etc/chatscripts/verizon-connect* and */etc/chatscripts/verizon-disconnect* scripts, shown in Example 9-7 and Example 9-8.

Example 9-7. PPP connect script for Verizon Wireless and Motorola v120e

```
# File: /etc/chatscripts/verizon-connect
#
TIMEOUT 10
ABORT   'BUSY'
ABORT   'NO ANSWER'
ABORT   'NO CARRIER'
SAY 'Starting CDMA connect script\n'

# Get the modem's attention and reset it.
''   'ATZ'

# E0=No echo, V1=English result codes
OK      'ATE0V1'

# Dial the number
SAY 'Dialing...\n'
```

Example 9-7. PPP connect script for Verizon Wireless and Motorola v120e (continued)

```
OK   'ATD#777'
CONNECT ''
```

Example 9-8. PPP disconnect script for Verizon Wireless and Motorola v120e

```
# File: /etc/chatscripts/verizon-disconnect
#
""   "\K"
""   "+++ATHO"
SAY "CDMA disconnected."
```

After you've set up these scripts, issue the command pppd call verizon as root (if you haven't configured Linux to automatically load the *acm.o* module, you must issue the command modprobe acm first). Usage charges will apply according to your data plan. When you are done, press Ctrl-C to invoke the disconnect script and hang up the PPP connection.

GSM/GPRS Phone with Data Cable

The Nokia 6200 (Figure 9-4) was the first phone on the market to support EDGE, an enhancement to GSM that increases the data rate per timeslot up to 48 kbps (higher in ideal network conditions). With two EDGE timeslots for uploads and downloads, the Nokia 6200 can achieve data rates of 96 kbps or higher. The Nokia 6200 is offered by AT&T Wireless.

EDGE-capable phones are compatible with GSM/GPRS networks. If the cellular base station you connect to does not support EDGE, the phone will fall back to regular GSM data rates.

Unfortunately, the Nokia 6200 does not support Bluetooth, so you must use either IrDA or a data cable. Linux does not recognize the Nokia data cable (DKU-5), but it does recognize the cable that comes with the Smith-Micro QuickLink Mobile for Mac OS X kit (available for $59.95 at *http://www.smithmicro.com*) as a Prolific 2303. However, we had trouble with some of the 2.4 kernels that we had tested with 2.4.20 through 2.4.22: the driver (*pl2303.o*) would trigger a kernel oops when hanging up the connection. However, we tested a prerelease version of 2.4.23 (rc3), which solved this problem.

To connect to the Internet with this phone, you must set up a PPP connection that sets the APN (see "Some Cellular Carriers" earlier in this chapter) and dials the number (*99***1#) for making a GPRS connection. In theory, you can use this phone to connect to a dialup service (see "CSD" earlier in this chapter).

Figure 9-4. The Nokia 6200 EDGE/GPRS phone

To set up your PPP connection, first create the */etc/ppp/peers/attws* file shown in Example 9-9. Be sure the device name corresponds to that of your phone (use dmesg to look at the device that the phone was assigned to), although it will probably be */dev/ttyUSB0*.

Example 9-9. PPP peer settings for AT&T Wireless and the Nokia 6200

```
/dev/ttyUSB0   # USB-serial port
230400         # speed
defaultroute   # use the cellular network for the default route
usepeerdns     # use the DNS servers from the remote network
nodetach       # keep pppd in the foreground
crtscts        # hardware flow control
lock           # lock the serial port
noauth         # don't expect the modem to authenticate itself

connect    "/usr/sbin/chat -v -f /etc/chatscripts/attws-connect"
disconnect "/usr/sbin/chat -v -f /etc/chatscripts/attws-disconnect"
```

Next, create the */etc/chatscripts/attws-connect* and */etc/chatscripts/attws-disconnect* scripts, shown in Example 9-10 and Example 9-11. If you are using a

GPRS cellular provider other than AT&T Wireless, you will probably have to change the APN (proxy in Example 9-10).

Example 9-10. PPP connect script for AT&T Wireless and the Nokia 6200

```
# File: /etc/chatscripts/attws-connect
#
TIMEOUT 10
ABORT   'BUSY'
ABORT   'NO ANSWER'
ABORT   'NO CARRIER'
SAY     'Starting GPRS connect script\n'

# Get the modem's attention and reset it.
''      'ATZ'

# E0=No echo, V1=English result codes
OK      'ATE0V1'

# Set Access Point Name (APN)
SAY     'Setting APN\n'
OK      'AT+CGDCONT=1,"IP","proxy"'

# Dial the number
SAY     'Dialing...\n'
OK      'ATD*99***1#'
CONNECT ''
```

Example 9-11. PPP disconnect script for AT&T Wireless and the Nokia 6200

```
# File: /etc/chatscripts/attws-disconnect
#
""      "\K"
""      "+++ATH0"
SAY     "GPRS disconnected."
```

After you've set up these scripts, issue the command pppd call attws as root. Usage charges will apply according to your data plan. Press Ctrl-C to invoke the disconnect script and hang up the PPP connection.

 If your carrier requires a username and password, set the user and remote_name options, as shown in Example 9-5 and create a *chap_secrets* file, as shown in Example 9-6.

GPRS PC Card

T-Mobile once operated in the United States under the VoiceStream brand. In fact, you still see voicestream.com on T-Mobile's APNs, and a USENET group that discusses T-Mobile is alt.cellular.gsm.carriers.voicestream. Back when it operated as VoiceStream, it offered a great cellular card that was branded iStream (see Figure 9-5). Under the hood, it's a Novatel Wireless Merlin G100 GPRS PCMCIA modem. We like this card because it's cheap (we picked ours up for $50 on eBay) and we have received faster downloads with it than with other GPRS phones that we've used.

Figure 9-5. The (VoiceStream branded) Novatel Wireless Merlin G100 GPRS card

Linux automatically detects this as a serial card; when you insert the card, look for messages in the system log or the output of dmesg to see the port it's assigned to. On our system, it shows up as */dev/ttyS2* (dmesg reports "ttyS02 at port 0x03e8," and ttyS02 corresponds to */dev/ttyS2*).

To connect to the Internet with this phone, you must set up a PPP connection that sets the APN (see "Some Cellular Carriers" earlier in this chapter) and dials the number (*99***1#) for making a GPRS connection. In theory, you could dial the number of a dialup ISP (see "CSD" earlier in this chapter).

To set up your PPP connection, first create the */etc/ppp/peers/tmobile* file shown in Example 9-12 Be sure the device name corresponds to that of the PCMCIA card.

Example 9-12. PPP peer settings for T-Mobile and the Merlin G100

```
/dev/ttyS2      # G100 modem
115200          # speed
defaultroute    # use the cellular network for the default route
usepeerdns      # use the DNS servers from the remote network
nodetach        # keep pppd in the foreground
crtscts         # hardware flow control
lock            # lock the serial port
noauth          # don't expect the modem to authenticate itself
local           # don't use Carrier Detect or Data Terminal Ready
debug

# Use the next two lines if you receive the dreaded messages:
#
#   No response to n echo-requests
#   Serial link appears to be disconnected.
#   Connection terminated.
#
lcp-echo-failure 4
lcp-echo-interval 65535

connect    "/usr/sbin/chat -v -f /etc/chatscripts/tmobile-connect"
disconnect "/usr/sbin/chat -v -f /etc/chatscripts/tmobile-disconnect"
```

Next, create the */etc/chatscripts/tmobile-connect* and */etc/chatscripts/tmobile-disconnect* scripts, shown in Example 9-13 and Example 9-14. If you are using a GPRS cellular provider other than T-Mobile, you will probably have to change the APN (internet3.voicestream.com). Also, T-Mobile offers two options on its T-Mobile Internet plan. By default, you should use the internet2.voicestream.com APN. However, if you've opted for VPN support (you receive a public IP address), use internet3.voicestream.com.

Example 9-13. PPP connect script for T-Mobile and the Merlin G100

```
# File: /etc/chatscripts/tmobile-connect
#
TIMEOUT 10
ABORT    'BUSY'
ABORT    'NO ANSWER'
ABORT    'ERROR'
SAY      'Starting GPRS connect script\n'

# Get the modem's attention and reset it.
""       'ATZ'

# E0=No echo, V1=English result codes
OK       'ATE0V1'

# Set Access Point Name (APN)
SAY      'Setting APN\n'
OK       'AT+CGDCONT=1,"IP","internet3.voicestream.com"'
```

Example 9-13. PPP connect script for T-Mobile and the Merlin G100 (continued)

```
# Dial the number
ABORT    'NO CARRIER'
SAY      'Dialing...\n'
OK       'ATD*99***1#'
CONNECT ''
```

Example 9-14. PPP disconnect script for T-Mobile and the Merlin G100

```
# File: /etc/chatscripts/tmobile-disconnect
#
""               "\K"
""               "+++ATH0"
SAY      "GPRS disconnected."
```

After you've set up these scripts, issue the command pppd call tmobile as root. Usage charges will apply according to your data plan. Press Ctrl-C to invoke the disconnect script and hang up the PPP connection.

 If your carrier requires a username and password, set the user and remote_name options, as shown in Example 9-5 and create a *chap_secrets* file, as shown in Example 9-6.

Sending a Fax

You can send a fax from your cell phone if both your cellular carrier and your cell phone support it. You can figure out quickly whether your phone supports it by making a Kermit connection (see "Phones and Cards" earlier in this chapter). Here's a session with a Motorola v120e in which the phone acknowledges that it's capable of Class 2 fax modem commands:

```
bjepson@debian:~$ kermit -l /dev/ttyACM0 -b 115200
C-Kermit 7.0.196, 1 Jan 2000, for Linux
 Copyright (C) 1985, 2000,
   Trustees of Columbia University in the City of New York.
Type ? or HELP for help.
(/home/bjepson/) C-Kermit>connect
Connecting to /dev/ttyACM0, speed 115200.
The escape character is Ctrl-\ (ASCII 28, FS)
Type the escape character followed by C to get back,
or followed by ? to see other options.
-----------------------------------------------------
AT+FCLASS=?
0,2.0

OK
```

However, the following session with the Nokia 6200 shows that it doesn't have any fax modem capabilities:

```
bjepson@debian:~$ kermit -l /dev/ttyUSB0 -b 115200
C-Kermit 7.0.196, 1 Jan 2000, for Linux
 Copyright (C) 1985, 2000,
  Trustees of Columbia University in the City of New York.
Type ? or HELP for help.
(/home/bjepson/) C-Kermit>set carrier-watch off # required for some phones
(/home/bjepson/) C-Kermit>connect
Connecting to /dev/ttyUSB0, speed 115200.
The escape character is Ctrl-\ (ASCII 28, FS)
Type the escape character followed by C to get back,
or followed by ? to see other options.
----------------------------------------------------
AT+FCLASS=?
0

OK
```

To send a fax with your cell phone, install a package such as efax (*http://www.cce.com/efax/*) and configure it for your modem. In the case of efax, you must edit */etc/efax.rc*. At a minimum, you should set the device (DEV), your phone number (FROM), and name (NAME):

```
DEV=ttyACM0

# Your fax number in international format, 20 characters maximum.
# Use only digits, spaces, and the "+" character.

FROM="+1 401 555 1234"

# Your name as it should appear on the page header.

NAME="Brian Jepson"
```

Once you've done this, you can use a client program, such as *fax* (included as part of the efax package), to send a file:

```
bjepson@debian:~$ fax send 4015555678 Letter.ps
Letter.ps is postscript or pdf ...
efax: Sun Nov 23 16:39:16 2003 efax v 0.9a-001114 Copyright 1999 Ed Casas
efax: 39:16 opened /dev/ttyACM0
efax: 39:21 using in class 2.0
efax: 39:22 dialing T4015555678
efax: 39:43 remote ID -> "       401 555 5678"
efax: 39:43 connected
efax: 39:51 session 196lpi  4800bps 8.5"/215mm 11"/A4 1D     -     - 0ms
efax: 39:51 header:[2003/11/23 16:39 +1 401 555 1234 Brian Jepson p. 1/1]
efax: 41:52 sent 20+2156 lines, 61097+0 bytes, 121 s   4039 bps
efax: 41:52 sent -> Letter.ps.001
efax: 41:57 done, returning 0 (success)
```

Text Messaging

Some phones and modems let you send a text message via Short Message Service (SMS) using AT commands. To find out whether your device supports this (nearly all GSM devices do), connect with Kermit, as shown in Example 9-1, and issue the query AT+CSMS=0 (the three columns indicate whether the device is capable of receiving messages, sending messages, or sending broadcast messages):

```
AT+CSMS=0
+CSMS: 1,1,1

OK
```

If your cell phone supports this capability, you can work with text messages using AT commands. You can list your text messages with AT+CMGL=4 (the 4 indicates all messages: use 0 for unread, 1 for read, 2 for unsent, and 3 for sent messages) and read a message with AT+CMGR=MESSAGE_NUMBER:

```
AT+CMGL=4
+CMGL: 1,1,,28
07919170389103F2040B91XXXXXXXXXXF100013011320211500A0AD3771D7E9A83DEEE10
+CMGL: 2,1,,25
07919170389103F2040B91XXXXXXXXXXF100013011329135610A06C8F79D9C0F01

OK
AT+CMGR=1
+CMGR: 1,,28
07919170389103F2040B91XXXXXXXXXXF100013011320211500A0AD3771D7E9A83DEEE10

OK
```

However, you'll want to put the phone into text mode, so the responses that you receive are human-readable. Use AT+CMGF=1 for this, and try reading the message again:

```
AT+CMGF=1
OK
AT+CMGR=1
+CMGR: "REC READ","+14015559000",,"03/11/23,20:11:05-20"
Soup's on!

OK
```

You can send a message with AT+CMGS="PHONE_NUMBER" (but make sure you've set responses to be human-readable with AT+CMGF=1). You'll be prompted for the message; type it and press Ctrl-Z when you are finished:

```
AT+CMGF=1
OK
AT+CMGS="4015559000"
> Hello, world!^Z
OK
```

You can also use the gsmsendsms utility from gsmlib (*http://www.pxh.de/fs/ gsmlib/index.html*) to send the message:

```
bjepson@debian:~$ gsmsendsms -d /dev/ttyUSB0 4015559000 "Hello, World"
```

Acceleration

Although GPRS and CDMA are pretty slow, some providers have put compression servers on their network to compress documents before they make it to your computer.

Verizon Wireless uses a two-tier proxy server called Venturi (*http://www. venturiwireless.com/products.html*). One tier of the proxy server sits on the cellular carrier's network and compresses documents before they come down to your machine. The other tier is a local proxy server that runs on your machine and decompresses the content on the fly before presenting it to your web browser or any other application. (Venturi can compress data sent over a number of protocols including SMTP and POP3.) AT&T Wireless uses something similar, but we do not know what it is. At the time of this writing, there isn't a Linux client for either Venturi (or whatever it is that AT&T Wireless uses). But that shouldn't stop you from asking customer support about it, because it may have changed (at the very least, you should let them know the demand exists).

Sprint and T-Mobile have transparent acceleration on their networks. The nice thing about this approach is that it should, in theory, obey web standards without requiring any fiddling on the client side; so it doesn't matter what operating system you're on. To compress HTML, the compression server can use gzip compression; to compress images, it can reduce the image quality. Figure 9-6 shows the T-Mobile Internet Accelerator configuration page (*http://getmorespeed.t-mobile.com*). You will not be able to reach this page unless you are connected to the *internet2.voicestream.com* or *internet3.voicestream.com* APNs on T-Mobile's GPRS network.

Figure 9-7 shows detail from an image that was sent across T-Mobile's network with compression disabled. Figure 9-8 shows that same detail with maximum compression. Although some artifacts appear in the image, the differences should not annoy most users. This 799×599 pixel image started out at 96 KB; compression reduced it to 48 KB.

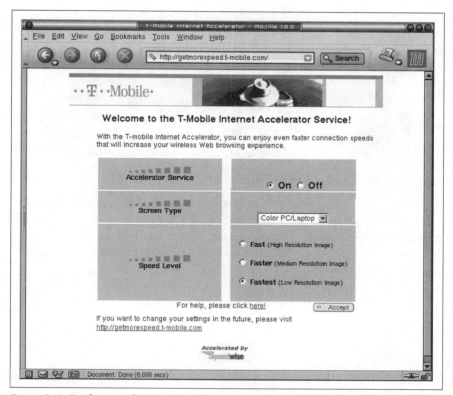

Figure 9-6. Configuring the T-Mobile Internet Accelerator

Figure 9-7. Photograph with no compression

Your mileage will vary using acceleration; in theory, it should speed things up. We've found this to be the case most of the time.

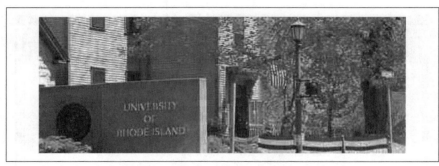

Figure 9-8. Photograph with maximum compression

However, we've also found cases where the compression server was having a bad day, and the amount of time it took to do its thing exceeded the acceleration we received from the compression. Try it out and see how it works, and disable it if it's a problem. Contact your cellular carrier for instructions on turning compression on and off.

## CHAPTER 10

The Global Positioning System (GPS) consists of 27 earth-orbiting satellites (of which 24 are operational and 3 are backups) circling the earth twice each day. These satellites are arranged in six orbital paths, as shown in Figure 10-1.

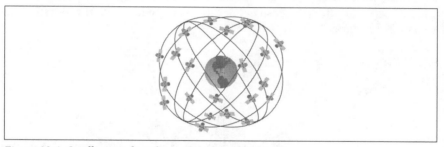

Figure 10-1. Satellites circling the earth in six orbital paths

These satellites continuously emit coded *positional* and *timing* information using low-power radio waves at frequencies around 1,500 MHz. GPS receivers on earth can pick up the signals and calculate the exact (we discuss what we mean by "exact" later in this chapter) positioning on earth. The orbits of the satellites are arranged in such a manner that at least four satellites are visible at any given time. Thus, a GPS receiver is able to receive signals from these four satellites and, based on the various signals transmitted by them, derive positional information on earth.

So how does the GPS receiver calculate its position? It does so by measuring the distance between itself and the satellites. Signals emitted by the satellites are received by the GPS receiver after a time lag, and based on the speed of light, the GPS receiver calculates the distance from itself to the satellite. But obtaining the distance from one satellite is not enough, because it tells you only that you are somewhere on the surface of the sphere (think in terms of three-dimensional space). Figure 10-2 shows that you can be anywhere on a sphere with a radius equal to the estimated distance to the satellite.

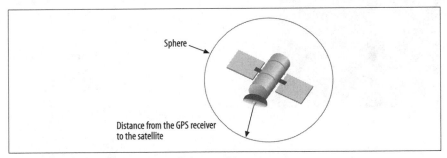

Figure 10-2. A sphere containing all the possible positions

To pinpoint your exact location, GPS uses at least three satellites to triangulate an exact location on earth. Figure 10-3 shows that if you have two satellites, then you can narrow down your location to the intersection of the two spheres. In this case, you can be anywhere on the dotted line (which is an ellipse).

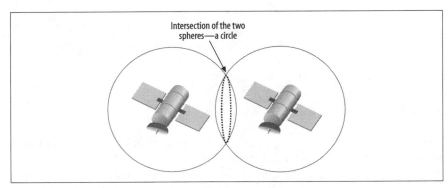

Figure 10-3. Intersection of two spheres forming an ellipse

This is not precise enough. With a third satellite, you can reduce the possibilities to two (see Figure 10-4). But one of these two points is in space, which is not likely the position you are in. Hence, you can effectively derive your position from three satellites, but four or more satellites are needed to get a decent altitude fix.

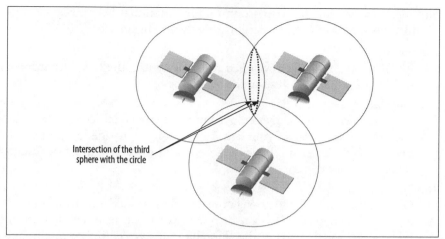

Intersection of the third
sphere with the circle

Figure 10-4. Intersection of the ellipse (formed by the two intersecting spheres) with a third sphere

GPS Accuracy

GPS was originally developed in the 1980s by the U.S. Department of Defense for military use. Because it was designed primarily for the military, the U.S. Department of Defense introduced Selective Availability (SA) to degrade the signal accuracy and to encrypt sensitive information, so that civilian usage could be restricted. The satellites would deliberately broadcast wrong and randomly inaccurate signals, which would cause the precision of the GPS data to be within 100 meters. The accurate information could be decoded only by the military.

Because of the great commercial potential of GPS, in May 2000, President Clinton announced that the U.S. would no longer degrade the accuracy of GPS. With SA turned off, the accuracy of the GPS data could be within five meters.

 Most GPS receivers use information from three or more satellites to increase the accuracy of the positional information.

Uses of GPS

The function of GPS is fairly straightforward—with a GPS receiver, you can obtain your positional information in the form of longitude, latitude, and altitude. It is the way that you use this information that is important. Some useful applications of GPS are described in the following list:

Military use

As GPS was originally developed for military use, the U.S. Department of Defense is the main user of the technology.

Location-Based Services (LBS)

GPS has been increasingly deployed in the commercial scene. LBS make use of the knowledge of your precise location to provide location-sensitive services. For example, you can use LBS to receive a list of restaurants near your current location.

Navigation services

GPS is popularly used for navigational purposes, such as driving and flying. A GPS-enabled PDA can help a driver navigate unfamiliar cities. GPS is also widely used in the shipping industry, as well as in airplane navigational systems. Courier companies, such as UPS and FedEx, make extensive use of GPS in their delivery infrastructures.

Tracking

Using GPS to track the whereabouts of people or objects is rapidly gaining acceptance. This is useful in the medical sector: patients suffering from diseases such as Alzheimer's can wear a GPS watch, and, when needed, they can press a panic button to reveal their exact location to their family members.

Mapping

GPS is also popularly used in mapping software, allowing you to combine a GPS receiver with mapping software to display your current location. This is useful for travelers or explorers who need navigational aids.

A GPS Glossary

Here are some GPS terms that you will encounter when you use GPS and GPS software:

8/12 channels receiver

An 8-channel receiver uses 8 channels to access 8 different satellites at any one time. A 12-channel receiver can access 12 satellites at once.

Bearing

The direction you are aiming for.

CEP, RMS, and 2D RMS

Circular Error Probable (CEP), Root Mean Square (RMS), and 2D RMS are all measures of the accuracy of a GPS receiver. CEP represents the radius of a circle containing 50% of the GPS readings. RMS represents the radius of a circle containing 68% of the GPS readings. 2D RMS represents the radius of a circle containing 98% of the GPS readings. If three GPS receivers each claims to have 2m CEP, 2m RMS, and 2m 2D RMS respectively, then the third one is the most accurate, because it has readings accurate to within a 2-meter radius 98 percent of the time.

DGPS

Differential GPS is an enhancement to the satellite-based GPS that makes use of receivers on fixed reference points on the ground and improves accuracy to within 3–5 meters. These receivers transmit error-correcting information to DGPS receivers to enhance the information supplied by the satellites.

Fix

A location returned by the GPS receiver after processing the readings of at least three satellites.

Heading

The actual direction you are traveling towards. It is not the same as bearing. Bearing is your desired direction, but you may not be heading towards the desired direction due to factors such as obstacles (e.g., water, fences, and mountains). Therefore, you have to momentarily head in another direction in a bid to get to your destination.

Latitude, longitude, and altitude

The coordinates of a specific location on earth. These three pieces of information together define a point in the three-dimensional space.

National Marine Electronics Association (NMEA)

The NMEA-0183 standard has been universally adopted by GPS manufacturers and virtually every GPS product for exchanging navigational information between devices. NMEA-0183 defines a "sentence" format (using printable ASCII text) describing navigational information.

Route

A collection of waypoints representing the path that you would like to take.

Selective Availability (SA)

The degradation of GPS data for nonmilitary use. See the sidebar "GPS Accuracy" earlier in this chapter for more information on SA.

Time to First Fix (TTFF)

The least amount of time required to obtain a fix by the minimum number of satellites required for triangulation. Normally, it takes a few minutes before you can receive a fix.

WAAS

WAAS is an enhancement similar to DGPS that uses fixed reference stations on the ground to enhance accuracy to under 3 meters.

Waypoint

A location that you store in your GPS system (as coordinates). Examples of waypoints are a hiking location, camping ground, church, or any place of interest to a GPS user. You normally add a waypoint to your GPS before you start your traveling. You can also add one during your travel when you locate a place of interest.

GPS Devices

There are two main types of GPS receivers on the market at the moment:

- Plain GPS receivers
- GPS receivers with maps

A plain GPS receiver simply interprets the readings from the satellite and returns the result in latitude, longitude, and altitude. Figure 10-5 shows the PocketMap (*http://www.pocketmap.com*) PMG-220 Compact Flash (CF) GPS receiver. You can use the PMG-220 on a handheld or your notebook computer (which may require a PCMCIA adapter for the CF card).

Figure 10-5. The PocketMap PMG-220 CF GPS receiver with a CF-to-PCMCIA adapter

Figure 10-6 shows the Deluo Laptop GPS receiver. This is an affordable receiver ($99) that's available from Deluo (*http://www.deluo.com*) in serial or USB configurations. We used the Deluo USB model in our testing for this chapter.

Figure 10-7 shows two standalone GPS receivers equipped with their own mapping software. The Magellan Meridian Gold and the Garmin StreetPilot

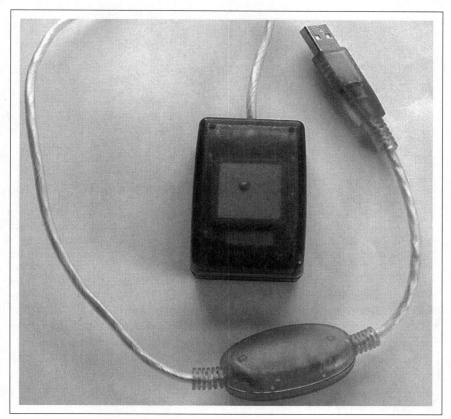

Figure 10-6. The Deluo Laptop GPS receiver

III contain built-in screens to display maps. There is no need to connect the receivers to any device for them to work. Standalone GPS receivers are useful for travelers who need a lightweight GPS solution.

Listening to a GPS

Listening to a GPS from a Linux box is as simple as listening to any serial device: plug it in, make sure the driver (if any) is loaded, open the port, and read the stream. We tried connecting both the PocketMap CF GPS (using a CF-to-PCMCIA adapter) and the Deluo USB GPS. The PocketMap GPS was detected automatically as a serial port; we needed to load the Prolific 2303 USB/Serial module (*modprobe pl2303*) for the Deluo GPS to be recognized (it appeared on */dev/ttyUSB0*, as did the Nokia 6200 described in Chapter 9).

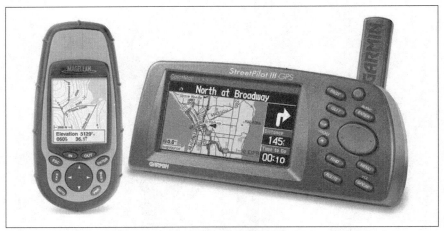

Figure 10-7. The Magellan Meridian Gold GPS (left) and the Garmin StreetPilot III (Magellen used by permission, Thales Navigation, Inc. 2003; Garmin courtesy of Garmin Ltd.)

Most GPS devices use a format called NMEA 0183; however, many of them include proprietary extensions. The NMEA standard specifies a transport of RS-232 at 4,800 kbps, 8 data bits, 1 stop bit, and no parity, but some devices support higher speeds. The Deluo GPS that we used sends standard NMEA sentences in the sequence GPGGA-GPGSA-GPGSV-GPRMC. Each sentence is a line of comma-separated text that begins with $*TYPE* (where *TYPE* is the NMEA 0183 sentence type) and ends with a checksum value, as shown in Example 10-1.

Example 10-1. Sample output from the Deluo GPS

```
$GPGGA,071110.000,3242.8536,N,11709.7626,W,1,05,01.5,00104.2,M,-34.0,M,,*50
$GPGSA,A,3,22,16,,14,20,,,,,25,,,02.5,01.5,02.1*05
$GPGSV,3,1,10,22,11,117,35,16,13,151,35,11,44,256,,14,26,056,35*78
$GPGSV,3,2,10,20,32,316,34,01,22,266,,30,09,052,,02,07,172,*76
$GPGSV,3,3,10,23,30,110,33,25,70,061,39*77
$GPRMC,071110.000,A,3242.8536,N,11709.7626,W,000.0,000.0,100204,013.0,E*7D
```

The checksum is a two-digit hexadecimal value that's created by XORing the ASCII values of each character in the sentence, except for the leading $ and * that precede the checksum itself. For example, the Perl code shown in Example 10-2 verifies the checksum of each line in Example 10-1.

Example 10-2. Verifying NMEA 0183 sentence checksums

```
#!/usr/bin/perl -w
#
# gpscksum.pl--verify each NMEA 0183 sentence in standard input
```

Example 10-2. Verifying NMEA 0183 sentence checksums (continued)

```
#

use strict;

my $count=1;
while (<>)
{
  my ($string, $cksum);
  if (/^\$(.*)\*([0-9A-Fa-f][0-9A-Fa-f])/)
  {
    $string = $1; # everything between leading $ and checksum
    $cksum  = $2; # hex checksum from NMEA sentence
  } else
  {
    die "Malformed NMEA 0183 sentence: $_\n";
  }

  # Calculate the checksum
  my $my_cksum;
  for (my $i = 0; $i < length ($string); $i++)
  {
    $my_cksum ^= ord(substr($string, $i, 1))
  }

  # Compare the checksums
  if ($my_cksum != hex($cksum))
  {
    print "Checksum for line $count doesn't match: ",
      $my_cksum, "!=", hex($cksum), "\n";
  }
  $count++;
}
```

The following tables describe the NMEA 0183 sentences listed in Example 10-1. Items in the Example column are drawn directly from Example 10-1. Table 10-1 describes the elements of the GPGGA sentence (GPS fix data). This sentence gives you information about the current position fix.

Table 10-1. GPGGA sentence

Column(s)	Example	Description
1	071110.000 (7:11:10)	Current time UTC (HHMMSS.mmm)
2, 3	3242.8536, N (32°42.8836′ N)	Latitude
4, 5	11709.7626, W (117°9.7626′ Wt)	Longitude

Table 10-1. GPGGA sentence (continued)

Column(s)	Example	Description
6	1	Fix quality (0=no fix, 1=GPS, 2=differential GPS)
7	05	Number of satellites used for fix
8	01.5	Horizontal dilution of precision
9,10	00104.2,M (104.2 meters)	Altitude
11,12	–34.0, M (–34 meters)	Difference between mean sea level and the ellipsoid modeled by WGS-84 (*http://www.wgs84.com/*)
13	(empty)	Age of differential GPS data (if any)
14	(empty)	Differential station ID
15	50	Checksum (preceded by * rather than a comma)

Table 10-2 describes the GPGSA (active satellites) sentence. This sentence summarizes information about the satellites used to determine your current fix.

Table 10-2. GPGSA sentence

Column(s)	Example	Description
1	A	Selection mode (A=Automatic, M=Manual)
2	3	Fix mode (1=no fix; 2=2-dimensional; 3=3-dimensional)
3–14	22,16,,14,20,,,,,25,,	Satellite IDs (blanks indicate satellites not in view)
15	02.5	Positional dilution of precision
16	01.5	Horizontal dilution of precision
17	02.1	Vertical dilution of precision
18	05	Checksum (preceded by * rather than a comma)

Table 10-3 describes the GPGSV (satellites in view) sentence, which may appear multiple times. This sentence provides detailed information about each satellite, describing up to four satellites per line.

Table 10-3. GPGSV sentence

Column(s)	Example	Description
1	3	Number of GPGSV sentences
2	1	Current sentence number
3	10	Number of satellites in view
4	22	Satellite number
5	11	Satellite elevation in degrees
6	117	Satellite azimuth in degrees

Table 10-3. GPGSV sentence (continued)

Column(s)	Example	Description
7	35	Signal-to-noise ratio
8–11	16,13,151,35	Repeat of 4–7 for another satellite
12–14	11,44,256,	Repeat of 4–7 for another satellite
15–18	14,26,056,35	Repeat of 4–7 for another satellite
19	78	Checksum (preceded by * rather than a comma)

Table 10-4 describes the GPRMC (transit information) sentence, which provides navigational data such as ground speed and course traveled.

Table 10-4. GPRMC Sentence

Column(s)	Example	Description
1	071110.000 (7:11:10)	Time of fix
2	A	Navigation receiver warning (A=OK; V=receiver warning)
3,4	3242.8536, N (32°42.8836' N)	Latitude
5,6	11709.7626, W (117°9.7626' W)	Longitude
7	000.0	Ground speed in knots
8	000.0	Course made good (degrees)
9	100204 (10 February 2004)	Date of fix
10,11	013.0, E (13°E)	Magnetic variation
12	7D	Checksum (preceded by * rather than a comma)

References

Peter Bennett's NMEA FAQ
  http://vancouver-webpages.com/peter/nmeafaq.txt
Walter Piechulla's Understanding NMEA 0183
  http://www.walterpiechulla.de/nmea0183.html

GPSd

GPSd listens to a GPS receiver and republishes the GPS information on the network in an easy-to-read format. It's included with GpsDrive, described later in this chapter, but you can also download it and install it yourself from the GPSd home page at *http://www.pygps.org/gpsd/gpsd.html*.

To launch GPSd, specify the serial port with -p and (optionally) the speed with -s. If you use the -D option to specify a debugging level above 1, GPSd will stay in the foreground and display debugging info (if you are using an RS-232 connection for your GPS, the port will be a standard serial port such as */dev/ttyS0*):

```
$ sudo gpsd -D9 -p /dev/ttyUSB0 -s 4800
command line options:
  debug level:        9
  gps device name:    /dev/ttyUSB0
  gps device speed:   12
  gpsd port:          2947
  latitude:           3600.000N
  longitude:          12300.000W
```

It doesn't start reading from the GPS until it gets a connection from a client. The simplest way to connect is via telnet to port 2947. GPSd understands several simple commands followed by a carriage return, as shown in Table 10-5.

Table 10-5. Commands supported by GPSd

Command	Response from GPSd
P	Latitude and longitude
D	Date and time
A	Altitude in meters
V	Speed in knots
S	Status (0=no GPS; 1=no fix; 2=2D fix; 3=3D Fix)
M	Mode (0=no GPS; 1=GPS; 2=differential GPS)
R	Enter raw mode (dumps NMEA 0183 sentences)

The first time you ask for latitude and longitude after launching GPSd, you might not get a valid result (and it may take a while to get a fix anyhow). But on subsequent requests, you should get valid data:

```
bjepson@debian:~$ telnet localhost 2947
Trying 127.0.0.1...
Connected to debian.
Escape character is '^]'.
P
GPSD,P=0.000000 0.000000
P
GPSD,P=32.714227 -117.162708
```

Here's a sample session showing some of the other commands:

```
bjepson@debian:~$ telnet localhost 2947
Trying 127.0.0.1...
Connected to debian.
Escape character is '^]'.
d
GPSD,D=02/10/2004 07:11:14
a
GPSD,A=103.500000
v
GPSD,V=0.000000
r
GPSD,R=1
$GPGSA,A,3,22,16,,14,20,,,,,25,,,02.5,01.5,02.1*05
$GPGSV,3,1,10,22,11,117,36,16,13,151,35,11,44,256,,14,26,056,36*78
$GPGSV,3,2,10,20,32,316,30,01,22,266,,30,09,052,,02,07,172,*72
$GPGSV,3,3,10,23,30,110,35,25,70,061,39*71
$GPRMC,071119.000,A,3242.8539,N,11709.7626,W,000.0,000.0,100204,013.0,E*7B
r$GPGGA,071120.000,3242.8539,N,11709.7626,W,1,05,01.5,00103.1,M,-34.0,M,,*58
$GPGSA,A,3,22,16,,14,20,,,,,25,,,02.5,01.5,02.1*05

GPSD,R=0
```

But to really have fun with GPSd, you can use GPSd-aware applications such as Kismet and GpsDrive, described in the following sections.

Mapping Wi-Fi Networks with Kismet

We introduced Kismet in Chapter 3 as a powerful network scanner. You can also use it in conjunction with GPSd to map out the locations of Wi-Fi networks. (For the basics of getting Kismet running, see Chapter 3.) Once you have Kismet and GPSd up and running, you can make them work together.

To map networks with Kismet and GPSd:

1. (Optional.) Load any modules needed for the serial port you're using for the GPS:

   ```
   $ sudo modprobe pl2303
   $ dmesg | grep tty
   ttyS00 at 0x03f8 (irq = 4) is a 16550A
   ttyS02 at 0x03e8 (irq = 4) is a 16550A
   usbserial.c: PL-2303 converter now attached to ttyUSB0 (or usb/tts/0 for
   devfs)
   ```

2. Start GPSd, specifying the serial port with -p and the speed with -s:

   ```
   $ sudo gpsd -D9 -p /dev/ttyUSB0 -s 4800
   ```

3. Telnet to GPSd and use p until you have a reliable fix; you can disconnect when you are done:

   ```
   $ telnet localhost 2947
   Trying 127.0.0.1...
   ```

Safety

If you plan to do some network mapping with Kismet, keep the following in mind:

- Put the computer somewhere safe and out of the way. Don't put it someplace where a sudden stop will send it into your lap or through a window.
- Forget that the computer is there while you are driving. If you have to fiddle with it, pull over first. If you can have a friend driving with you who can operate the computer, all the better. Do not let the computer distract you while you are driving.
- Make sure that the GPS gets a fix before you start driving. It may be hard for it to get a fix while you are in motion.
- Put the GPS somewhere where it can easily pick up the satellite signals. Your best bet is to get a magnetized external antenna that can attach to your roof. Be sure that there are no loose wires sticking out of your window. Don't slam the wires in the door!

Above all, when you are driving a car, your first responsibility is to drive safely. Pay attention to the road and drive carefully.

```
Connected to debian.
Escape character is '^]'.
p
GPSD,P=0.000000 0.000000
p
GPSD,P=41.485882 -71.524841
^]
telnet> q
Connection closed.
```

4. Launch Kismet with the -g (GPS) switch and specify the hostname and port that GPSd is listening on:

   ```
   $ sudo kismet -g localhost:2947
   ```

5. Go for a drive. Press Q when you are done with the drive to terminate Kismet.

When you shut down Kismet, it writes its log files. Check the logtemplate setting in *kismet.conf* to see where it puts its log files:

```
logtemplate=/var/log/kismet/%n-%d-%i.%l
```

Kismet writes several log files in the *logtemplate* directory (*I* starts at 1 and increments for each time you run Kismet on a given day):

Kismet-<MMM-DD-YYYY>-I.csv

Kismet log in semicolon-separated fields, one line per entry. The first entry contains the field names.

Kismet-<MMM-DD-YYYY>-I.dump

Kismet log in a *pcap(3)* format suitable for loading under Ethereal (*http://www.ethereal.com*).

Kismet-<MMM-DD-YYYY>-I.gps

Kismet log in a format designed to be read by the *gpsmap* utility, which is included with the Kismet distribution.

Kismet-<MMM-DD-YYYY>-I.network

A human-readable dump of the networks that Kismet encountered.

Kismet-<MMM-DD-YYYY>-I.xml

Kismet log in an XML format.

When you're done with Kismet, you must reassociate your Wi-Fi card with the network. This can sometimes be done by restarting PCMCIA card services or removing and reinserting the card, but it resulted in a kernel panic in some of our tests. Our workaround was to use a second network card for network connectivity and let Kismet have its way with the Prism-based card on *wlan0*.

To generate a map, run *gpsmap* on the *.gps* log file. See the *gpsmap* manpage for all the drawing and mapping options. If you choose to use a downloaded map (the default), you must be online. Figure 10-8 shows a map generated by the following command:

```
$ gpsmap -S3 -p /var/log/kismet/Kismet-Feb-16-2004-5.gps
```

The -S option specifies which map server to use (0 = MapBlast;1 = Map-Point;2 = Terraserver; 3= Tiger Census). If you have trouble with one, try another (Tiger is loosely maintained by the Census Bureau and is not up 100 percent of the time). Use -p to show power levels or -e to plot simply the locations of the hotspots on the map (see the *gpsmap* manpage for more options).

GpsDrive

GpsDrive (*http://www.gpsdrive.cc/index.shtml*) is an open source GPS-aware navigation system that uses GTK+. It works with maps from a variety of sources, and plot waypoints, and even lets you share your position with friends and send SMS text messages with position information.

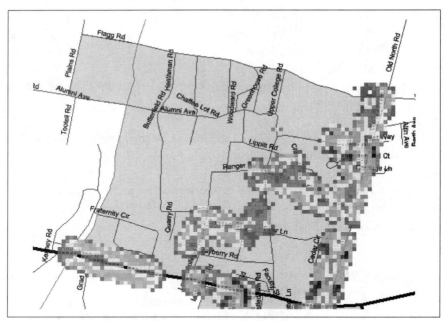

Figure 10-8. Wi-Fi power levels in the Kingston, Rhode Island area

If you launch GpsDrive while GPSd is listening on the localhost, it will pick it up and start reading coordinates from it. By default, GpsDrive displays a placeholder map that's not very detailed (see Figure 10-9). However, you can download new maps by clicking the Download Map button and selecting the map server from the dialog that pops up, as shown in Figure 10-10.

Using GpsDrive to download maps from a commercial map service may violate that site's Terms of Service (ToS). Be sure to consult that mapping site's ToS before proceeding.

The latest beta version as of this writing (2.08pre12) comes with support for NASA's Blue Marble (*http://earthobservatory.nasa.gov/Newsroom/BlueMarble/*) satellite images. You must download some extremely large files (over 1 GB uncompressed) and install them according to the *README.nasamaps* file that's included with the GpsDrive distribution. Figure 10-11 shows the NASA maps in action.

GpsDrive does not support route planning, but it does show your speed, position, and altitude. What's more, a version is available that runs on Linux-powered handhelds (*http://www.gpsdrive.cc/pda.shtml*), so you can load it up with waypoints for points of interest and use it while you wander around unfamiliar territory.

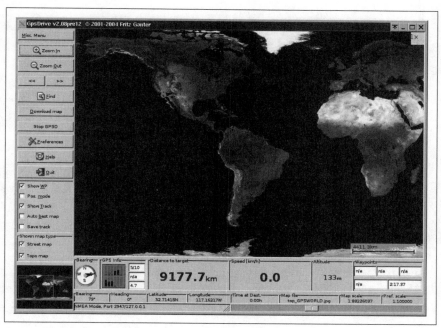

Figure 10-9. Default map from GpsDrive

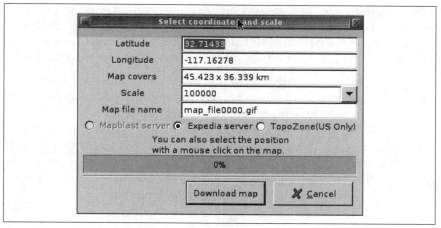

Figure 10-10. Selecting a map to download in GpsDrive

Other Applications

Linux is a playground for geographic information, and there are a lot of other applications out there for you to play with. GPStrans (*http://sourceforge.net/ projects/gpstrans*) and GARNIX (*http://homepage.ntlworld.com/anton.helm/*

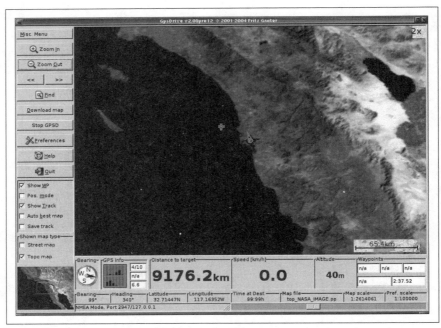

Figure 10-11. Using NASA's Blue Marble satellite maps with GpsDrive

garnix.html) are free applications that exchange information (track, route, waypoint, etc.) with a Garmin GPS. If you want to enjoy the increased accuracy of Differential GPS without having to buy a DGPS radio, see the DGPS over the Internet project at *http://www.wsrcc.com/wolfgang/gps/dgps-ip.html*.

If you're looking for a public map server with U.S. street maps, the U.S. Census Bureau makes street maps that date from 1998, available at the TIGER Map Server (*http://tiger.census.gov/cgi-bin/mapbrowse-tbl*). The maps on this site are public domain, and you can specify latitude, longitude, marker positions, and more in the URL. If you want to put a bunch of markers on the map (such as Wi-Fi hotspots), see the instructions at *http://tiger.census.gov/instruct.html#MURL*. The Tiger web server is loosely maintained by the Census Bureau and is not always in a working state.

One of the best resources for free/open source geographic information is the FreeGIS project (*http://www.freegis.org/*). This site contains an overview of the massive world of free Geographic Information Systems (GIS) software and provides software on CD-ROM. FreeGIS also acts as a central point for communication and collaboration on free GIS projects. You can browse the software by category at *http://www.freegis.org/browse.en.html* and its list of geographic data (including maps and other geographic models) at *http://freegis.org/geo-data.en.html*.

Index

We'd like to hear your suggestions for improving our indexes. Send email to *index@oreilly.com*.

F

Fast Infrared (FIR), 219
FatPort, 68
faxes, sending from cell
    phones, 261–262
FCC (Federal Communications
    Commission), 2
    bands defined by, 3
Fedora, installing Kismet, 72
File Transfer Profile (FTP), 181
fix (GPS), 271
flash RAM and access points, 128
flashing access points, 117
frag parameter (iwconfig), 46
FreeGIS project, 284
freeradius packages, 104
freq parameter (iwconfig), 45
freq parameter (iwlist), 49
frequency, 2
    allocation chart, 3
    range defined for various bands, 3
    (see also radio frequency)
Frequency Hopping, 6
Fujitsu Stylistic, using to build access
    points, 121

G

Garmin GPS, 284
Garmin StreetPilot III, 272
GARNIX, 283
General Packet Radio Service (GPRS), 1, 13
General Packet Radio Services (GPRS), 241
Generic Object Exchange Profile
    (GOEP), 181
Gentoo 1.4 and IrDA, 222
GHz (gigahertz), xii
gigahertz (GHz), xii
Global Positioning System (see GPS)
Global System for Mobile
    communications (GSM), 242
GN networks, 206
GNOME Bluetooth subsystem, 215
GNOME-Pilot, 233, 236–239
GPGSA (active satellites) sentence, 276
GPGSV (satellites in view) sentence, 276
GPRMC (transit information)
    sentence, 277
GPRS (General Packet Radio Service), 1,
    13, 242
    carrier, connecting to Internet, 244

PC card, 258–261
    getting online, 259
GPS (Global Positioning System), 267–284
    accuracy, 269
    communication rate, 274
    glossary, 270–272
    listening from a Linux box, 273–279
    pinpointing exact location, 268
    receivers, 272
        calculating position, 267–269
        with mapping software, 272
    uses of, 269
GPSd, 277–279
    commands supported by, 278
    launching, 278
    mapping networks with Kismet
        and, 279–281
GpsDrive, 281
gpsmap command, 281
GPStrans, 283
group ad-hoc network (see GN
    networks)
GRUB boot loader, 31
GSM Evolution (EDGE) network, 241
GSM (Global System for Mobile
    communications), 242
GSM/GPRS phone with data
    cable, 256–258
    getting online, 256
GTK+, 281

H

hands-free wireless headsets for mobile
    phones, 13
Hardcopy Cable Replacement
    (HCRP), 181
Hardware Abstraction Layer (HAL), 22
hciconfig tool, 191
    common usages, 192
    options, 195
hcid daemon, configuring, 194–195
heading (GPS), 271
Headset Profile (HS), 181
Hermes AP driver, 24
    custom access points, 149
Hertz (Hz), xii
Hidden Node problem, 8
High Frequency (HF) band, 1, 3
High Rate DS, 6
High Speed CSD (HSCSD), 241
hobo symbols, 78

About the Authors

Roger Weeks has nearly a decade of experience in systems and network administration and has been building Linux systems at home and in the enterprise since 1998. His first computer was an Atari 800, which was promptly taken apart so that he could add more memory before he attached the 300 kbps modem.

Most recently, he has been involved in building a community wireless network (*http://nocat.net*) and Internet co-op (*http://www.wscicc.org*) in Sonoma County, California. He lives with his wife, two dogs, and a cat in a small house that is saturated with radio waves in the 900 MHz, 2.4 GHz and 5 GHz frequencies.

Edd Dumbill is the managing editor of XML.com. He is an enthusiastic software developer, as well as a writer. Edd was also the chair of the XML Europe 2002 conference and chaired the O'Reilly XTech 2001 conference on XML.

Brian Jepson is an O'Reilly editor, programmer, and coauthor of *Mac OS X Panther for Unix Geeks* and *Learning Unix for Mac OS X Panther*, both available from O'Reilly. He's also a volunteer systems administrator and all-around geek for AS220, a nonprofit arts center in Providence, Rhode Island. AS220 gives Rhode Island artists uncensored and unjuried forums for their work. These forums include galleries, performance space, and publication. Brian sees to it that technology, especially free software, supports that mission.

Colophon

Our look is the result of reader comments, our own experimentation, and feedback from distribution channels. Distinctive covers complement our distinctive approach to technical topics, breathing personality and life into potentially dry subjects.

The image on the cover of *Linux Unwired* is cattle ropers. Ropers were cowboys who snared calves and dragged them to the fire for branding. Branding was the act of applying a red-hot branding iron to a calf's flank to mark the animal. Each ranch had a marking that identified cattle belonging to its herd, and this was thought to discourage theft.

Sarah Sherman was the production editor and copyeditor for *Linux Unwired*. Matt Hutchinson was the proofreader. Colleen Gorman and Claire Cloutier provided quality control. Julie Hawks wrote the index.

Emma Colby designed the cover of this book, based on a series design by Hanna Dyer and Edie Freedman. The cover image is a 19th-century engraving from *The Book of the American West* (Bonanza Books, 1963). Emma Colby produced the cover layout with QuarkXPress 4.1 using Adobe's ITC Garamond font.

David Futato designed the interior layout. The chapter opening images are from the Dover Pictorial Archive, *Marvels of the New West: A Vivid Portrayal of the Stupendous Marvels in the Vast Wonderland West of the Missouri River*, by William Thayer (The Henry Bill Publishing Co., 1888), and *The Pioneer History of America: A Popular Account of the Heroes and Adventures*, by Augustus Lynch Mason, A.M. (The Jones Brothers Publishing Company, 1884). This book was converted by Joe Wizda to FrameMaker 5.5.6 with a format conversion tool created by Erik Ray, Jason McIntosh, Neil Walls, and Mike Sierra that uses Perl and XML technologies. The text font is Linotype Birka; the heading font is Adobe Myriad Condensed; and the code font is LucasFont's TheSans Mono Condensed. The illustrations that appear in the book were produced by Robert Romano and Jessamyn Read using Macromedia FreeHand 9 and Adobe Photoshop 6. The tip and warning icons were drawn by Christopher Bing. This colophon was written by Sarah Sherman.